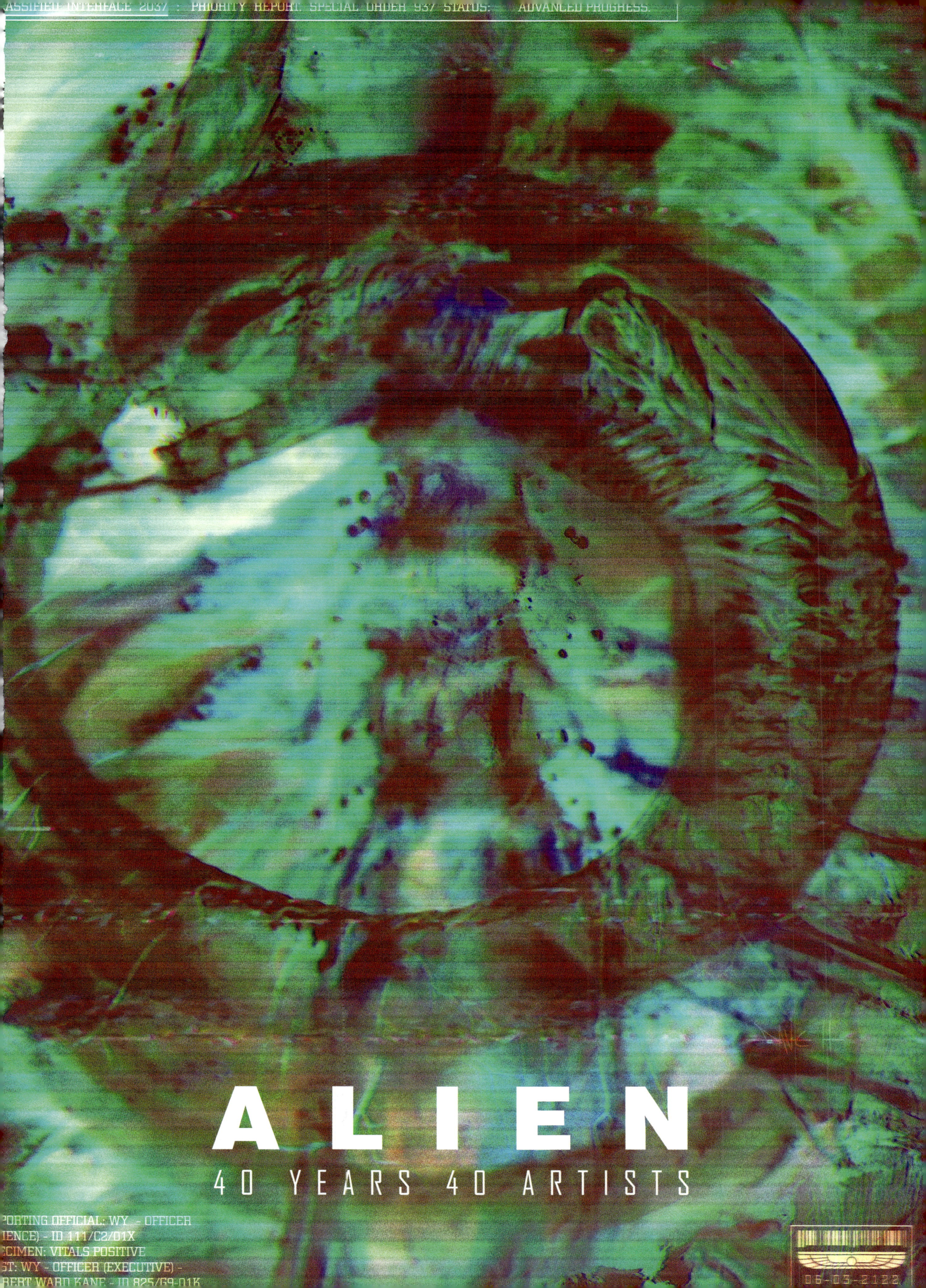
ASSIFIED INTERFACE 2037 : PRIORITY REPORT. SPECIAL ORDER 937 STATUS: ADVANCED PROGRESS.
ALIEN
40 YEARS 40 ARTISTS
PORTING OFFICIAL: WY - OFFICER
IENCE) - ID 111/C2/01X
CIMEN: VITALS POSITIVE
ST: WY - OFFICER (EXECUTIVE) -
BERT WARD KANE - ID 825/G9-01K
06-03-2122

ALIEN: 40 YEARS 40 ARTISTS
ISBN: 9781789091380

Published by
Titan Books
A division of Titan Publishing Group Ltd
144 Southwark Street
London
SE1 0UP

First edition: April 2020

2 4 6 8 10 9 7 5 3 1

Image Page 1: *Kane's Son* by Dane Hallett
Image Page 4: *ALIEN WIP 4* by Katherine Kuehne

www.titanbooks.com

Did you enjoy this book?
We love to hear from our readers.
Please e-mail us at:
readerfeedback@titanemail.com
or write to Reader Feedback at the above address.

To receive advance information, news, competitions, and exclusive offers online, please sign up for the Titan newsletter on our website:
www.titanbooks.com

A CIP catalogue record for this title is available from the British Library.

Printed and bound in China.

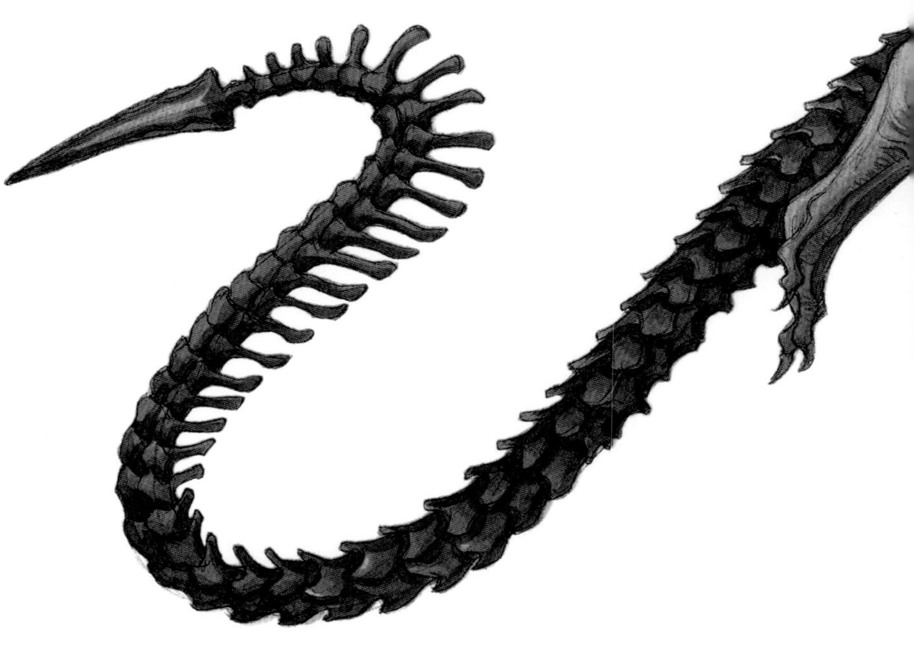

ALIEN

40 YEARS 40 ARTISTS

FOREWORD BY **CHRIS FOSS**

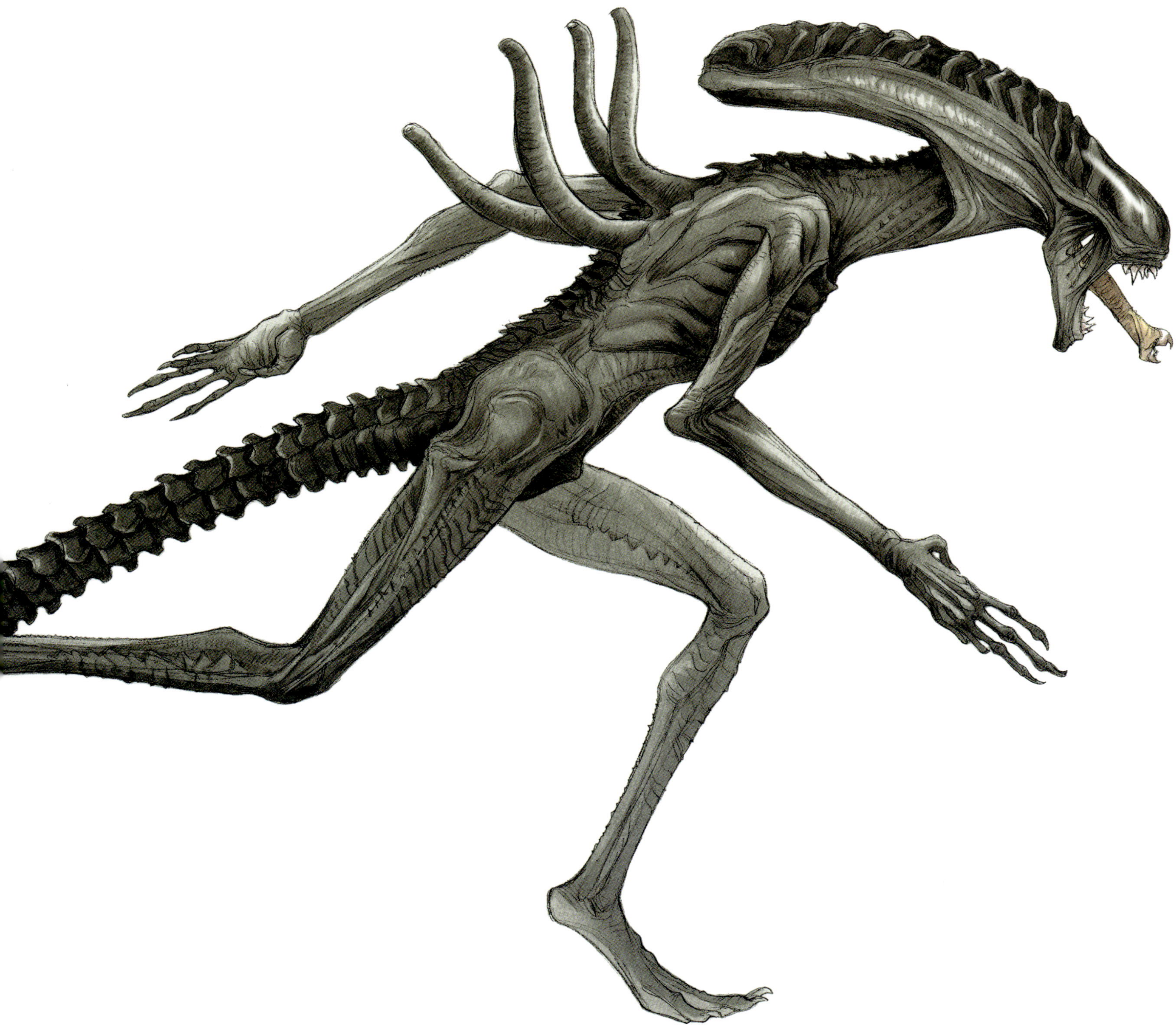

TITAN BOOKS

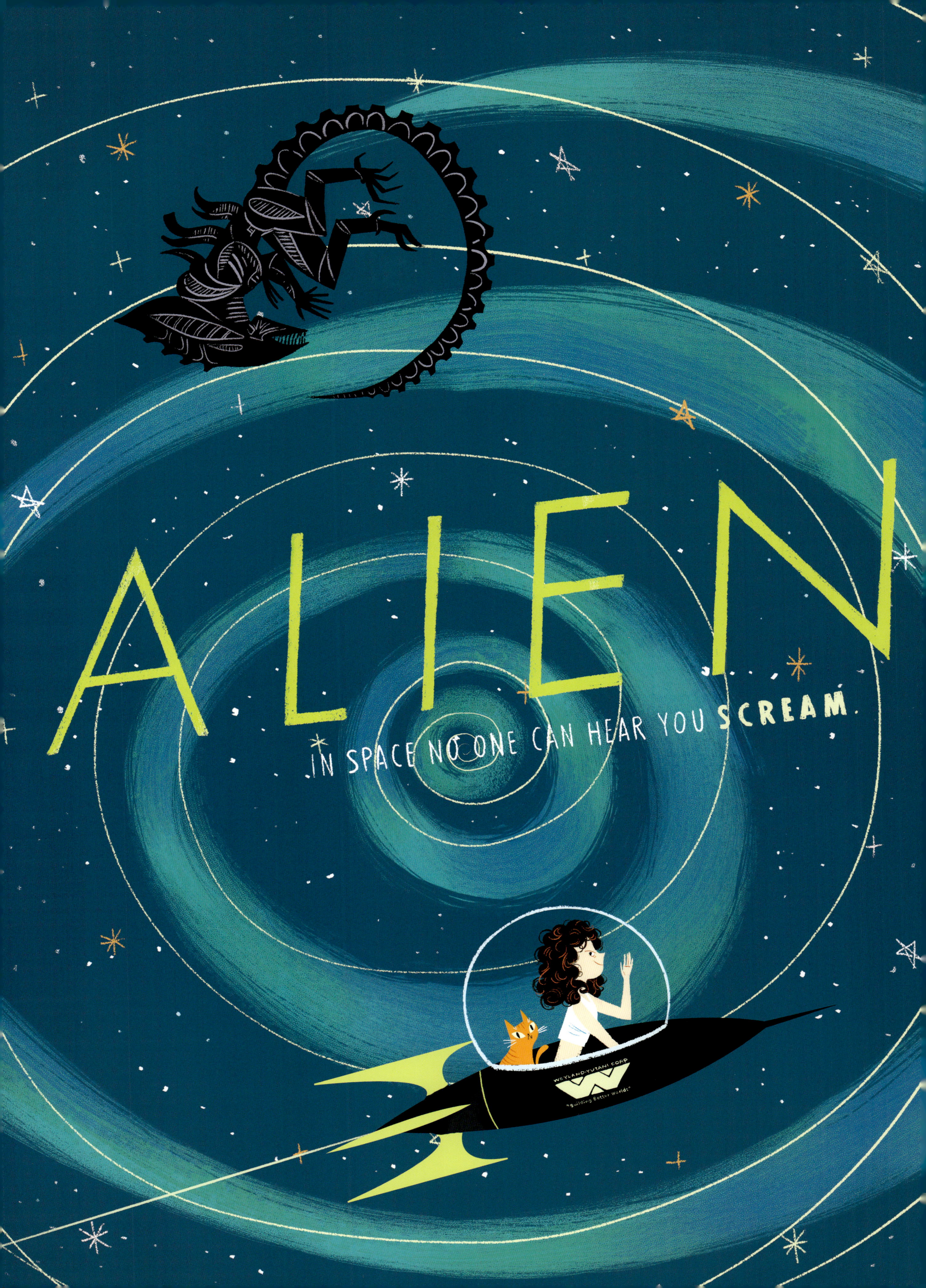
ALIEN
IN SPACE NO ONE CAN HEAR YOU SCREAM
WEYLAND-YUTANI CORP
"Building Better Worlds"

ALIEN: 40 YEARS 40 ARTISTS
CONTENTS

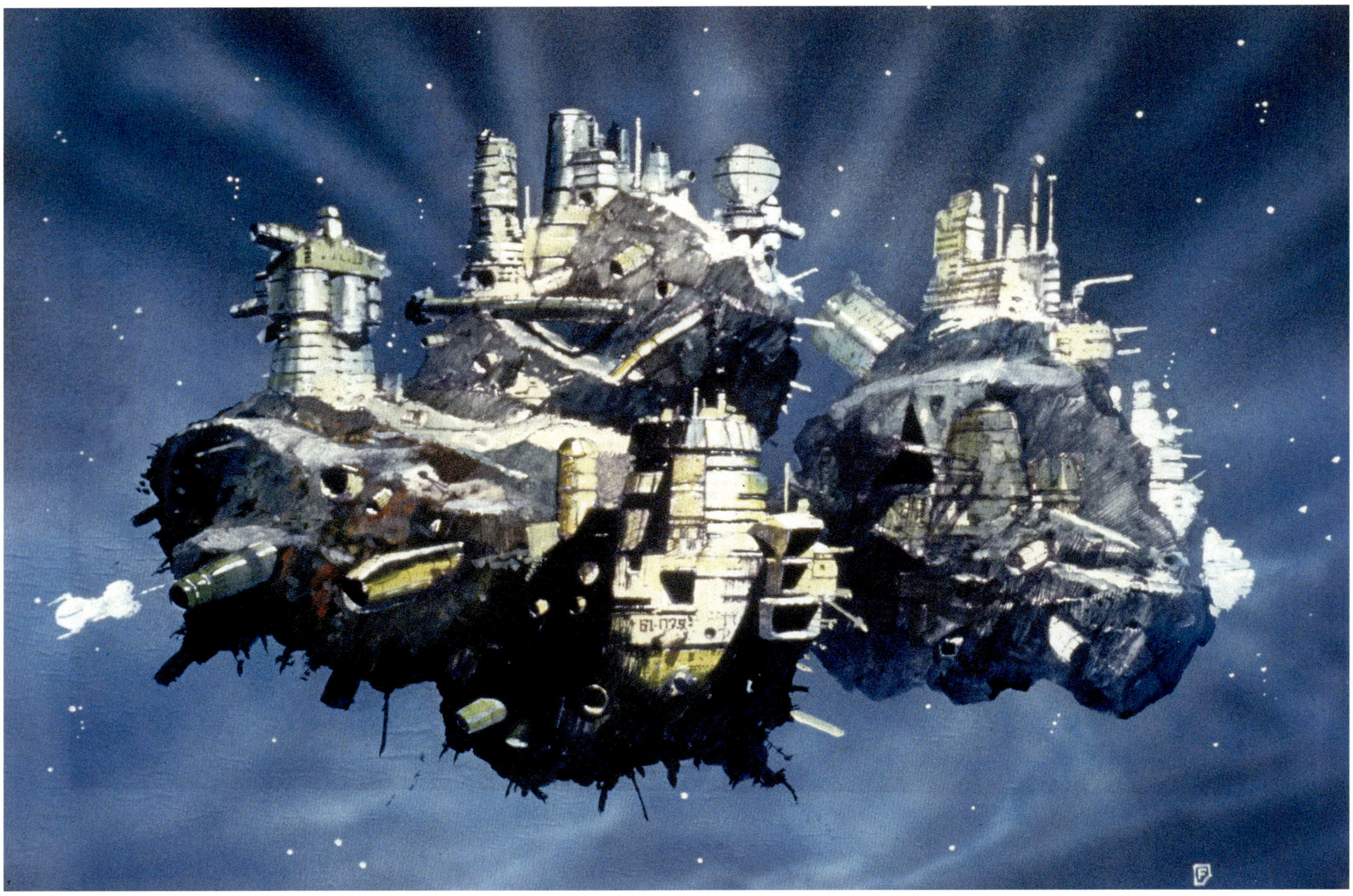

Above: A Chris Foss concept of the refinery.

Opposite: Chris Foss concepts of the *Nostromo*.

My introduction to working as a concept artist on films was in the mid-1970s with Alejandro Jodorowsky on his (ultimately unmade) *Dune* project. I didn't realise, because it was the first film I had ever worked on, how unique Jodorowsky was, and how unique his method of working was. There was certainly no comparison with any conventional studio. And he motivated us, got us all very excited. I then went on to work on *Superman*, before getting the call to go to America to work on *Alien*, a film that Dan O'Bannon – one of the great concept artists on *Star Wars* – put together. Dan was really keen to continue with the team from *Dune*. So, initially, I was full of enthusiasm and hope, based on the experience with *Dune*. But it slowly dawned on me that working for a Hollywood studio was a completely different experience.

At that time, Twentieth Century Fox – along with most of the big Hollywood studios – thought science fiction films were funny little things featuring people in silver paper hats. They didn't take them seriously. Then *Star Wars* was released and when the higher-ups at Fox saw the numbers on *Star Wars*, they said, "Hey, how can we capitalise on the current popularity of sci-fi?" And someone said, "Actually, you've got this small movie being produced on the back lot." That was *Alien*. And a bit like an old car, they jump-started it and *Alien* suddenly got rocketed right to the front of the production line.

On the whole, I enjoyed creating the artwork, particularly a lot of concepts for the *Nostromo*, but as a concept artist you want feedback, and there wasn't a lot of that at the pre-production stage. Dan O'Bannon had a very clear idea of what the film should look like and actually storyboarded and visualised the whole thing. He loved to give us input and he was very enthusiastic. Often though, you'd come in, do a day's work, and go again, and that was it. So it was very strange working all day in a sort of vacuum.

Mostly, Ron Cobb and I had to motivate ourselves. A big inspiration for me has always been industrial machinery – German fortifications around the coast of Guernsey, cranes at the dock, steam engines and the remnants of Victorian industry. But if you look at my designs for the *Nostromo*, I was actually obsessed with Picasso at that time. Picasso's bulls particularly fascinated me. If you look at some of my most distinctive space ship designs for *Alien*, they're all hunched up like a bull – big, strong, menacing; the arch of the neck, and then tailing away a bit. In fact, many of my designs are influenced by animals,

ALIEN: 40 YEARS 40 ARTISTS

CHRIS FOSS

FOREWORD

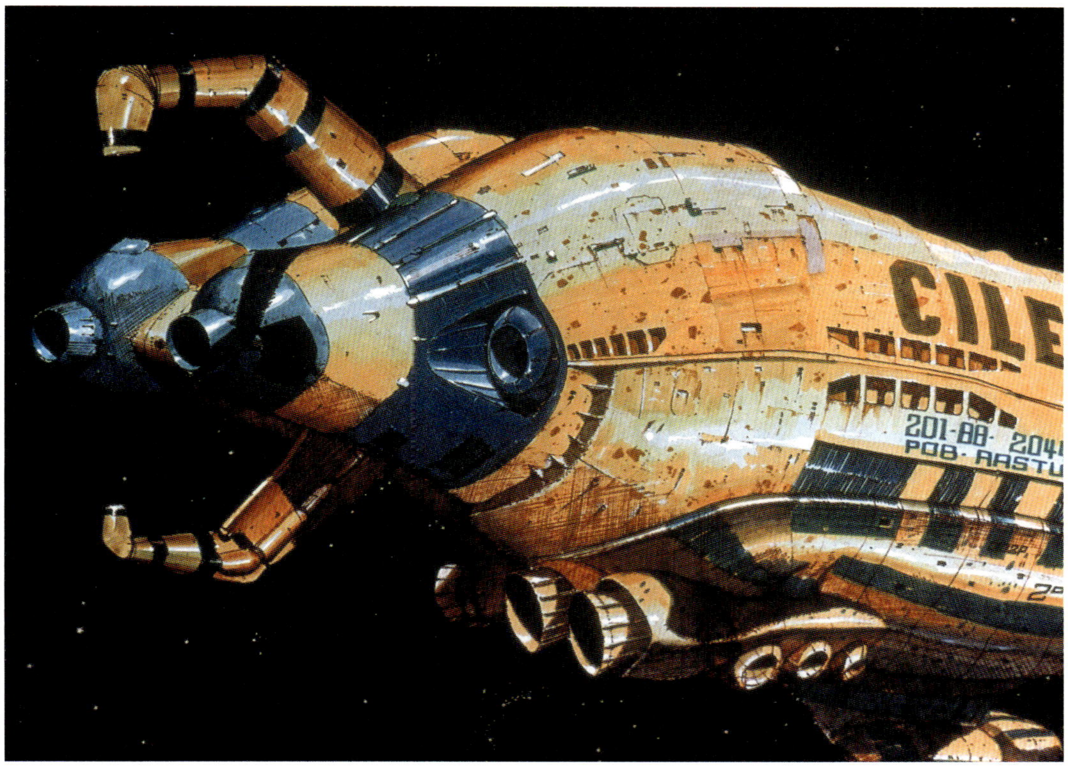

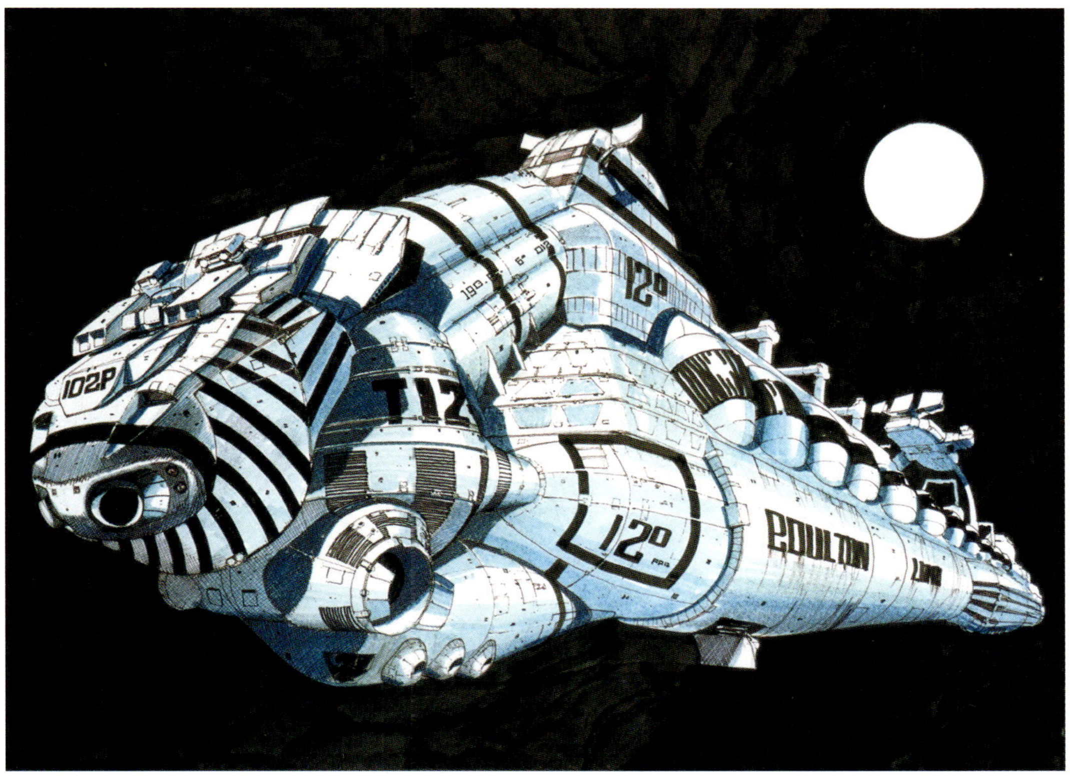

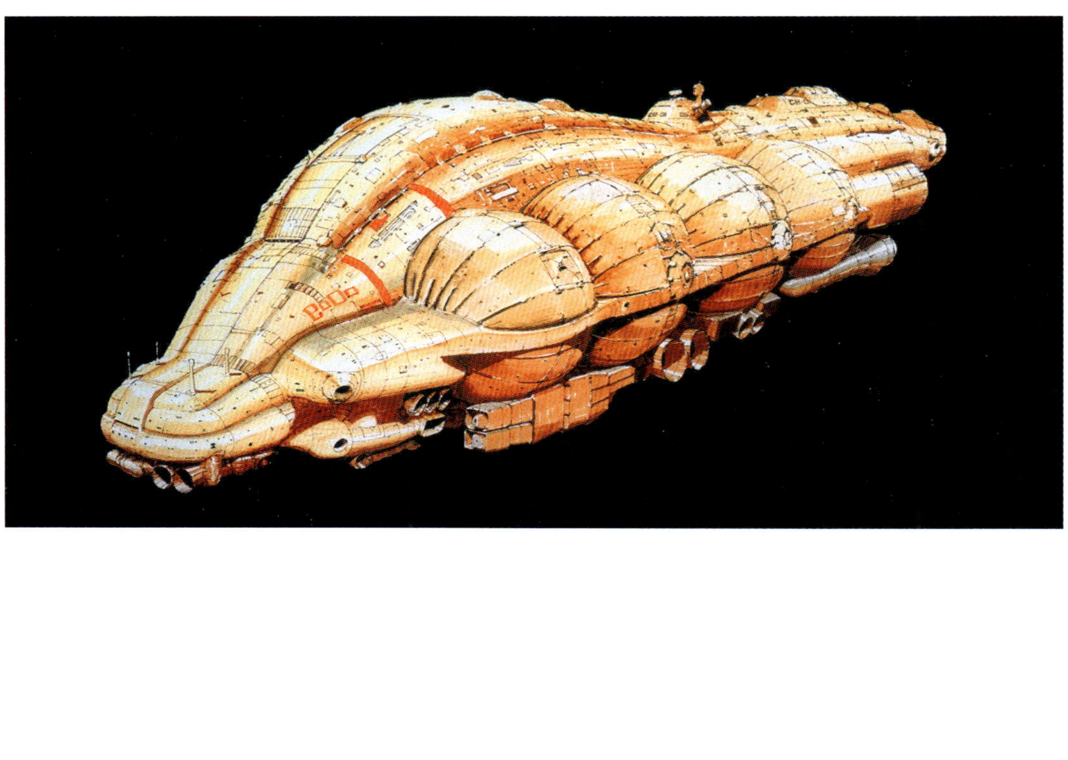

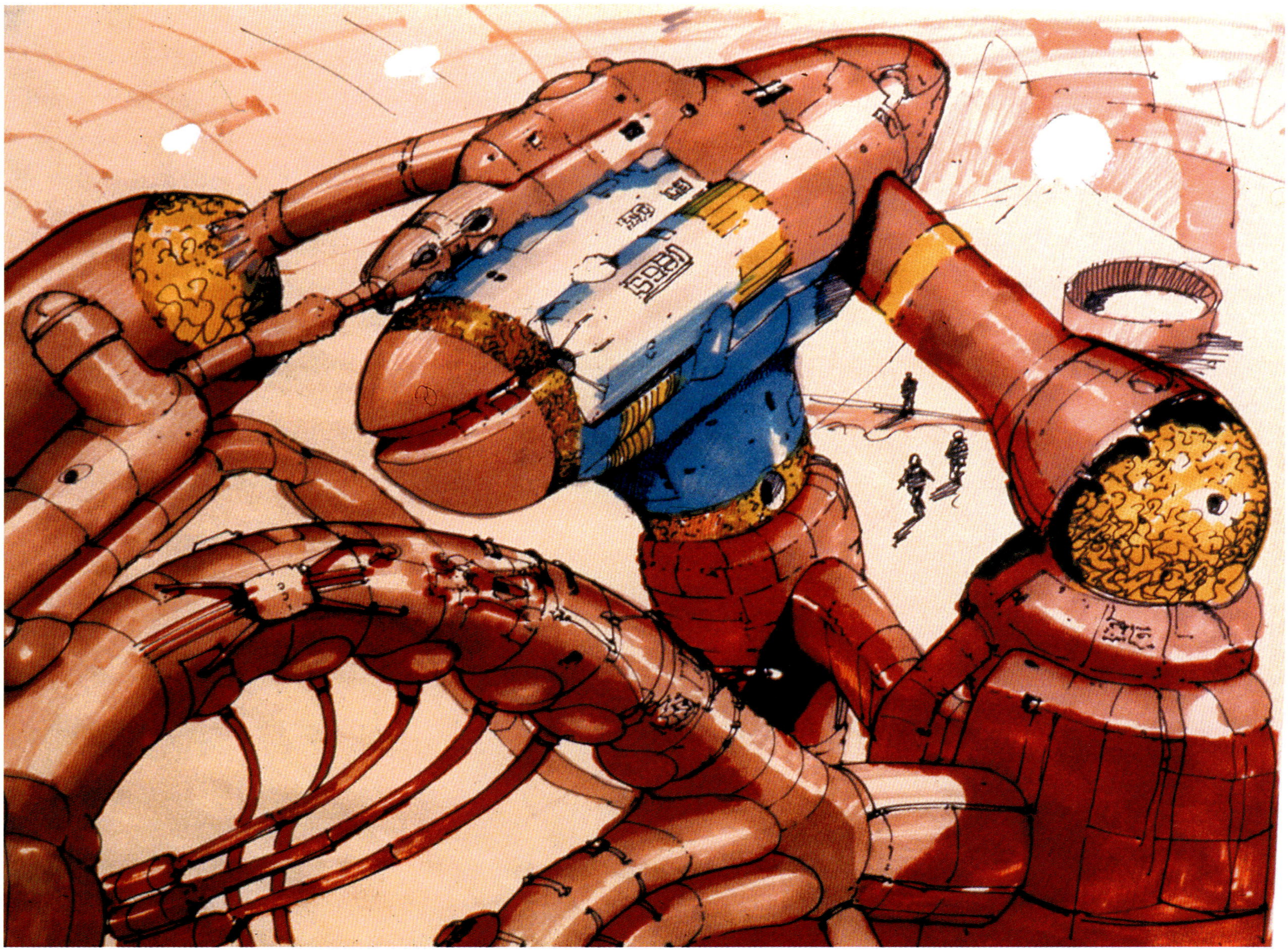

Above, Opposite Top Right & Opposite Middle: Chris Foss concepts of the Derelict exterior.

Opposite Bottom: A Chris Foss concept of the Derelict interior.

particularly the colouring and patterns on exotic animals. I grew up with the *National Geographic*, copies of the magazine were always around the house, and that's where I got the inspiration for the stripes and bars that appear in a lot of my concept designs.

I remember at one point they were debating what the *Nostromo* was pulling. The *Nostromo* was supposed to be like a tug. So I had great fun designing a complicated asteroid for the *Nostromo* to pull. Ridley took one look at it and said, "Bloody hell, we can't have that." I was quite upset. I asked, "Why not?" He said, "It's too interesting, Chris. People will want to know what's going on there."

I had a wonderful time staying with Ron and his wife Robin in LA. Ron and I had great fun exploring the studio backlot and pranking each other when we needed a break. And it goes without saying that *Alien* is only the film that it is because of H. R. Giger's genius and Giger's genius for design. Giger I already knew before *Alien*. He and I shared the same gallery in Paris. They, of course, thought he was bloody weird on the set, because he was up to his elbows in rotting sheep meat. But the alien itself, which has created a whole iconic look, that was genius.

Alien is a marvelous film, though I was a bit disappointed that the sharpness of Dan's original concept got diluted. Obviously, I terrifically enjoyed watching it. I think Sigourney Weaver was brilliantly cast. As was Harry Dean Stanton. The scene where the alien bursts out of the guy's chest was very well done. I used to like taking people to the cinema and not telling them about it. I would get bruises on my arm where my companion had gripped me in shock.

Starting out as a concept artist on *Alien* and those other films, I was in the right place at the right time. In the early days, the *Star Wars* days, everyone was saying, "How do we make space ships? How do we go about this?" That's when they hired people like me. Myself and my colleagues (and friends), like Dan O'Bannon and Ron Cobb, started out during the dawn of a new era in film. We were figuring out a new way of doing things. While now, of course, the whole world and its mother reckons they know exactly what to do, how to make a space ship, how to do everything.

I'm really beginning to feel my age these days, but I look back with pleasant surprise at the way I handled it all. Nowadays people are always professional, but in the old days it was a sort of off-hand happy time. Now it can be quite intense. On *Guardians of the Galaxy*, they were quite incredulous when I turned up with

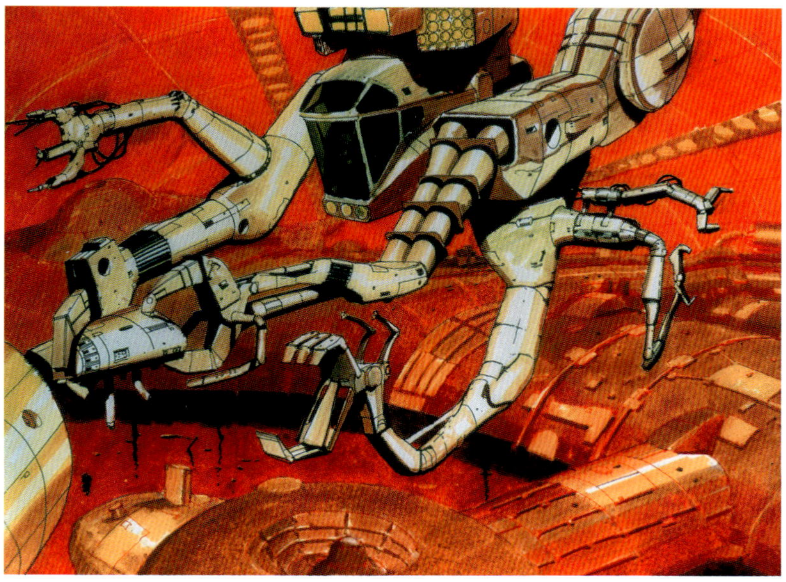

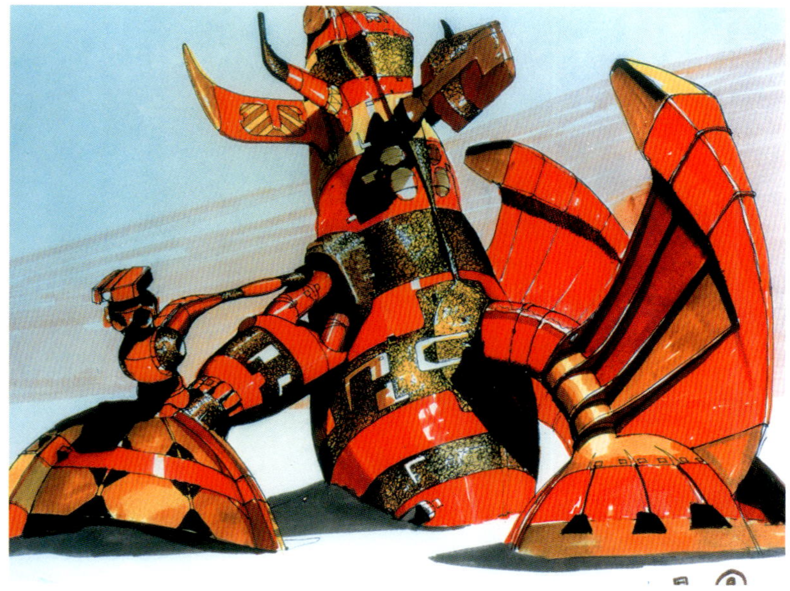

Above: A Chris Foss concept of a machine for *Alien*.

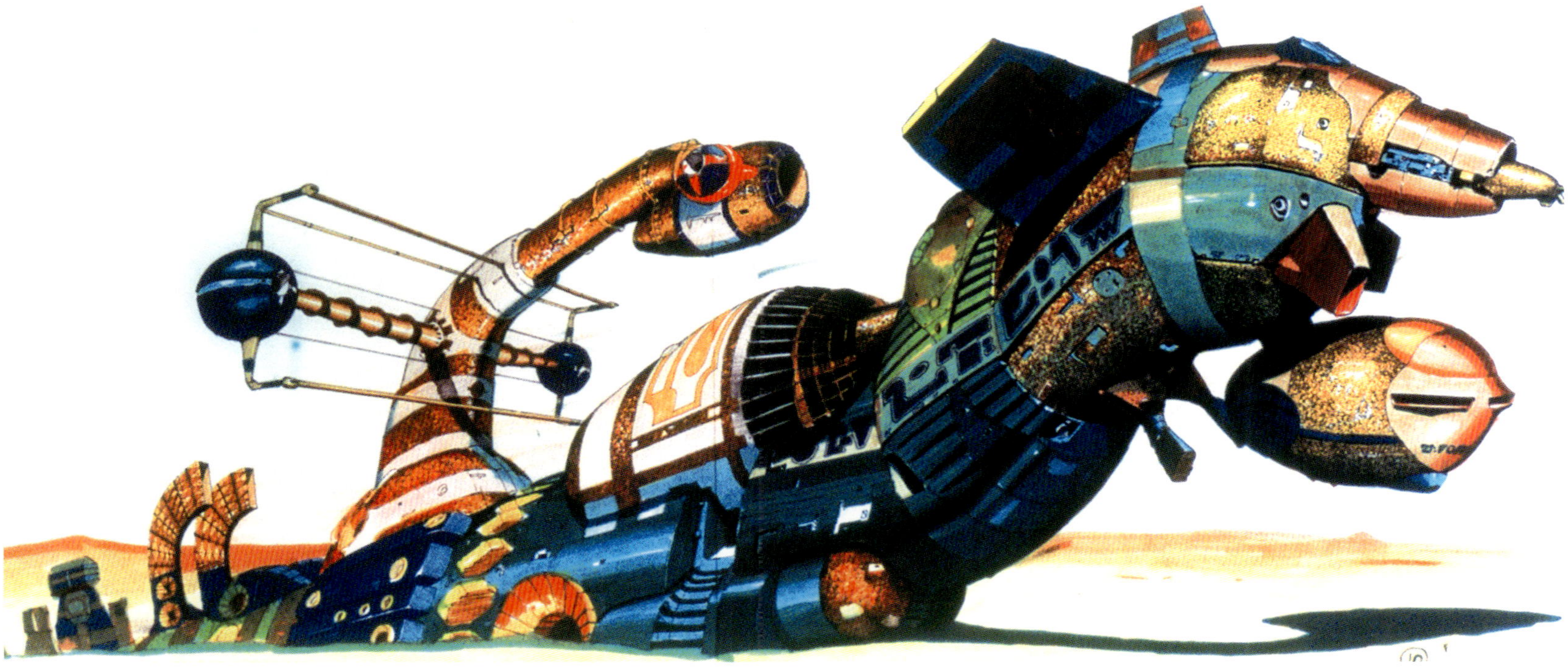

an airbrush and tubes of paint. All of the other concept artists worked digitally and had special trolleys, because they had to transport their computer screens and hard drives.

While I was working at *Guardians of the Galaxy*, several of the artists would pop into my room to say, "Chris, do you realise you started me off in this industry!" So I said, "Wow, right!" Then, of course, when they left, I thought, "My god, what can I do to live up to that!"

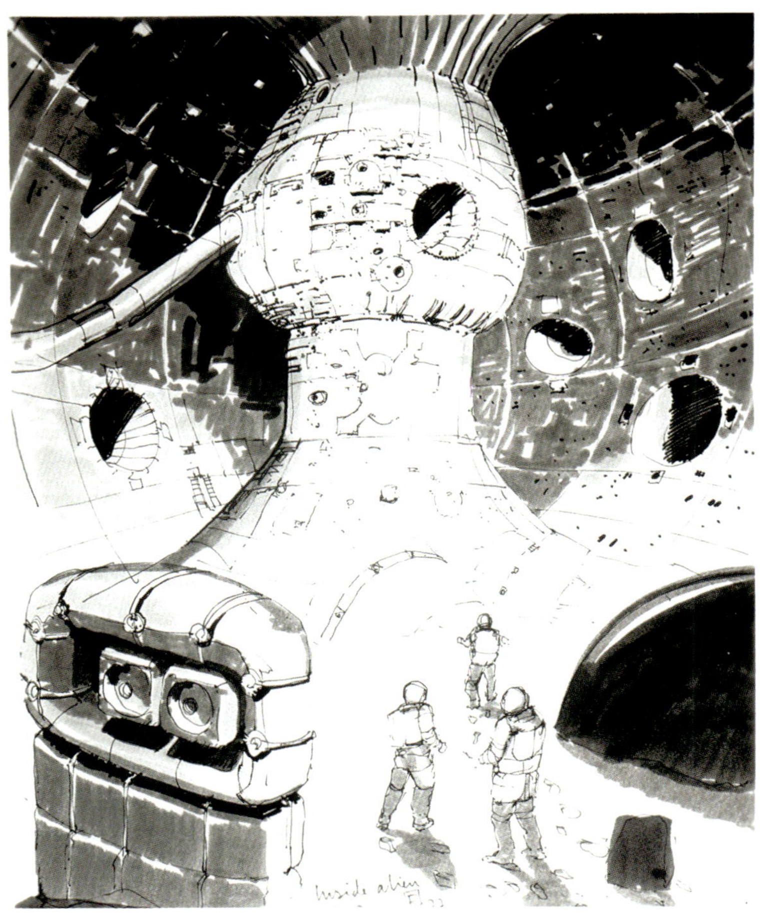

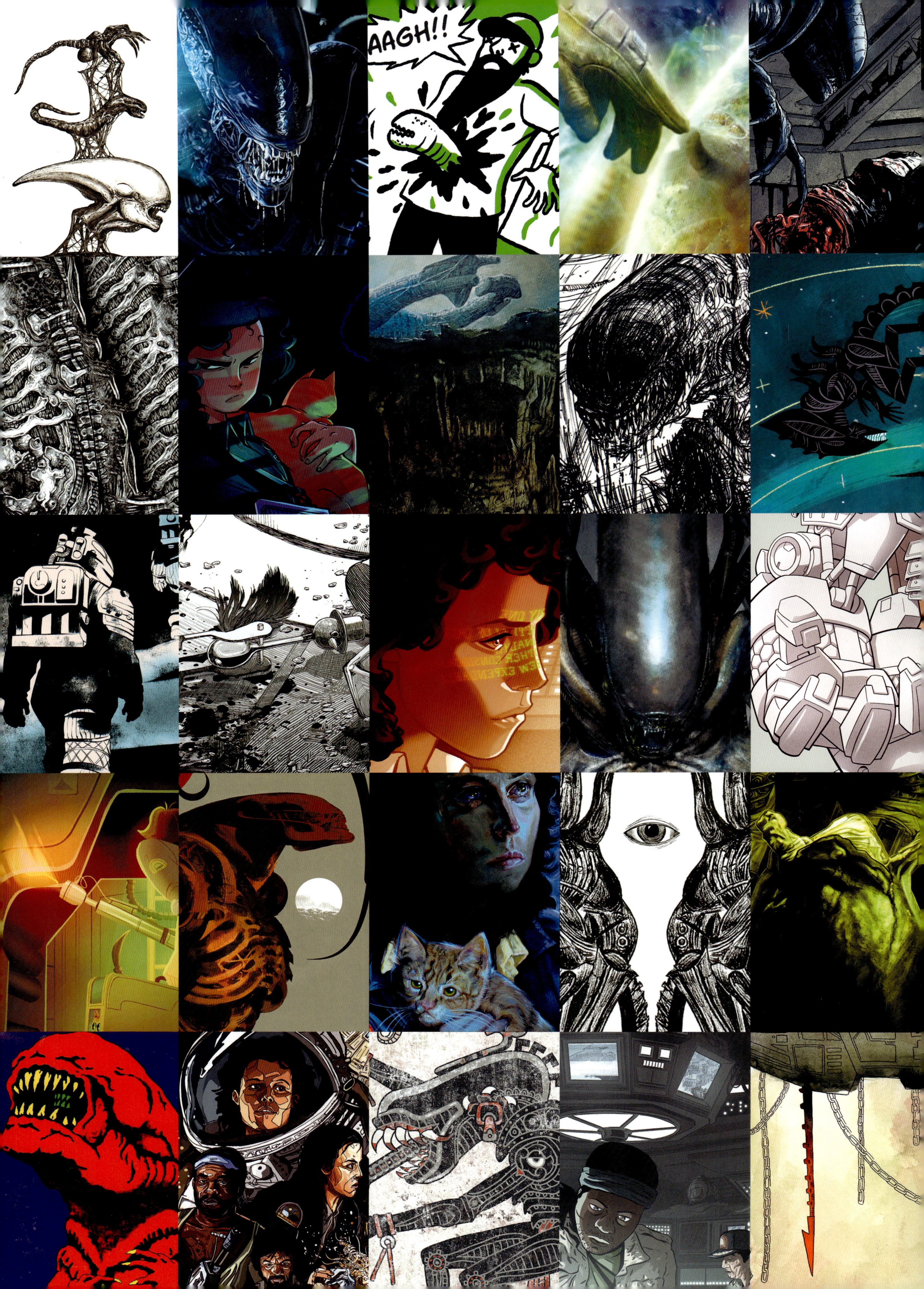
AAGH!!

ALIEN: 40 YEARS 40 ARTISTS

THE ART

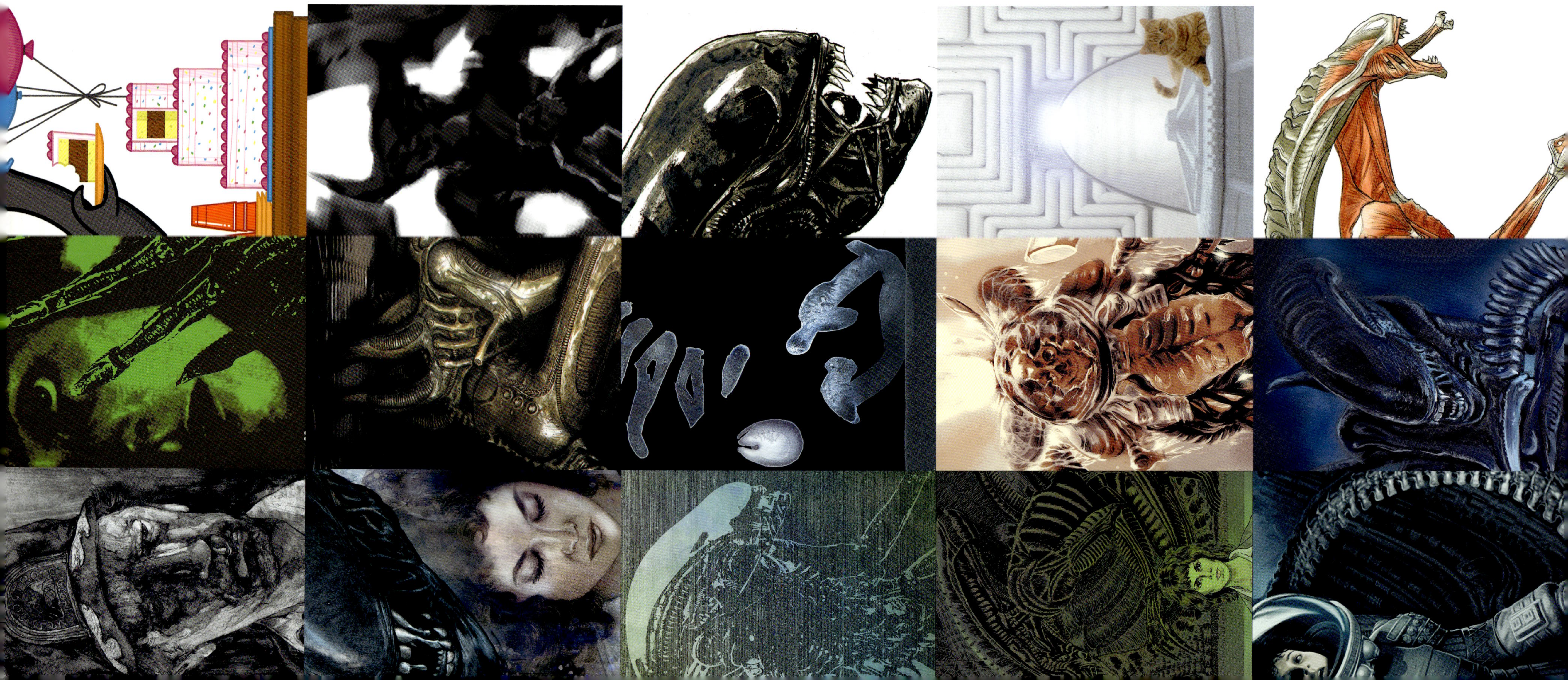

TOM HUMBERSTONE

Waiting | digital | 38 x 27.5 cm

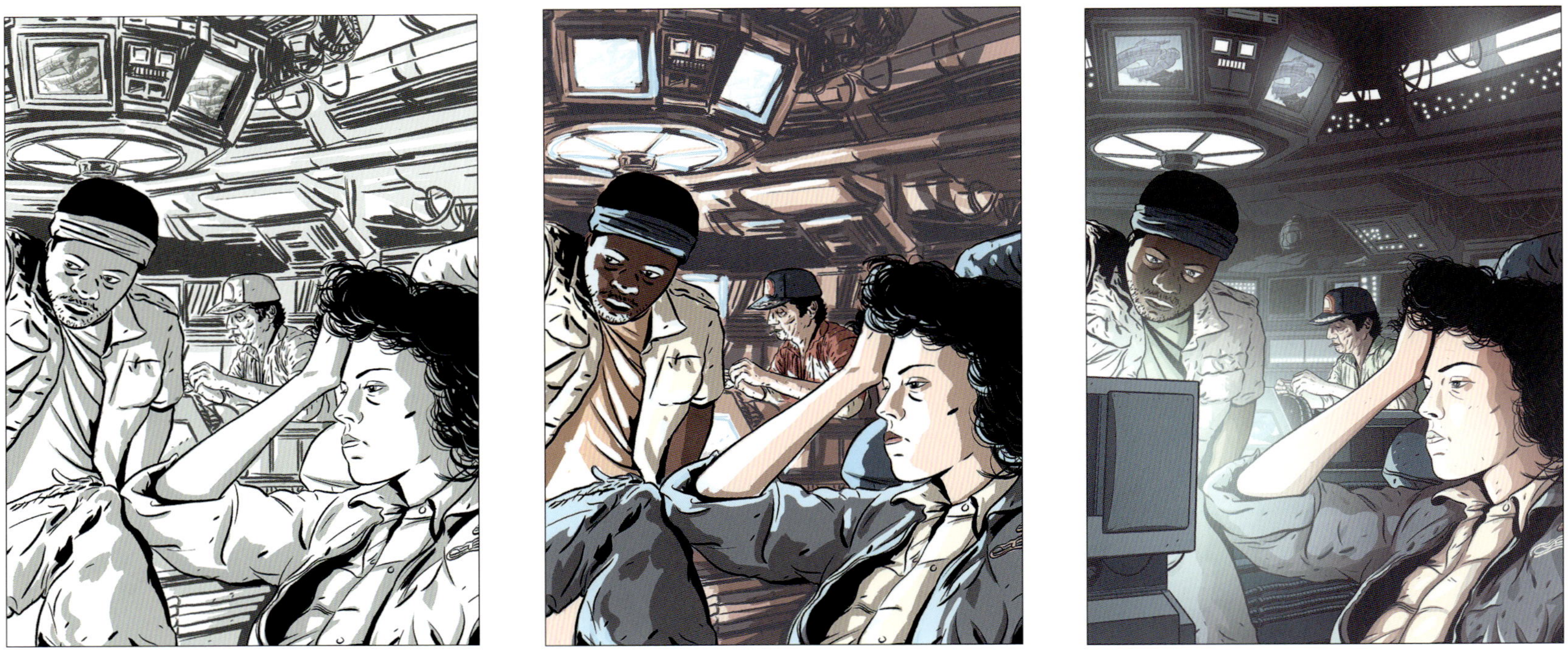

Most cinematic science fiction or fantasy protagonists are aspirational. They're often royalty, or high-status scientists, or colonial naval officers in space, or part of a religious order of warrior monks. More often than not, there's a chosen one. They are rarely working class.

Alien's crew of blue-collar space-truckers aren't special. In fact, they barely have any agency. They spend the majority of the film following orders from a faceless corporation that considers their lives forfeit to larger, bio-weaponry, concerns. Through deliberate and precise world-building we're given the impression that, in this future, shareholders and stock options are God. It isn't just the tight spaces and dark corners of the *Nostromo* that create *Alien*'s feeling of claustrophobia. If a terrifying Xenomorph doesn't get you, "The Company" will grind you down eventually.

What was so refreshing about *Alien* (and it's predecessor, *Dark Star*) was that it presented space travel as everyday. As ordinary. Boring even. None of the crew of the *Nostromo* seem the least bit awed by where they are or what they're doing. It's just another day on the job.

Let's go over the bonus situation…

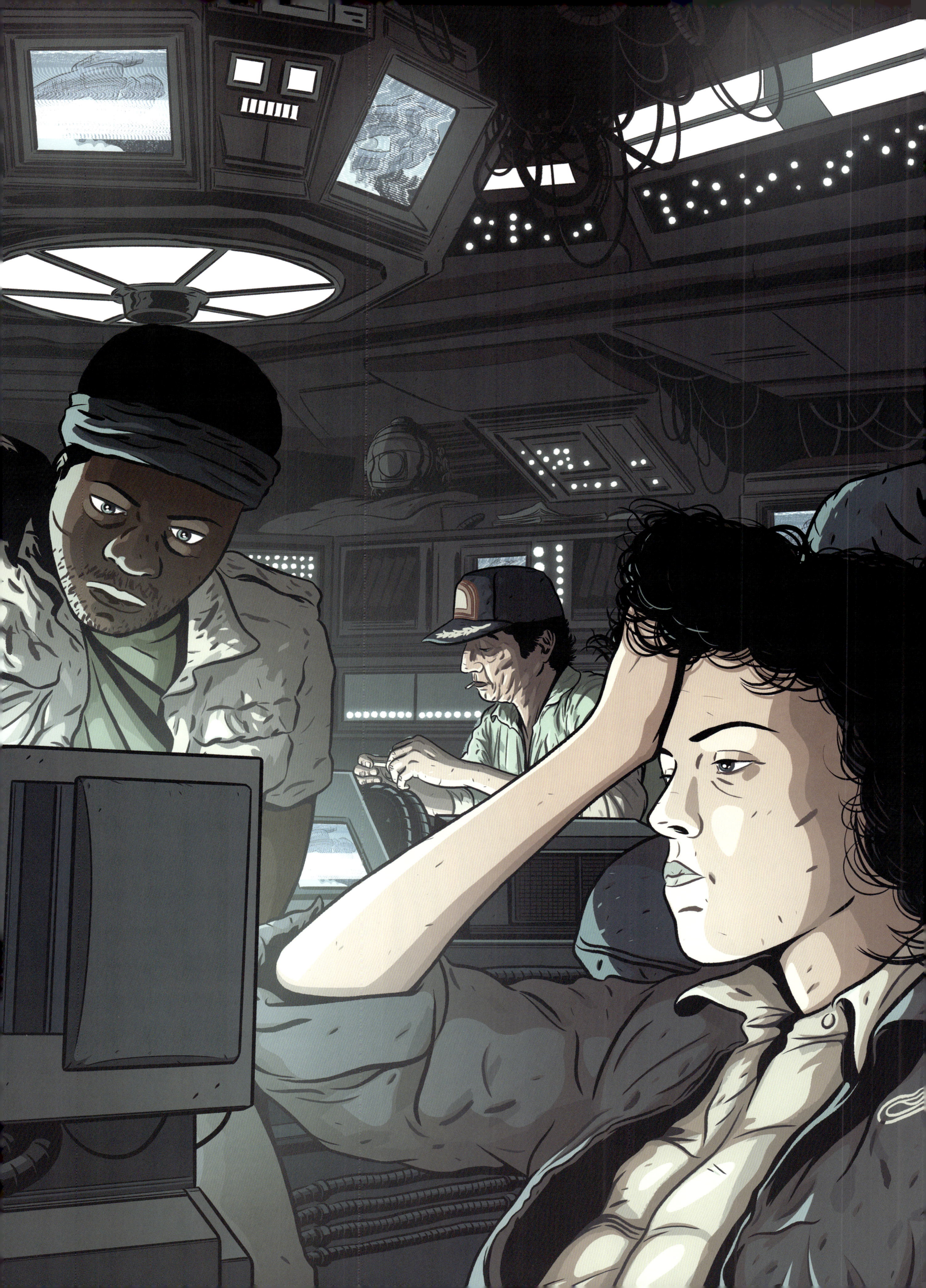

DAVID BENZAL

Beauty and the Beast | digital | 34.5 x 50 cm

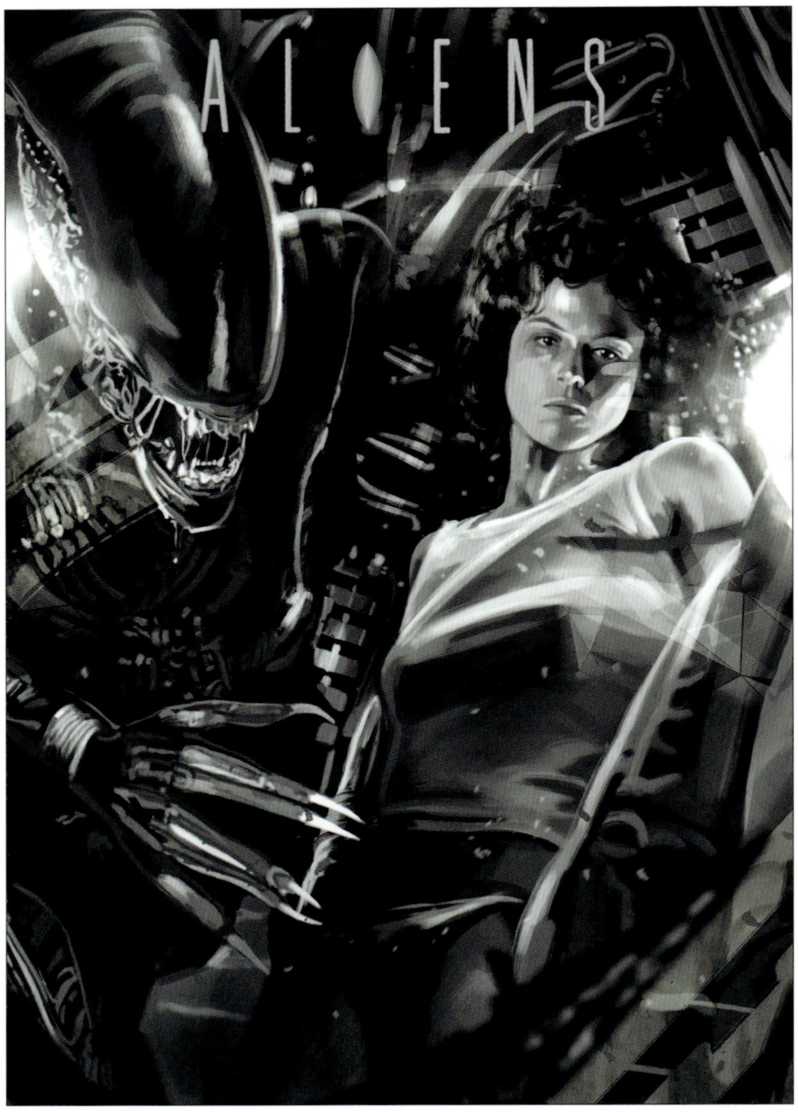

I am really happy to be part of this project, because *Alien: The Eighth Passenger* (as it was released in Spain) was always, for me, one of the best science fiction films of all time. A great reference, in terms of aesthetics – very advanced for its time, particularly in the design of characters, ships, and especially the great design that H. R. Giger did for the creature.

The truth is that the aesthetics of the *Alien* series, taking into account all the films, has always been a great source of inspiration for me, and it has often influenced works I have done related to science fiction, because for me it is one of the most solid pillars aesthetically and culturally in this genre. I also want to highlight the timelessness of *Alien*, the creature's personality and the film's genius is so great that it has remained a current movie.

In my final piece, I wanted to show the mythical relationship of Beauty and the Beast – characters from two different universes, with different natures, whose lives come together in a period of time. Taking into account the whole saga of *Alien* films, the two characters pass through many different vital and emotional states.

For me, *Alien* is the great masterpiece of science fiction cinema.

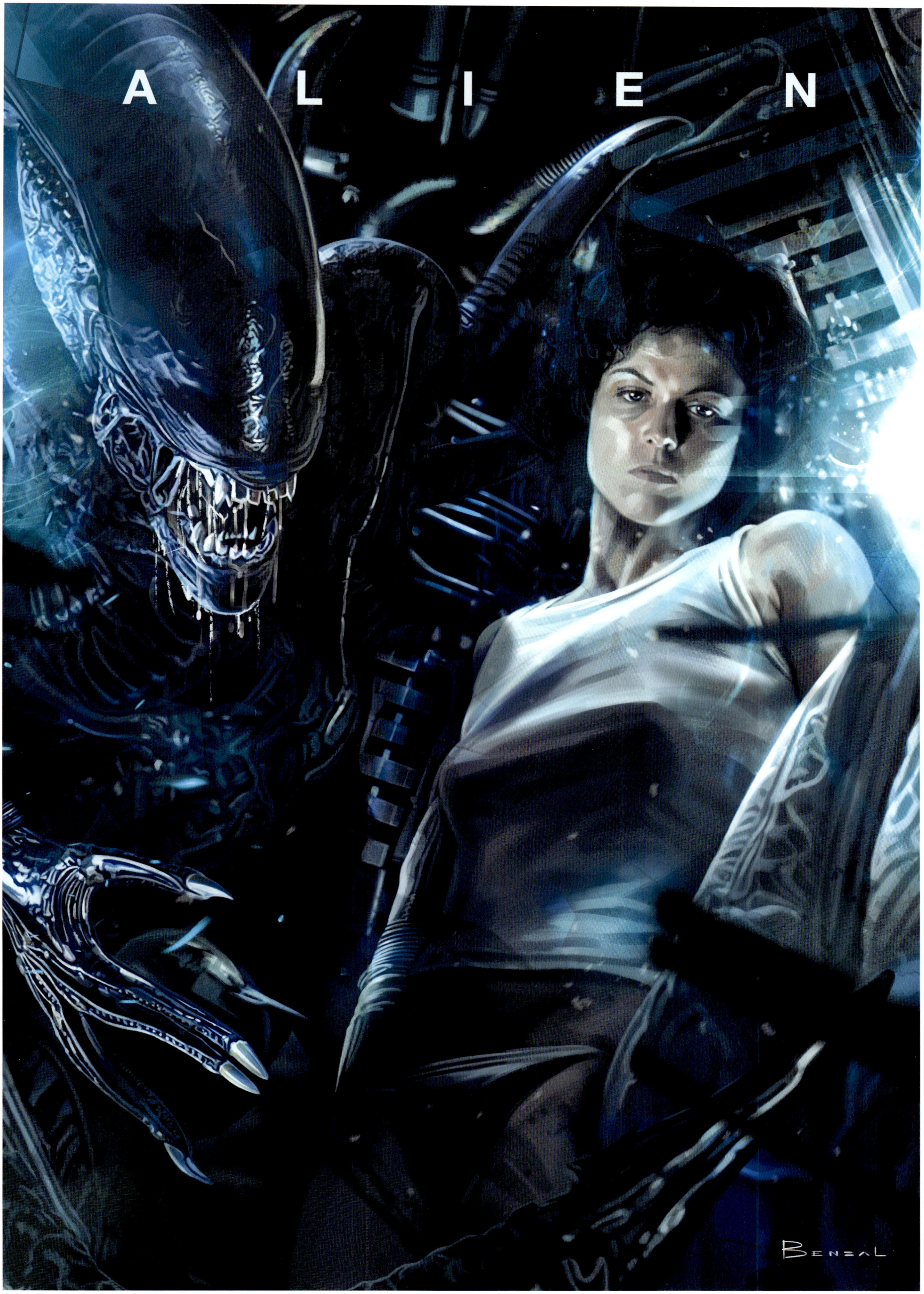
A L I E N
BENZAL

CHELSEA LOWE

In Space No One Can Hear You Scream | digital | 36 x 26 cm

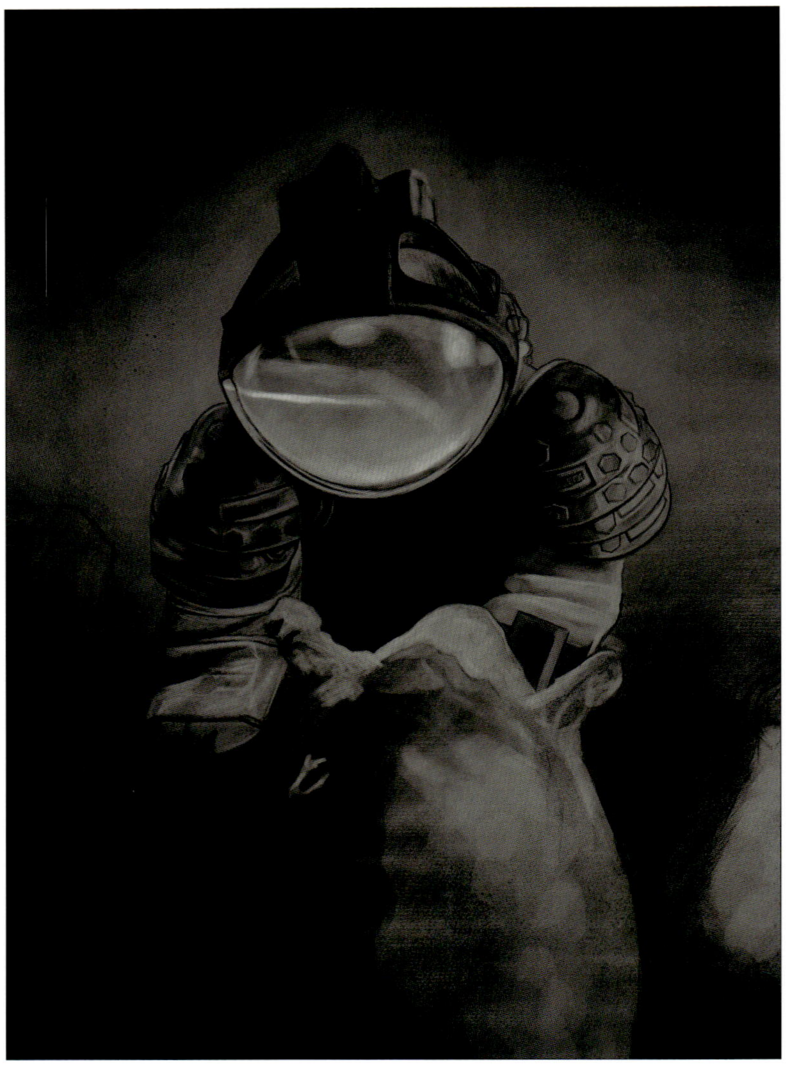

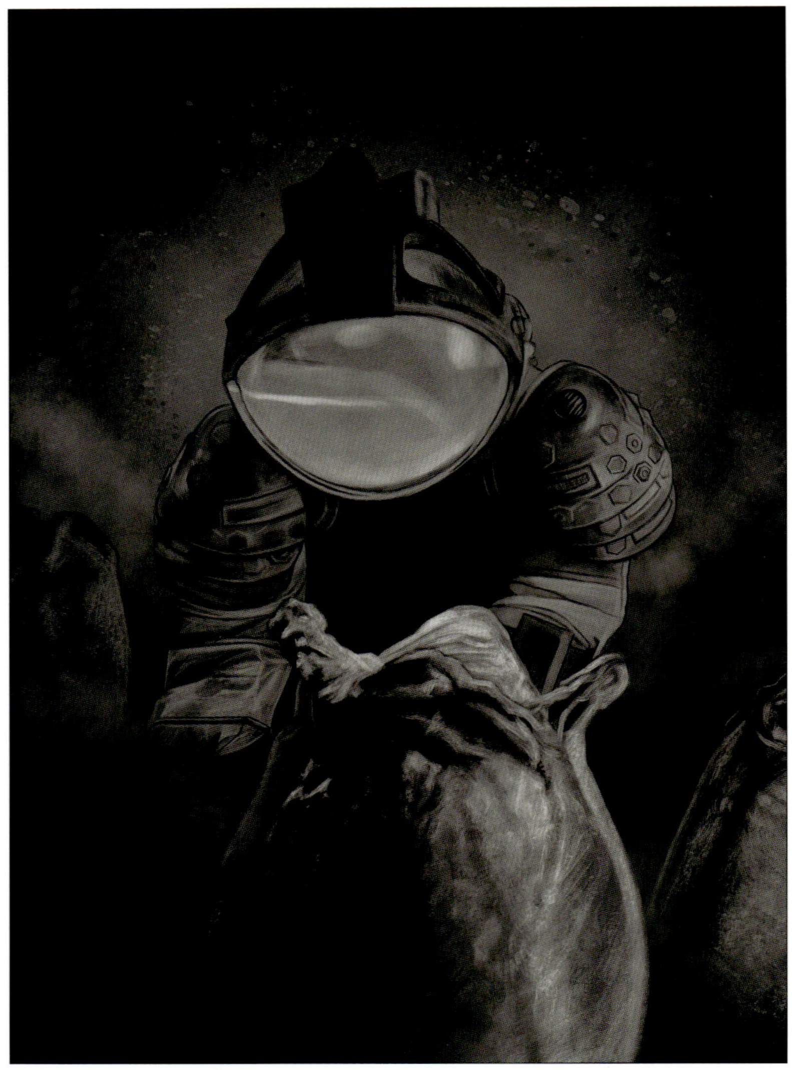

From the stellar cast to the beautiful cinematography and set design, it's easy to see why *Alien* has held up so well over the years. The storyline itself is a wonderful blend of horror, suspense, and psychological thriller. We see just enough of the monster to terrify us, and the plot's build-up is fantastic, as tensions rise while the Xenomorph hunts everyone one by one – all leading to that epic showdown with Ripley.

Upon creating my art, I knew I wanted to focus on an important visual that was central to *Alien*. After cycling through various ideas, I decided to choose the scene that started it all: when Kane discovers the nest of Xenomorph eggs. In my illustration I depict Kane right before things go downhill for him. He's crouching over one of the eggs, examining it curiously, when it opens up. This is the first of many moments that keep me on the edge of my seat as I anticipate the facehugger jumping out and latching onto him.

Most of the art was created in Procreate on the iPad Pro before I transferred it to Photoshop to finish it off. It was originally drawn as a grayscale illustration. I then started colorizing it. I decided to go with green as the central color scheme in order to give it an unsettling, creepy feeling. By doing this, I hope to have captured the uneasiness of the scene – leaving the viewer to remind themselves: *In space no one can hear you scream.*

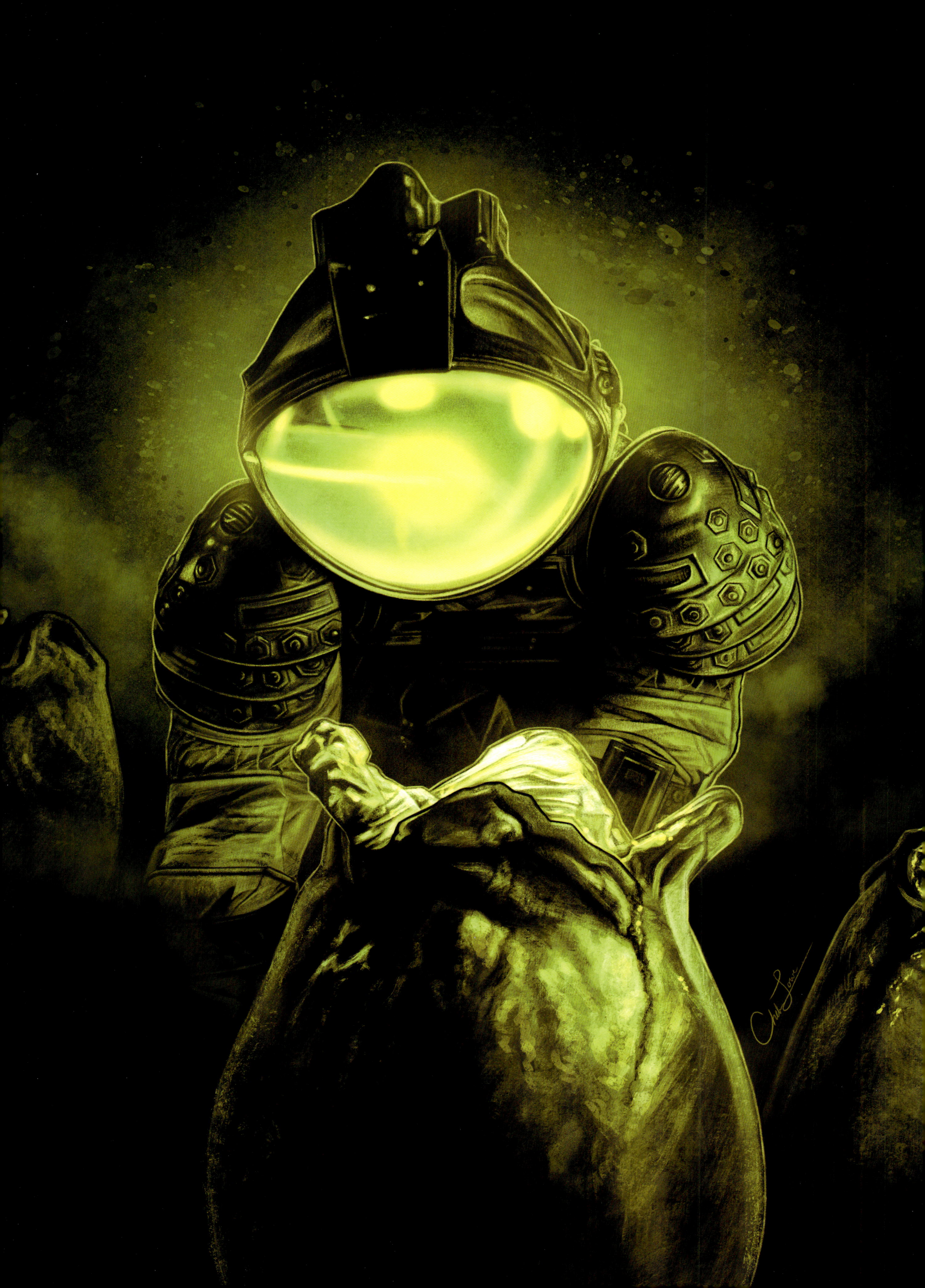

JORGE 'QUETZA' GARZA

Mesoamerican Alien | digital | 36.5 x 26 cm

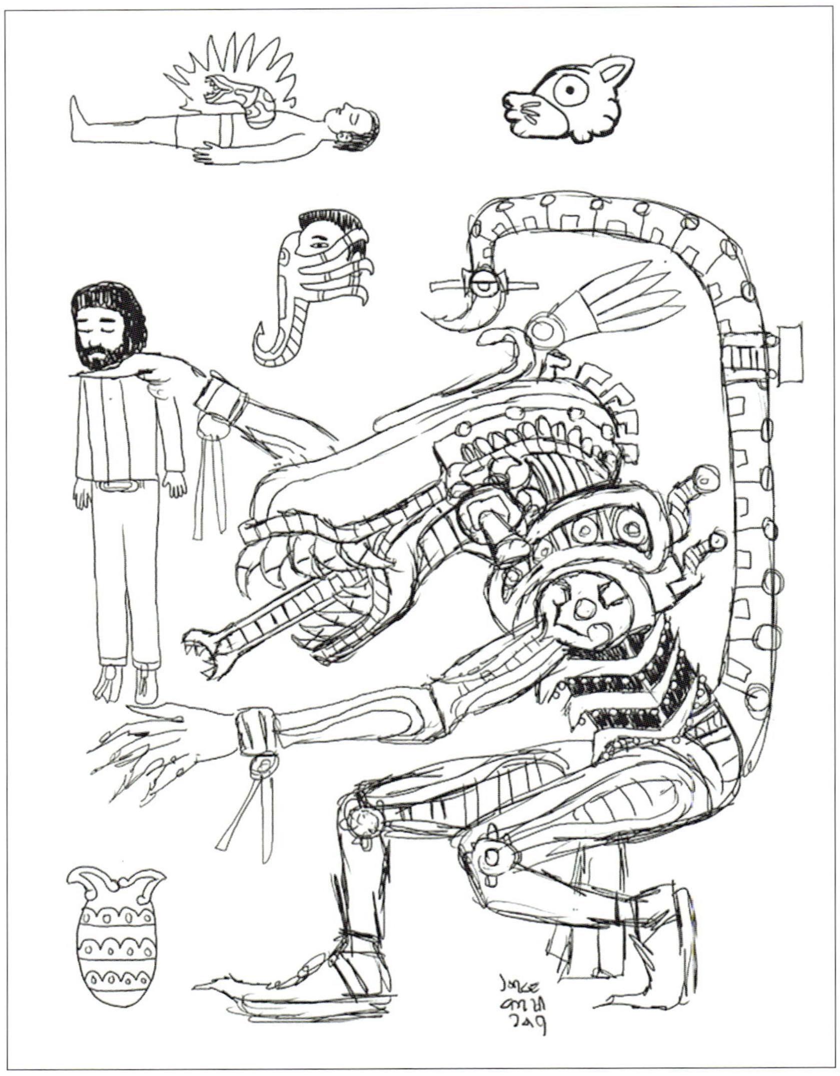

I have been into horror, sci-fi and comics for as long as I can remember. I remember hearing about *Alien* from classmates. It sounded cool, scary, and I really wanted to check it out. This film takes the sci-fi and horror theme into a new world! What I love about the film is, despite its futuristic setting, the creature seems to be very ancient. That history is touched on a little, but having that adds so much depth to the alien and background. I am very into ancient cultural art (specifically Mesoamerican) and it has influenced a lot of my work. I thought it would be cool to illustrate this in a style of a series of mine, as if the creature visited Earth long ago and was recorded. I illustrated the various stages of the alien, as if to serve as a warning for anyone who views this mural.

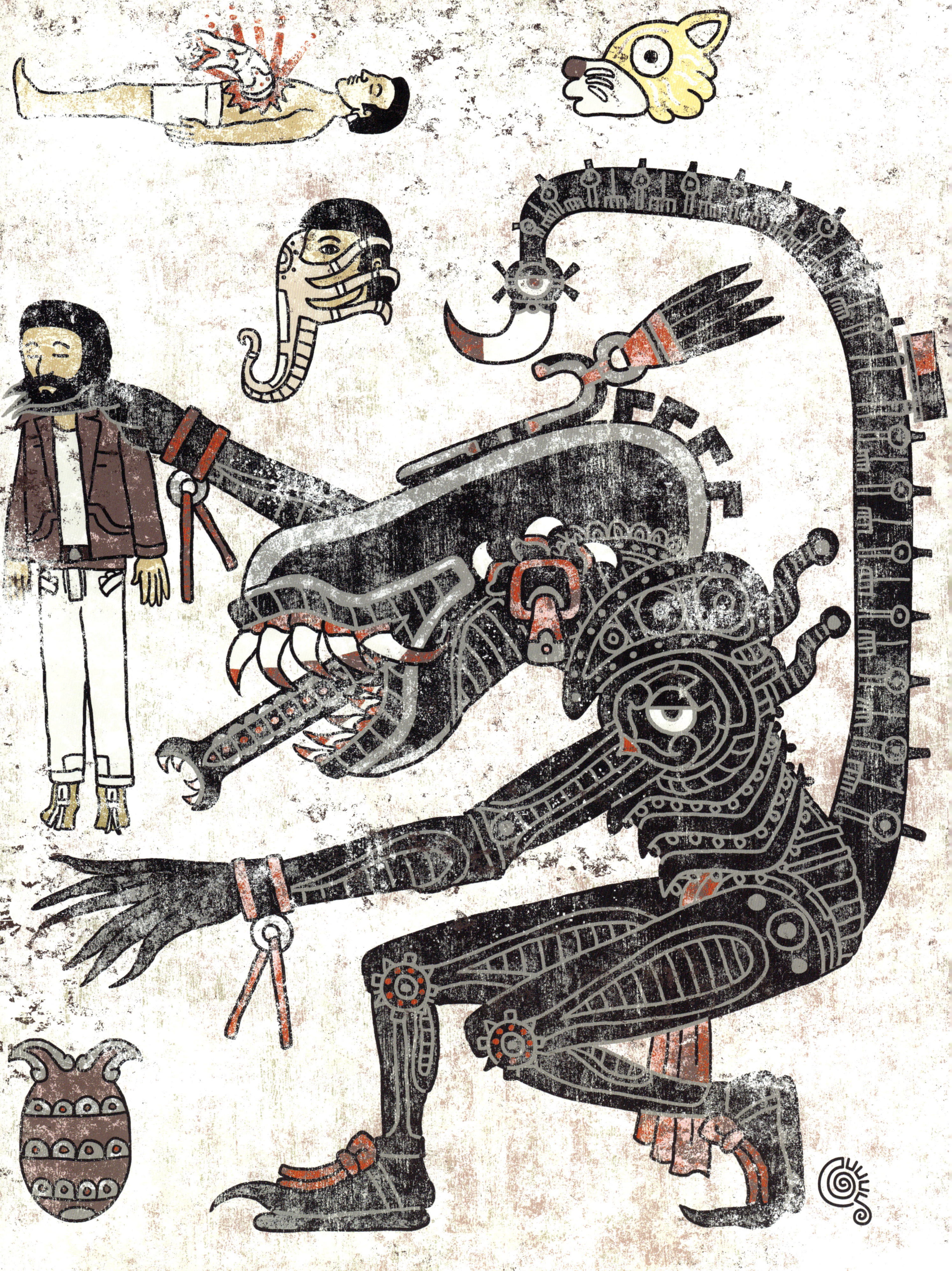

FERNANDO 'FRO' REZA

ALIEN | digital | 45 x 30 cm

I remember first seeing the H. R. Giger alien design as a child. Way before I was old enough to see the movie. It looked like nothing I had seen before. It was industrial, sleek, weird enough to feel alien, but intricately designed enough to give it a sense of grandeur. It was a mind expanding piece of design.

It would be years until I'd see the film and by then most of the iconic moments had become familiar through second-hand references and parodies. I expected the exoticness and twists to be too watered down by then to be effective. But when I sat down to watch it, I was blown away by how claustrophobic and atmospheric the film was. The Giger designs were the centerpiece in an unnerving dark ride. *Alien* is iconic and its impact can't be overstated, but it's a surprisingly small and intimate film. That's a weird thing to say about a killer-alien-in-space movie, but it's true. The horror comes from isolation and the anxiety of the unknown.

For my design I wanted to do something that captured the atmosphere of the film without relying too heavily on the more iconic imagery that has become so familiar. The film is about the unfamiliar, and as the franchise has grown it can be hard to see *Alien* as the genre defying curiosity it originally was.

In my artwork, the outer portion of the design is spectacle – the flames, the lights. The Giger-inspired textures drape the central figure. A human skeleton with its chest and rib cage busted out from within. Just like the film, a film that's expanded across pop culture, dressed in iconic production design, but at the center an effective claustrophobic piece of horror.

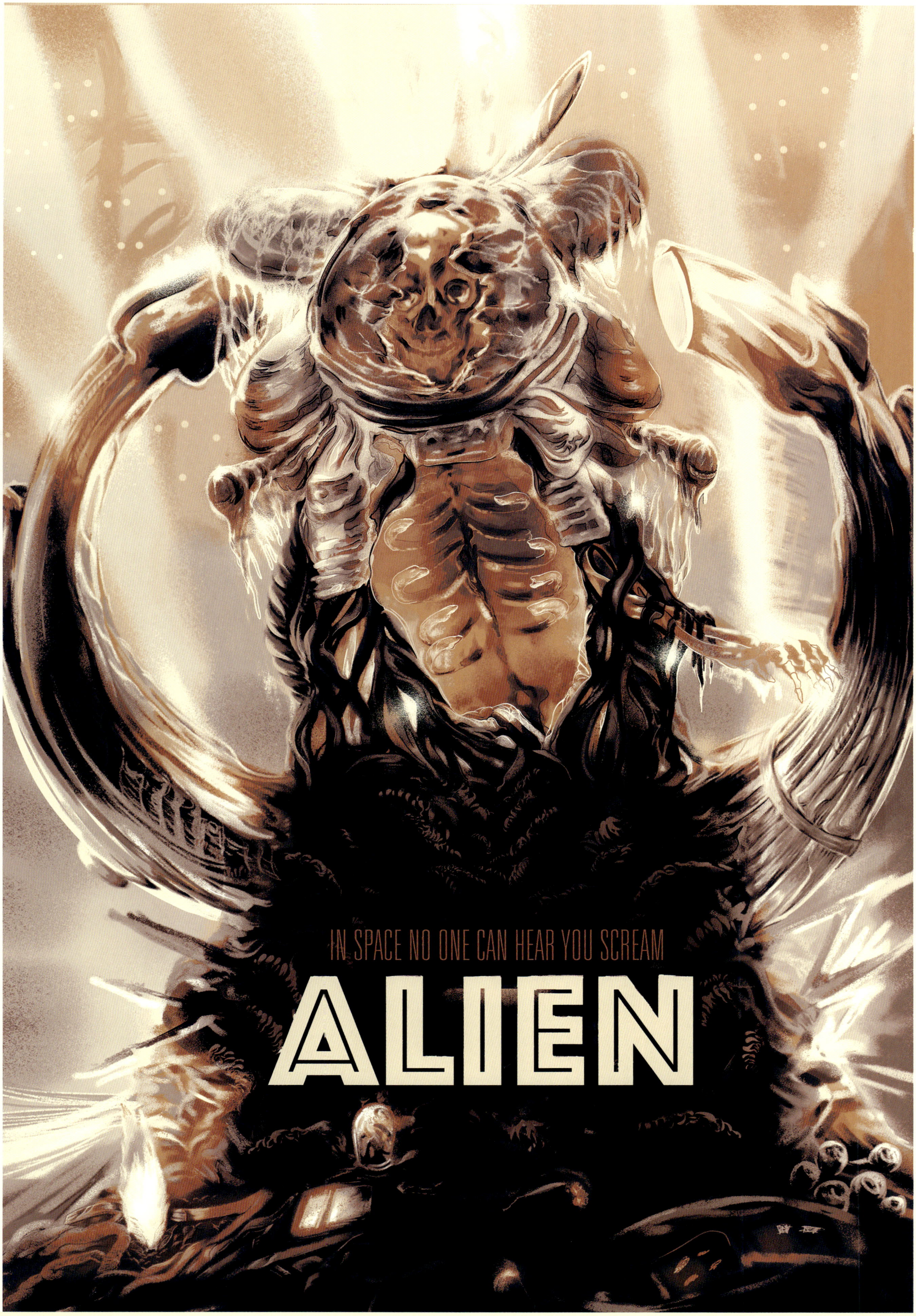
IN SPACE NO ONE CAN HEAR YOU SCREAM
ALIEN

LEONIE O'MOORE

The Perfect Organism | digital | 36 x 26 cm

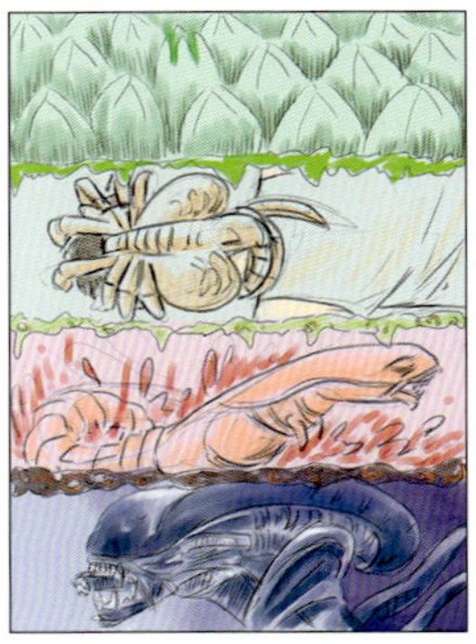

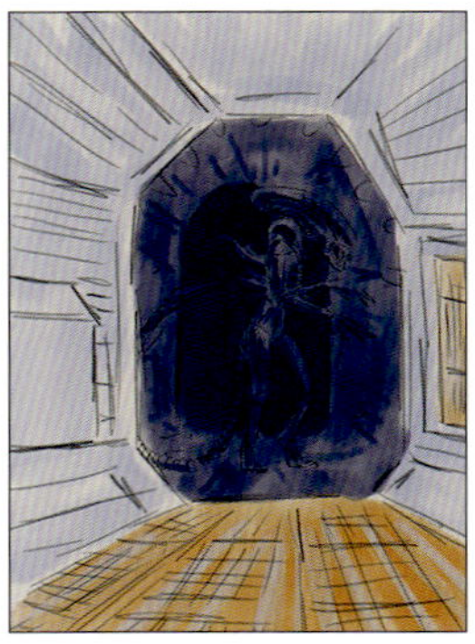

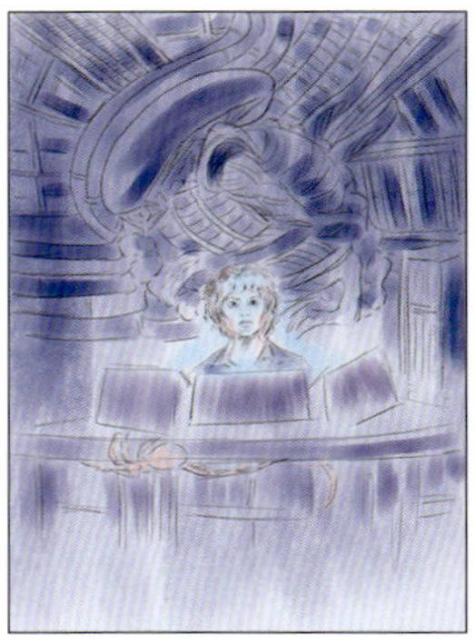

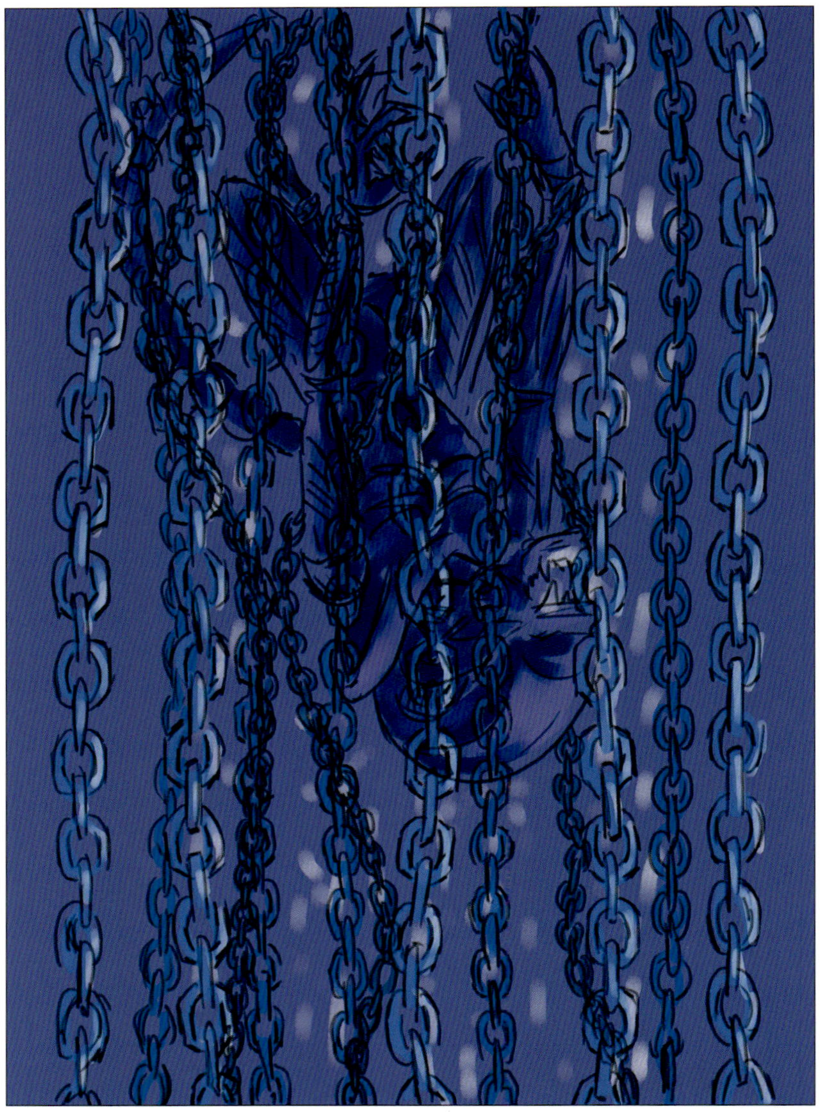

"The perfect organism. Its structural perfection is matched only by its hostility." — Ash

As someone who is passionate about both sci-fi and horror, *Alien* has always been a landmark film for me. Although I've watched it countless times over the years, each time brings a new appreciation.

There are so many intriguing elements to this movie – a space ship turned into a haunted gothic mansion, body horror, the simmering conspiracy. One of the most fascinating aspects for me is the life cycle of the alien, each stage of which brings its own sort of terror, both internal and external. Though Ripley is shown to be capable and smart, we still always feel that she is in danger.

The design throughout the film and the insanely talented line-up of creators involved has left an indelible mark on my own design sensibilities.

H. R. Giger's Xenomorph is a remarkable concept. Even though it's large and monstrous, it could be hiding anywhere. It is this lurking terror that I wanted to capture in my artwork. The piece plays with the combination of biological and mechanical design, contrasted with the human (Ripley). It's this tension of design in *Alien* that I find so captivating.

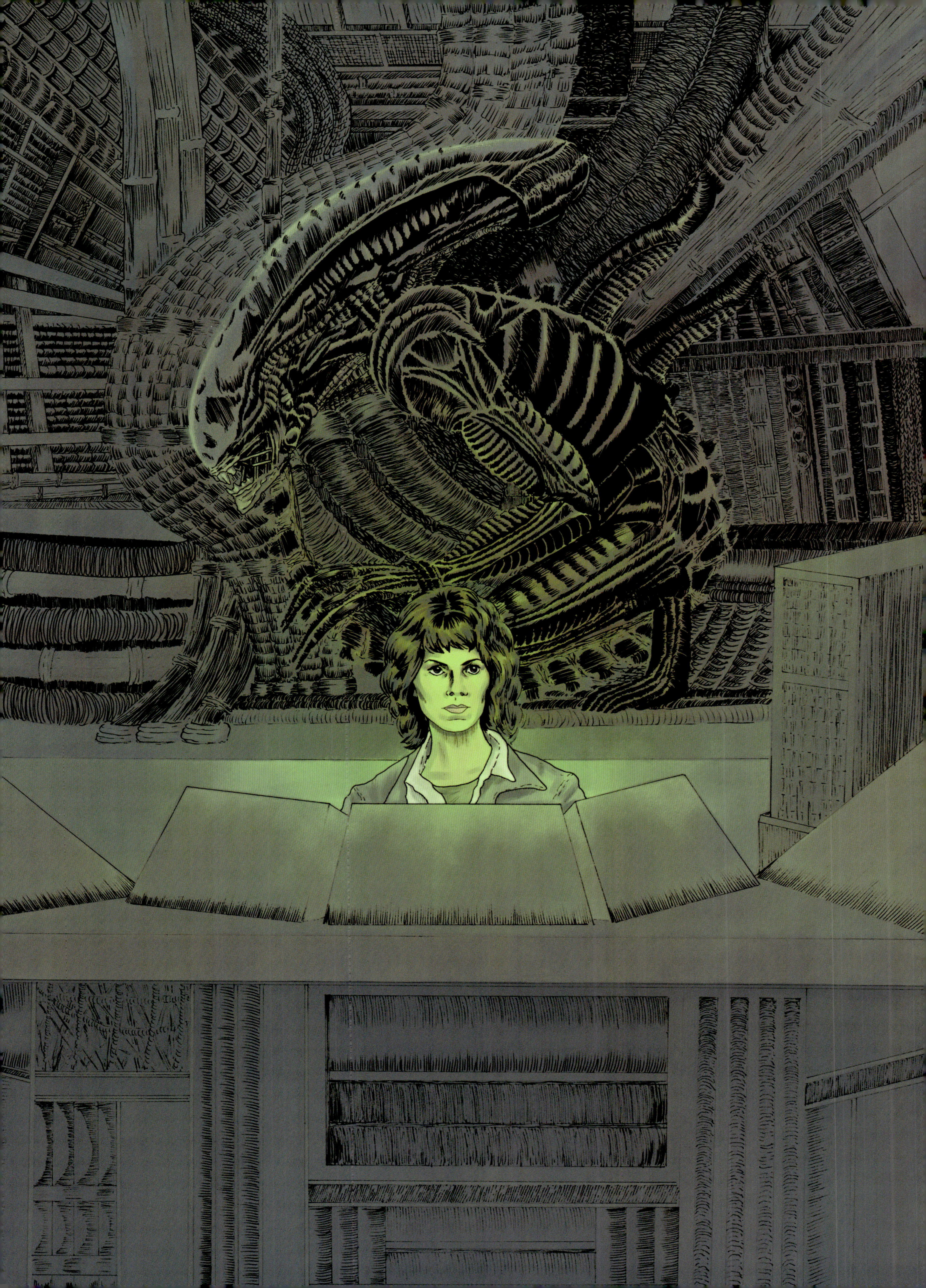

DANE HALLETT

Adam & In Utero | digital | 30 x 21 cm & 51 x 34 cm

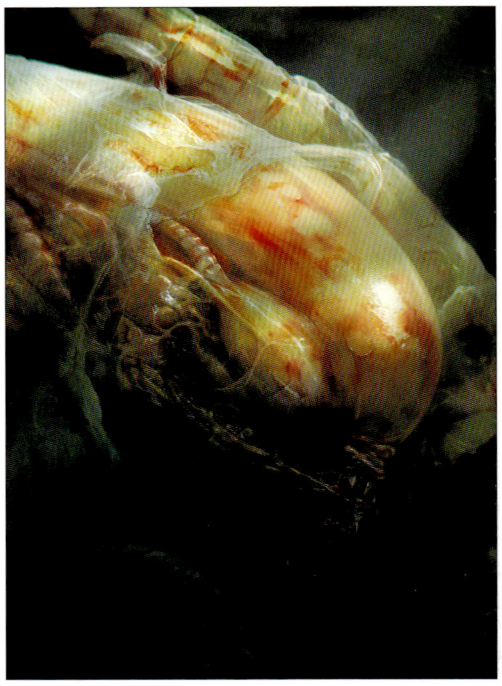

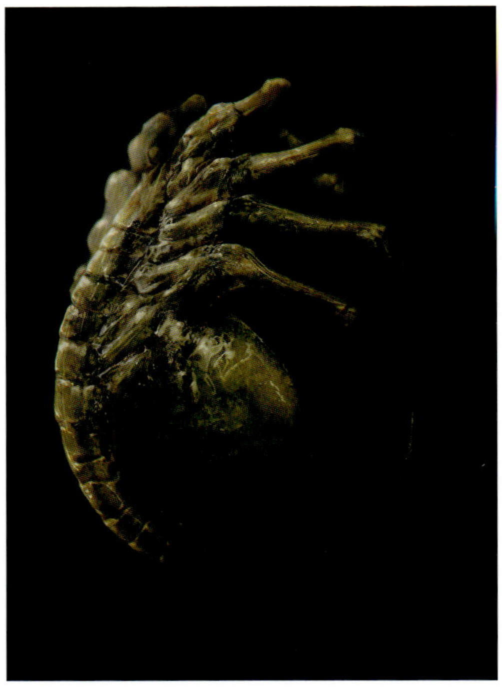

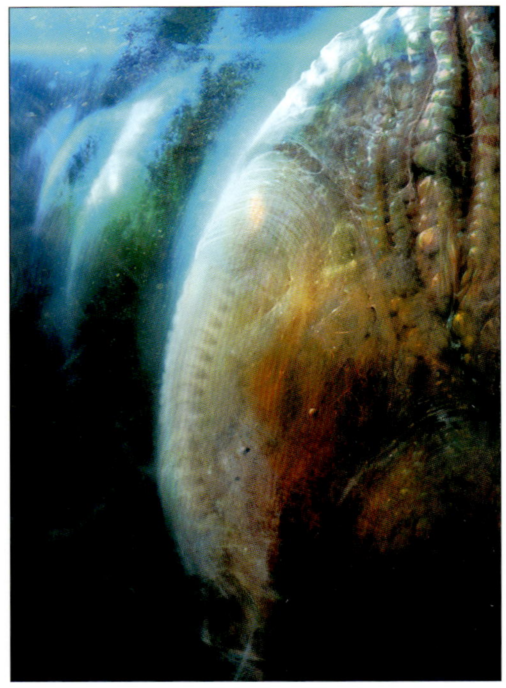

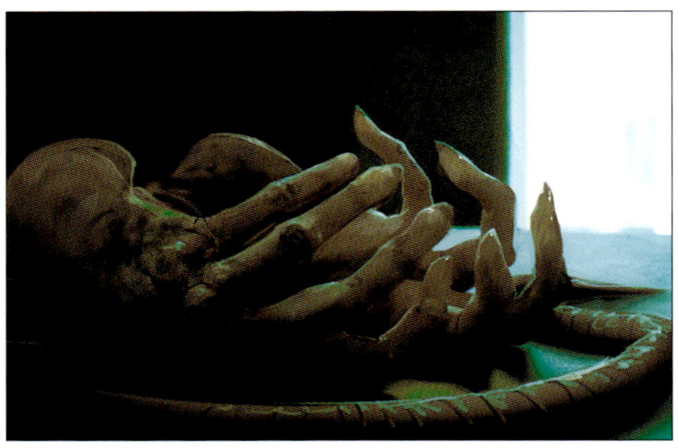

Alien somehow manages to exist in an impossible nebula; deftly weaving nightmare and fantasy, beauty and terror together as though they were always meant to exist as one. As a child, I couldn't understand it. I was utterly terrified of this surreal world. The monster haunted my dreams, the violence affected me and the fear of galactic isolation suddenly felt justified. And yet, I couldn't stop watching it. I *can't* stop watching it. *Alien* connected with me on such a deep level, it was almost chemical. Now, having played a small part in the mythology myself, I have been very lucky to have been in touch with so many people who have fallen under the very same enchantment (probably the same passionate folks reading this very sentence).

So many of the cultural facets we hold dear converge aboard the *Nostromo*. Art, history, sexuality, even architecture, come together to form a bio-gothic monolith. A seductive, mythic tapestry that won me over before I even had the chance to fall in love with such a perfect cast. And so, for the forty year anniversary, I wanted to produce artwork that could serve as love letters to our beloved *Alien* universe that existed somewhere in the vicinity of the great artistry that inspires me (and presumably the host of talented individuals that have already brought something to the franchise).

While riffing on Michelangelo seems like a pretty heavy handed place to start, I couldn't resist subverting the roles portrayed in the original *The Creation of Adam*. I called it *Adam* and put the facehugger in place of God, which felt particularly nasty. Funny, even.

In Utero was an idea I had after playing with all the X-ray art. Also an excellent opportunity to reference the classic Nirvana album...

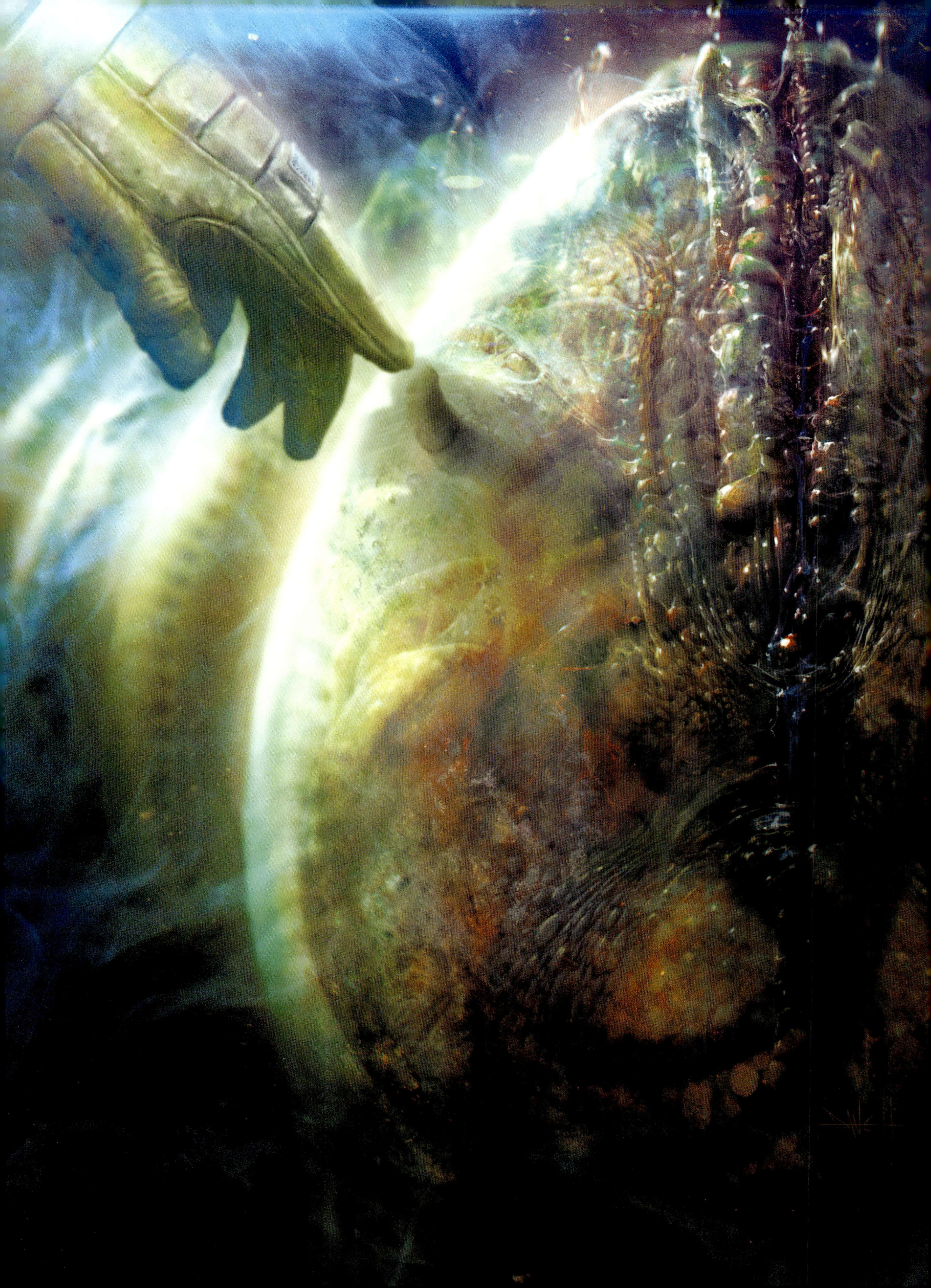

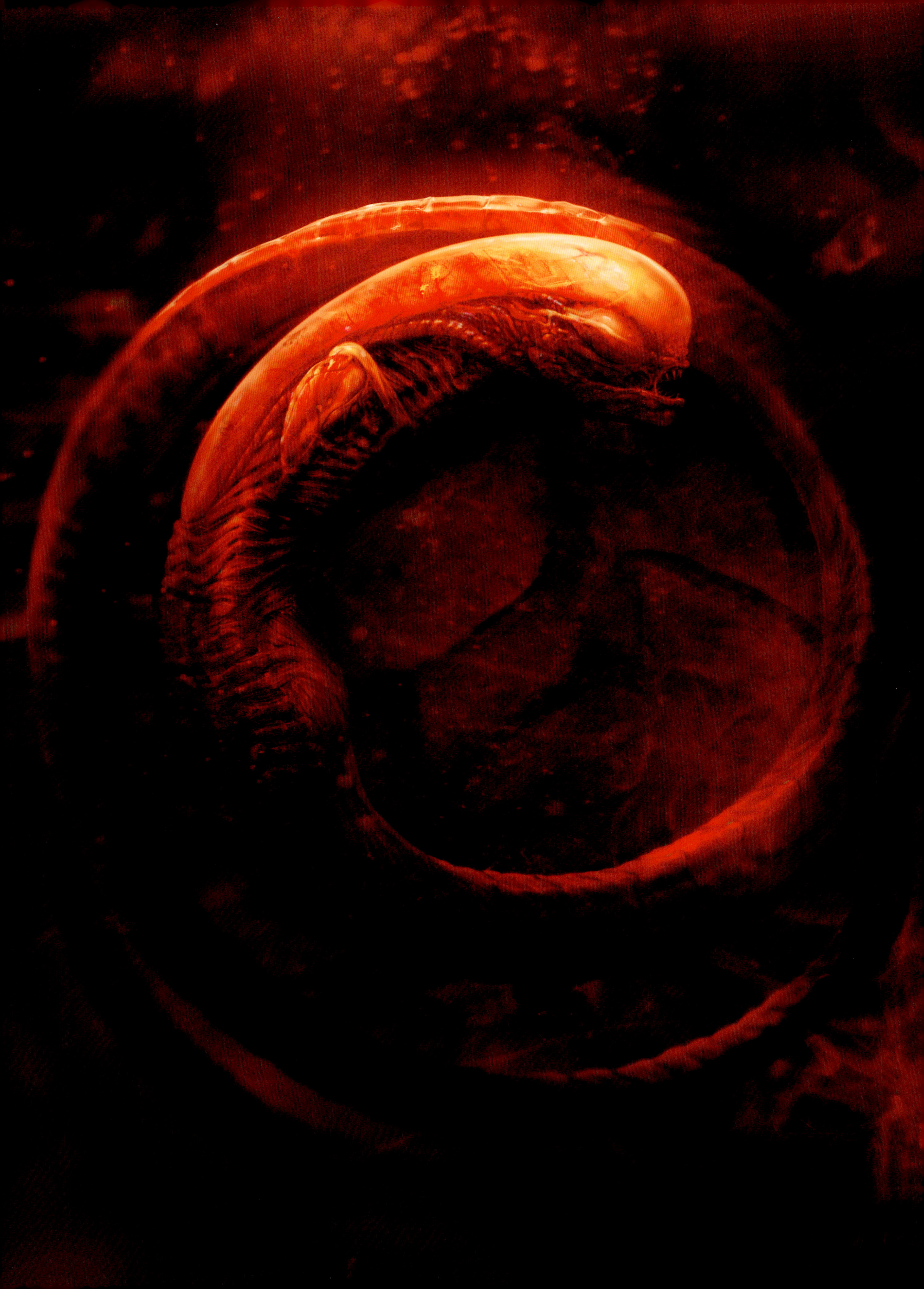

MATT HATTON

Juvenile Xenomorph (Back) & Juvenile Xenomorph (Front) | digital | 37.5 x 27 cm

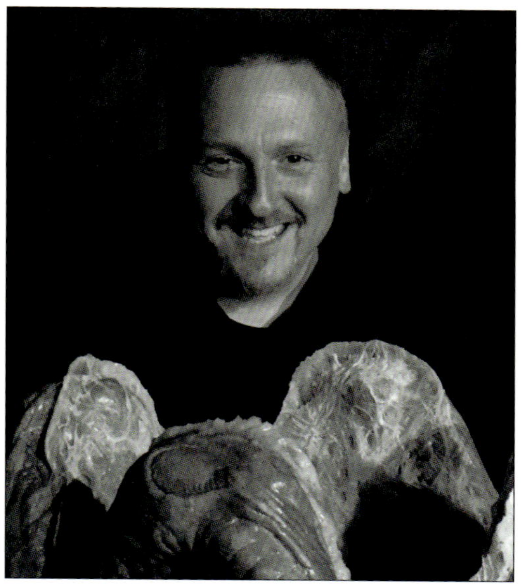

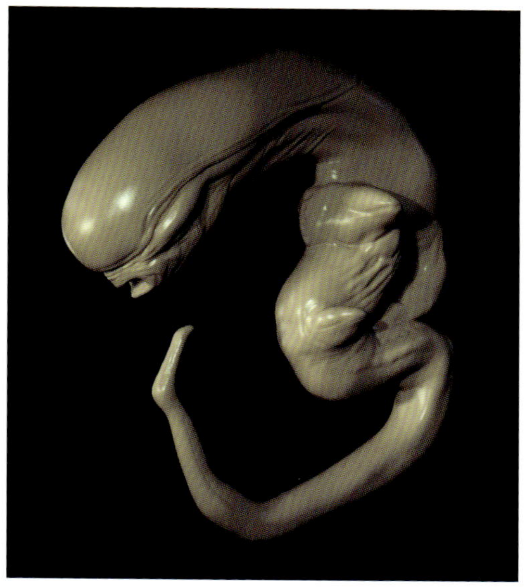

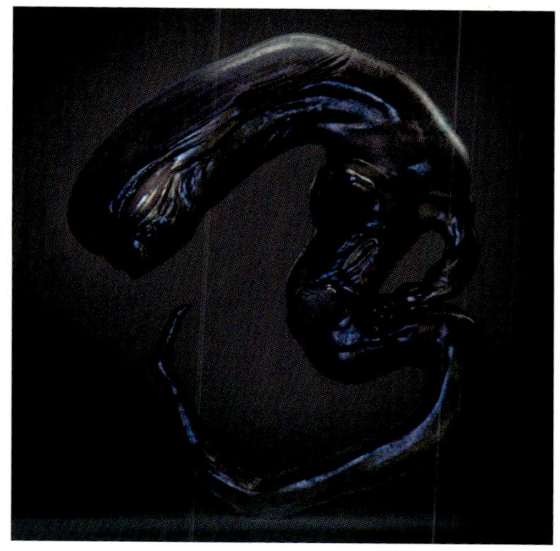

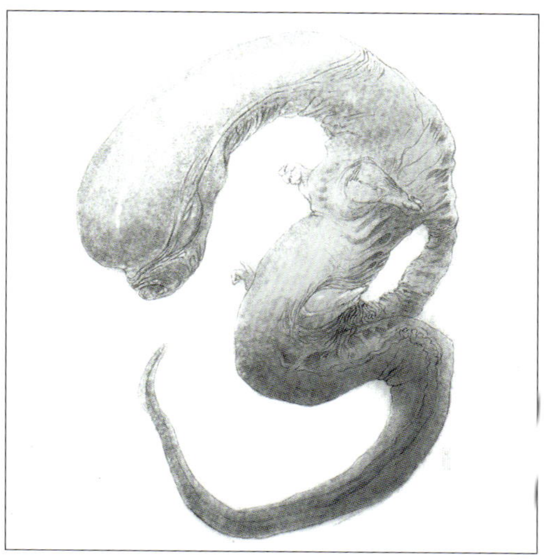

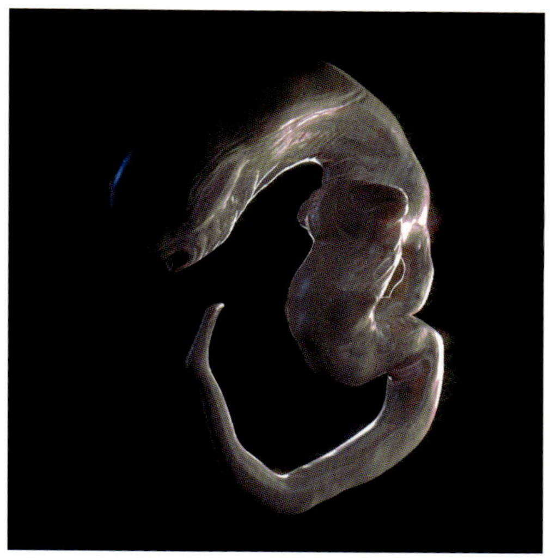

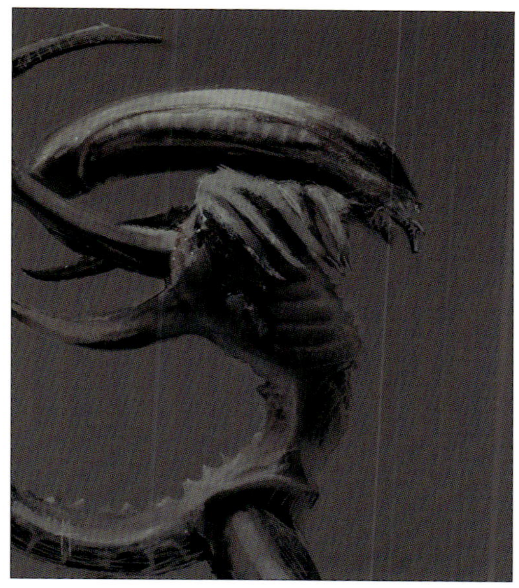

Like most, I saw *Alien* way too young. The story captivated me (I mean science fiction AND horror?!!), even if I was too young to digest the subtext. The visuals awed me, and H. R. Giger's aesthetic overwhelmed me, like many others. My uncle brought it home (when VHS was so new you rented not just the video, but the player, too) and obviously everyone missed the R rating. All I saw was "A L I E N" in classy widely kerned lettering. It must be great. The adults chatted, and I watched, transfixed. After the initial shock of the chestburster, I did think the slightly under-articulated puppet – which looked amazing until it moved – was absolutely hilarious when it took off like a (skinned) rabbit at a dog track. With Muppet tendencies, high voiced and all. And laughed at "Right, right." But that was about the extent of the humor for me.

I've watched it countless times and grown to appreciate it in so many ways. Above all, the combination of inescapable sexuality and threat makes it an uncomfortable and undeniably effective landmark among generally Puritanical (but sometimes hypocritical) Hollywood horror, where sex and violence are usually kept separate. But *Alien* offers no such shelter. And even if the main narrative wasn't new, the direction and the aesthetic still floors me. No one had seen anything like Giger's creations on film. The twin attacks, both visceral and allegorical, are punishing and hang heavy with every frame of the film. Even the beast is both horrible and beautiful. For someone who loves monsters, genre and straight-up great films, it's irresistible.

For my piece, I started out wanting to pay homage to the master Giger's elegant design. So I did many versions of a profile on a plain ground to play up the graphic strength of the silhouette and beautiful curves. Then it occurred to me others would probably be doing amazing and accurate versions of the beast. I thought about a triptych, as I love the idea of religious and sacrilegious imagery and venerating what are to me essentially a space-borne/biblical plague of locusts. Then I realised it was too hard to make that work in book format, but that a diptych would work, linking front and back paper-doll style. And going for a painterly/non-photographic look. *Then* it occurred that we never saw a juvenile version of the *Alien* in the first film, so why not do something a little different while still paying homage. I also wanted to incorporate amongst Giger-esque Egyptian and Nouveau elements a foetus version (that I'd previously done as a concept for a poster). I hope people like it!

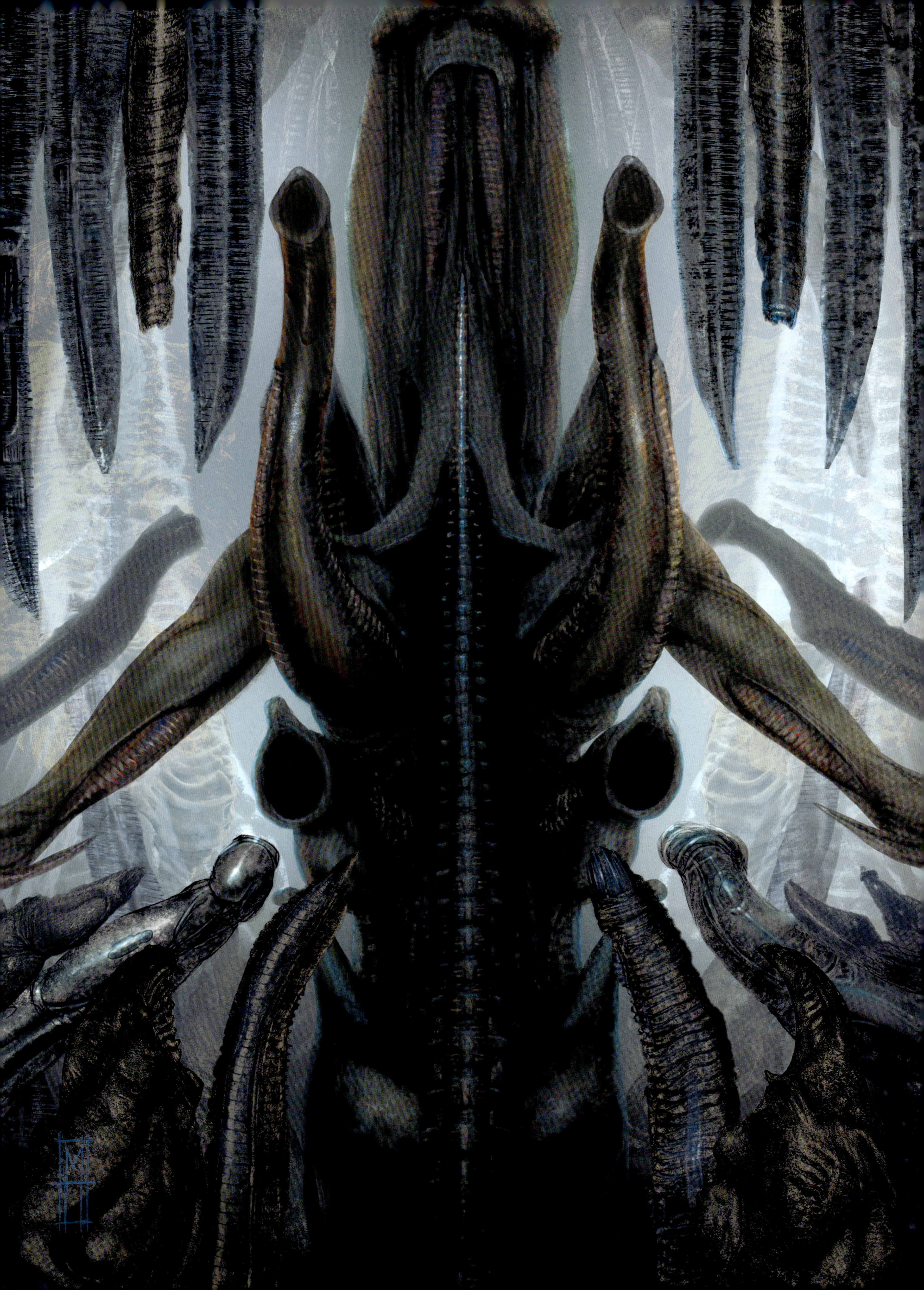

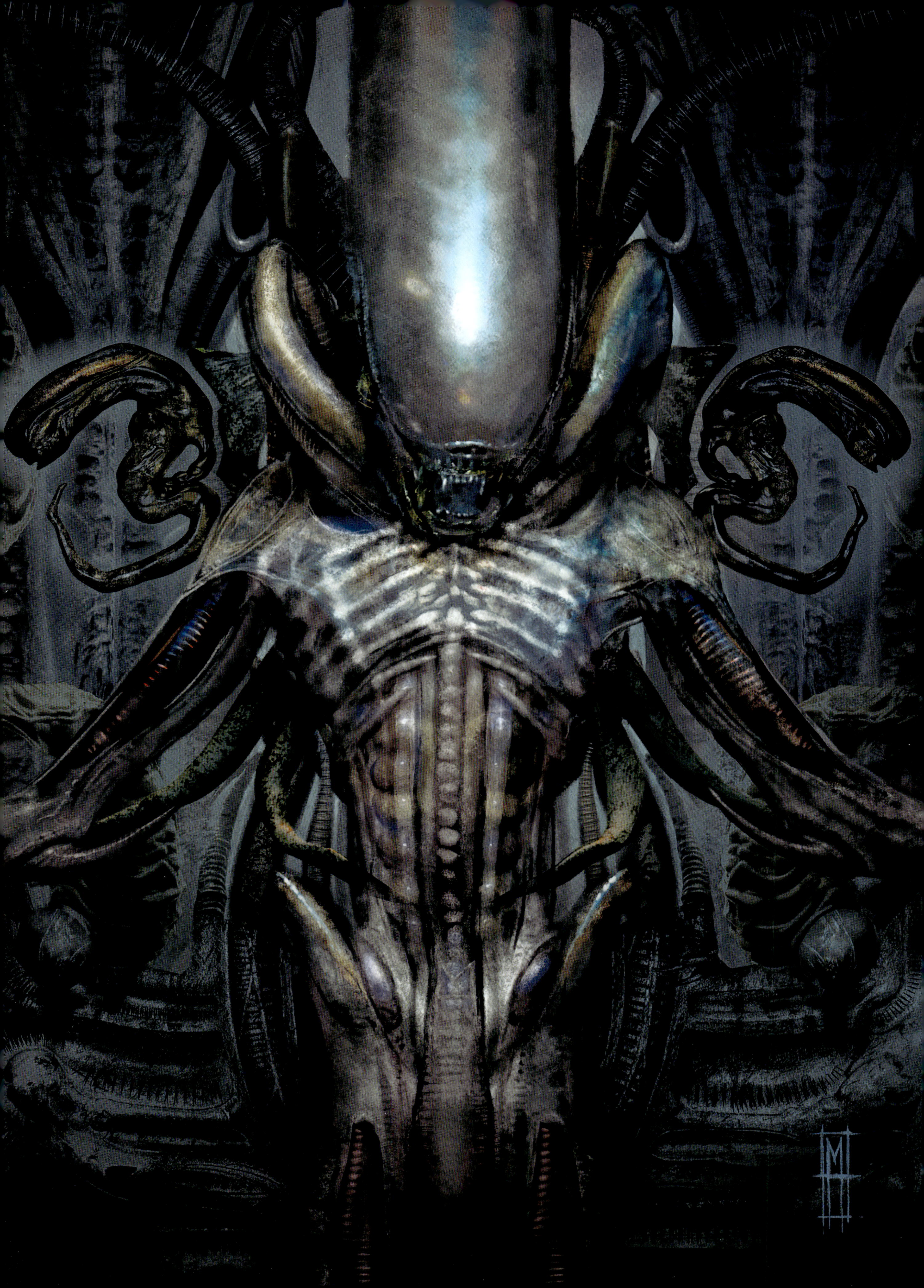

SWEENEY BOO

Ripley | digital | 36 x 26 cm

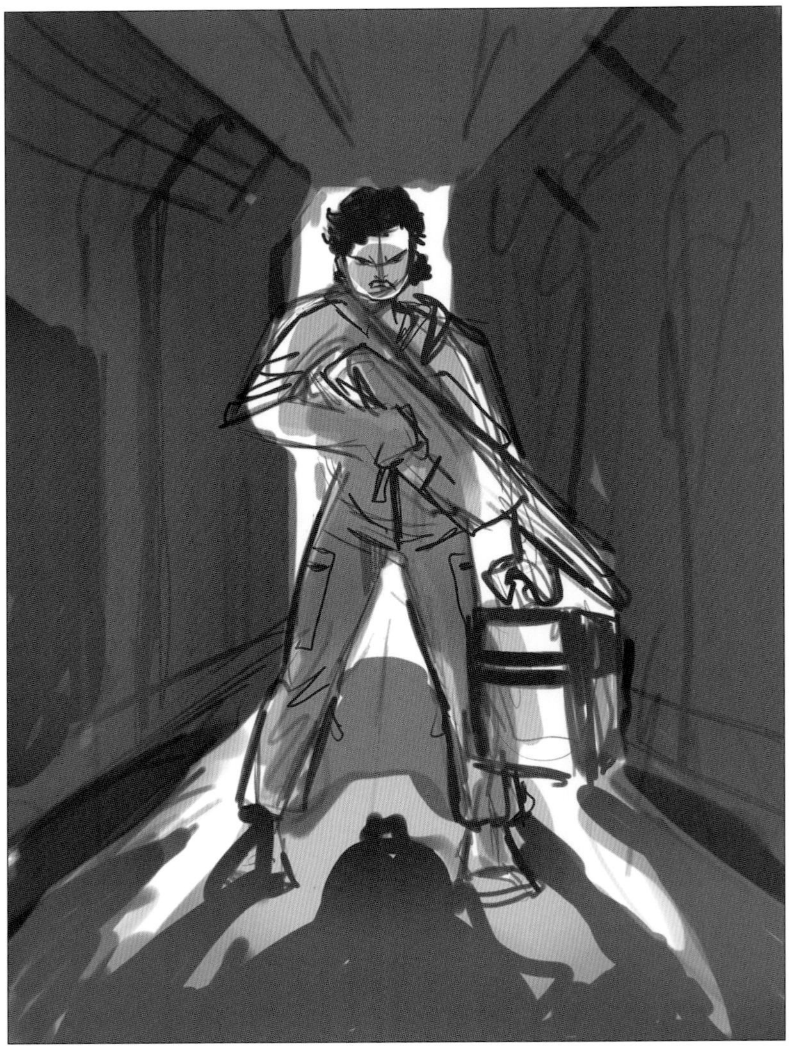

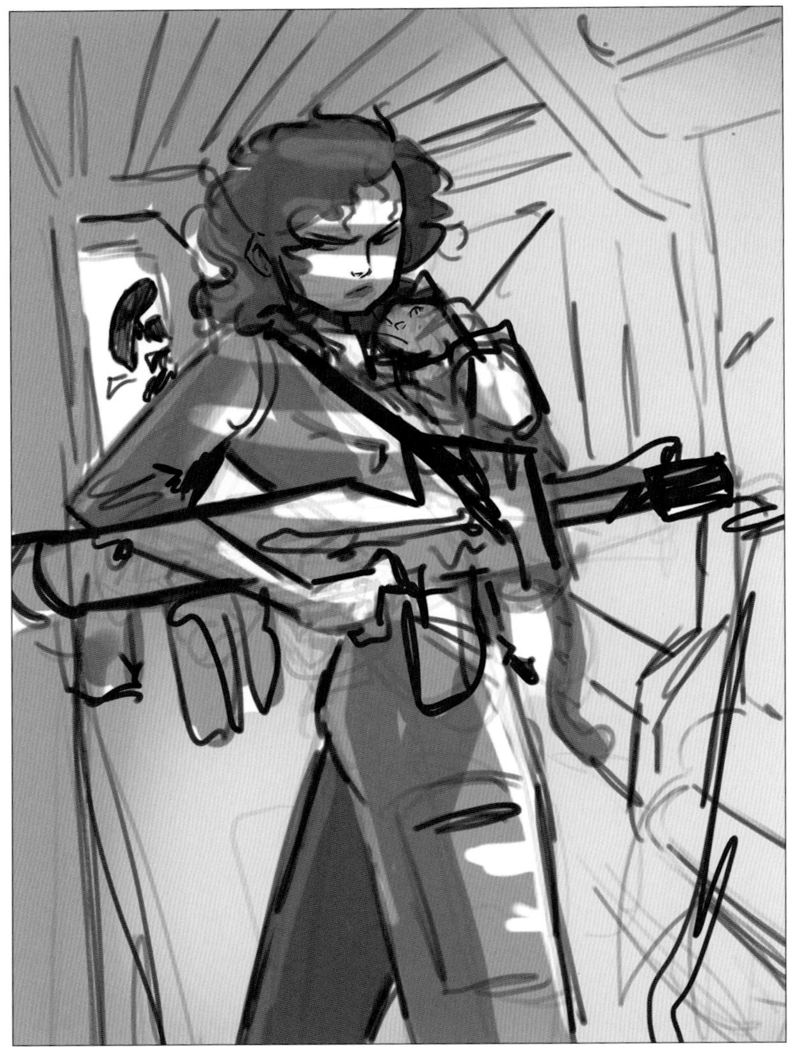

I didn't have the opportunity to watch *Alien* until 2018. And what struck me was that, even though the movie was already almost forty years old, Ripley's character is one of the strongest heroes I have ever seen. What I like the most about this movie are the characters and how they are portrayed simply as people and not as stereotypes. The characters' behaviour and reactions are real and human. Ripley's evolution into the hero is believable as we watch her cautious fear turn into dire heroism. Her bravery is a direct result of her fear, which helps create the instant connection we have with her. She isn't the sidekick, or the damsel in distress. She needs no one, and she'll help everyone in danger even if it puts her own life at risk. Even today, I can't really think of a female character such as Ripley. After forty years, she is still one of the best female heroes in a science fiction movie. And we need more of that.

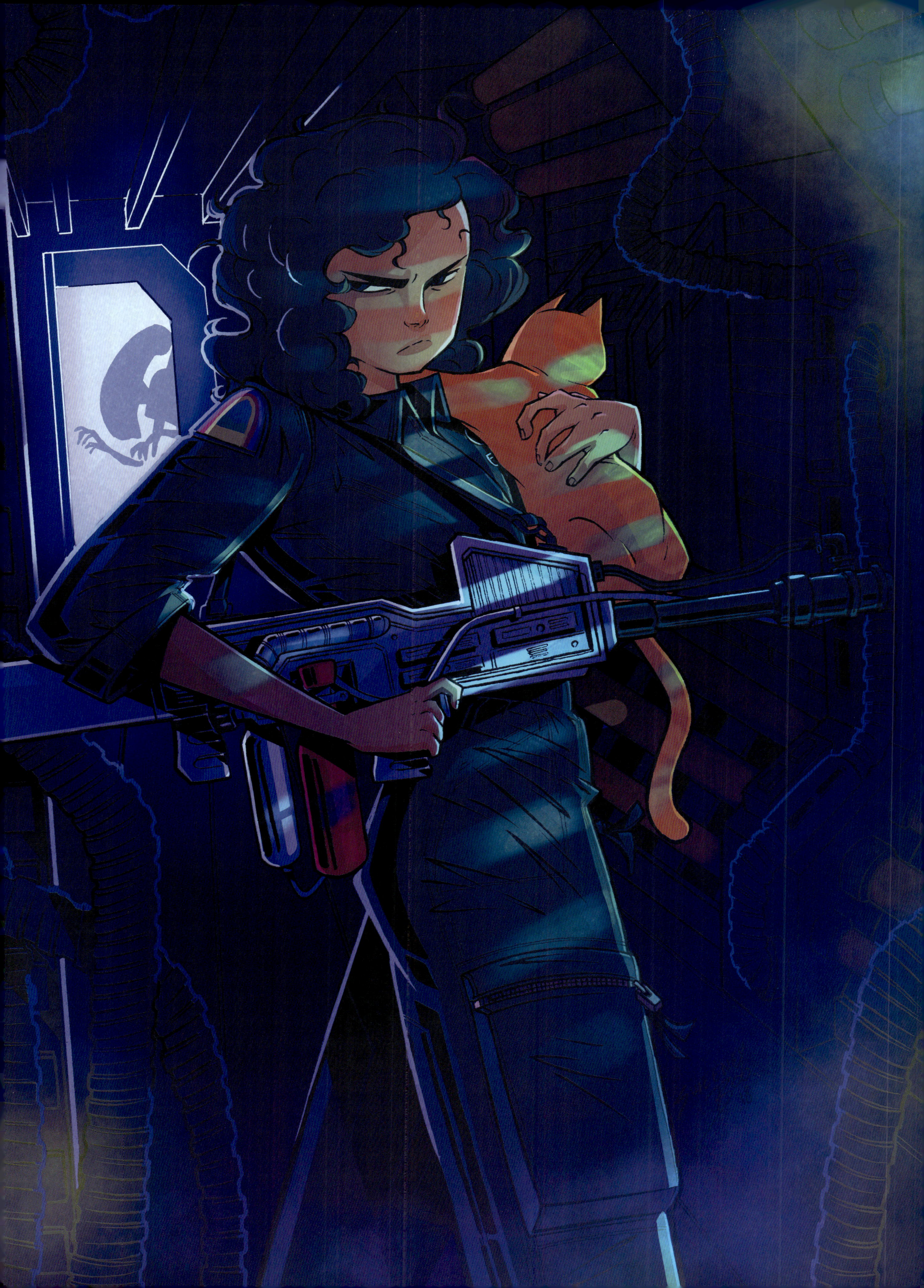

TERRYL WHITLATCH

Anatomical Analyses of the Xenomorph | digital | 36 x 52.5 cm

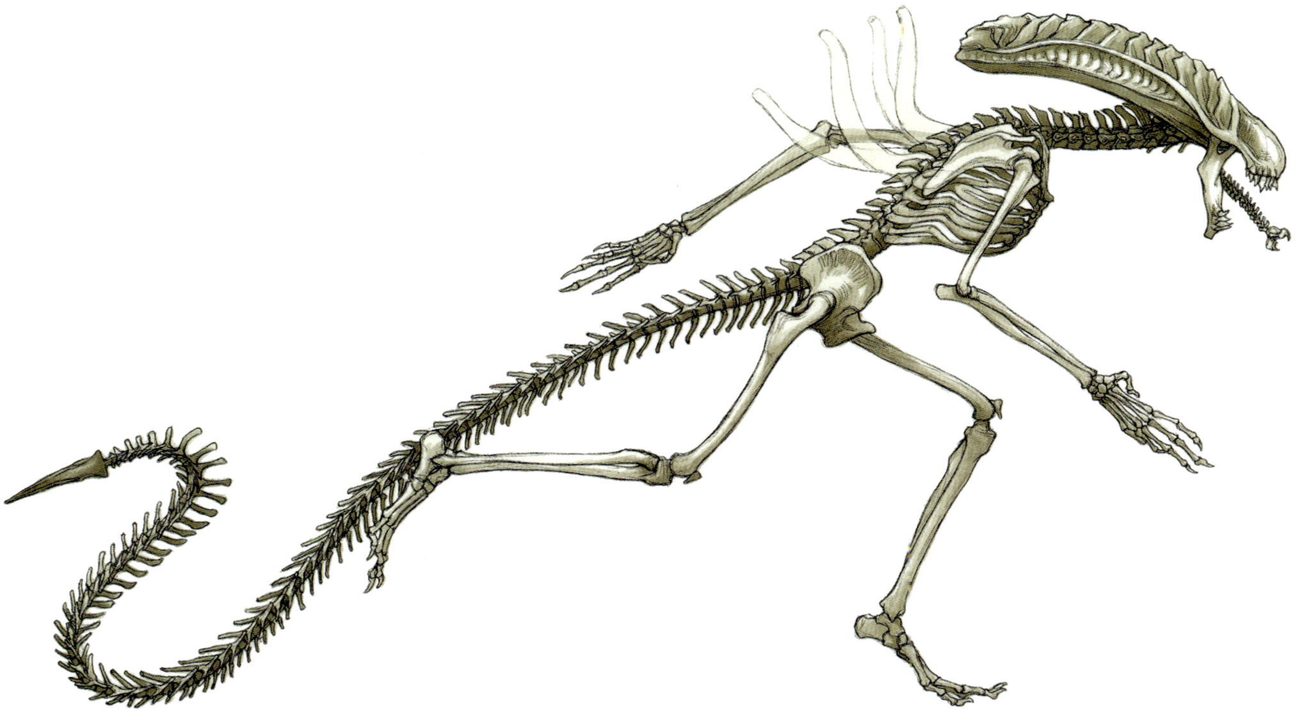

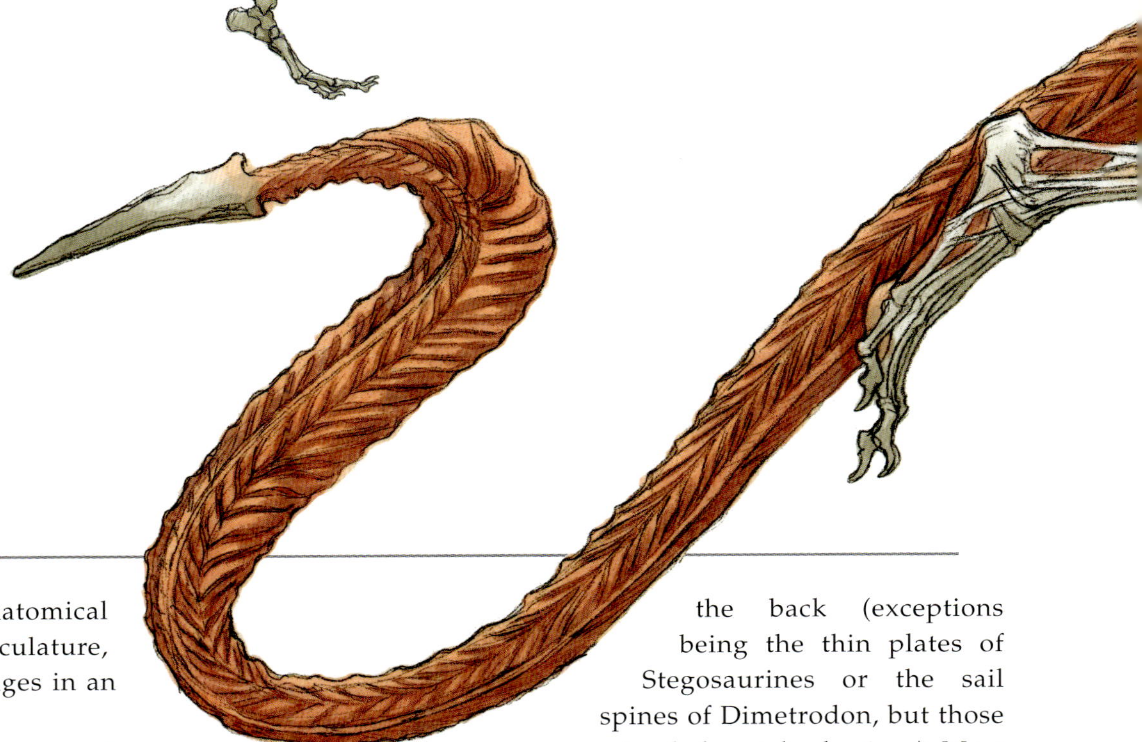

For my final pieces, I completed three anatomical analyses of the Xenomorph – skeletal, musculature, and surface. I then produced three full-color images in an exciting action pose.

The four spines on the back of the creature I have assumed are hard cartilage, possibly reinforced with dermal scutes/scales/denticles (as in sharks), without any bony internal structure, which is why they don't appear on my skeletal or musculature views. I was hard pressed in my research to determine if they had an official function – there are many theories, including that they may be reproductive chambers – so I looked to life on this planet as a guide. Most bony, horn-like structures in vertebrates seem to be by-and-large restricted to the head (ie Parasaurolophus) or the tail (ie Stegosaurus) rather than the back (exceptions being the thin plates of Stegosaurines or the sail spines of Dimetrodon, but those are extended vertebral spines). Most of the time, projecting dorsal structures seem to be composed of non-bony tissues that tend to decompose or disappear after death. The fact that the tubular spines of the Xenomorph are a quartet with pairs arranged on either side of the vertebral column suggests to me that they are not attached to or a part of the skeleton and are dermal, originating in the skin, in origin and structure.

It was a great deal of fun to play with this iconic creature.

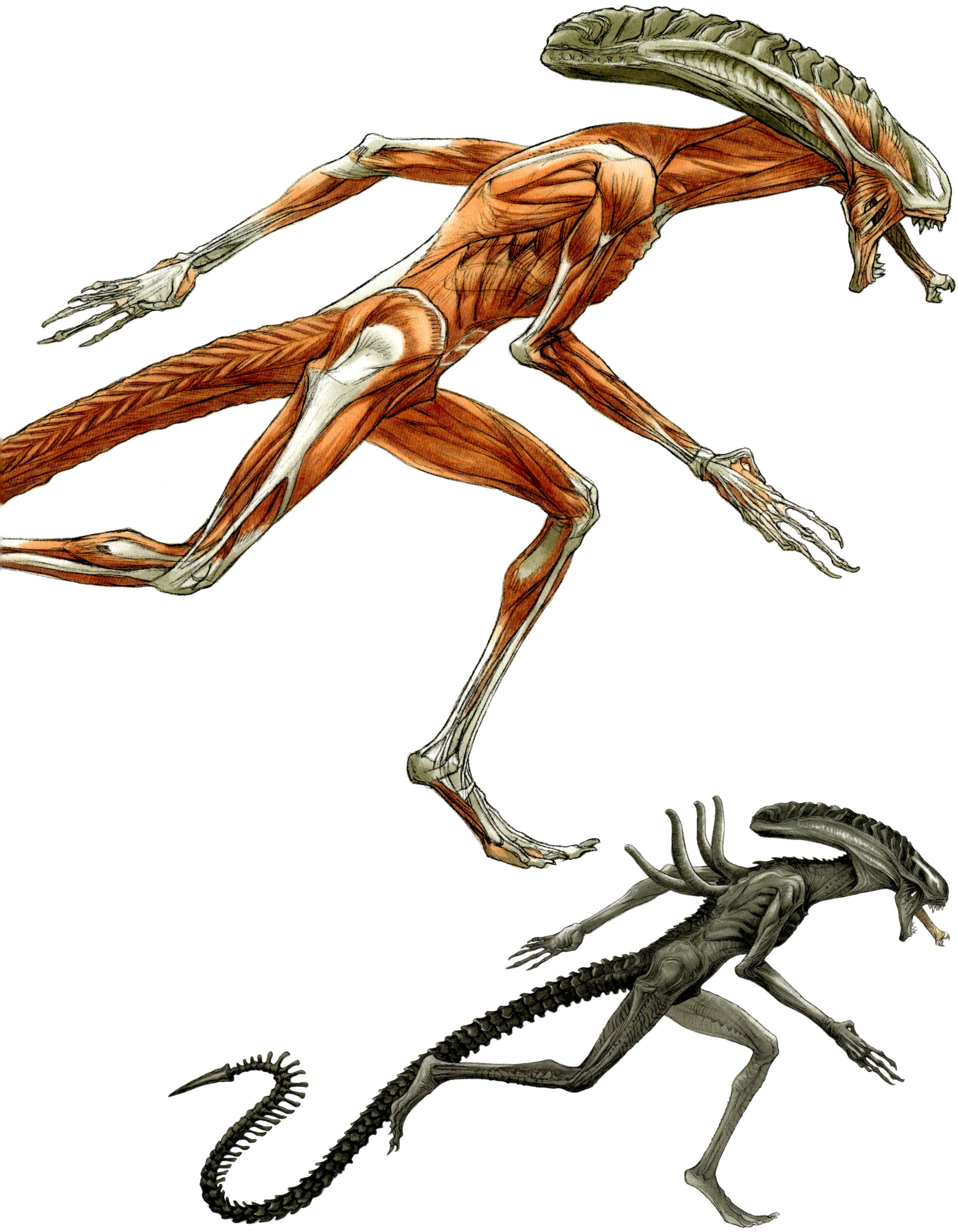

DAVID LUPTON

Brett's Demise | pen and ink on paper | 35 x 24 cm

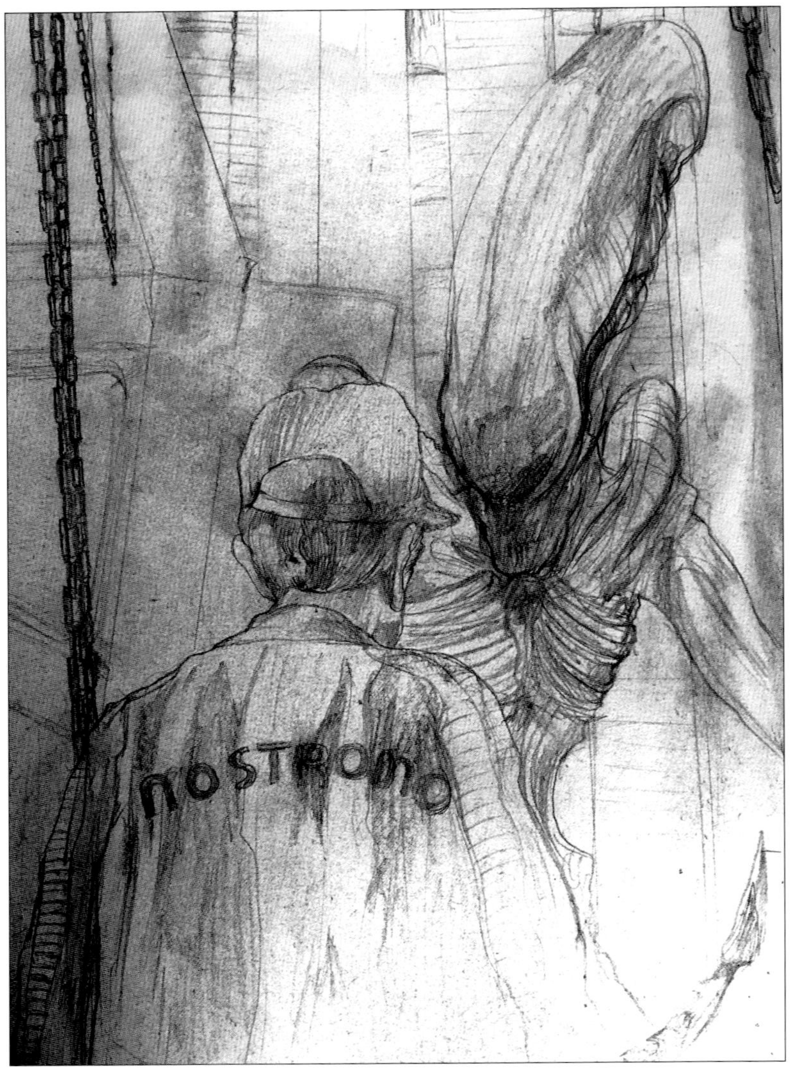

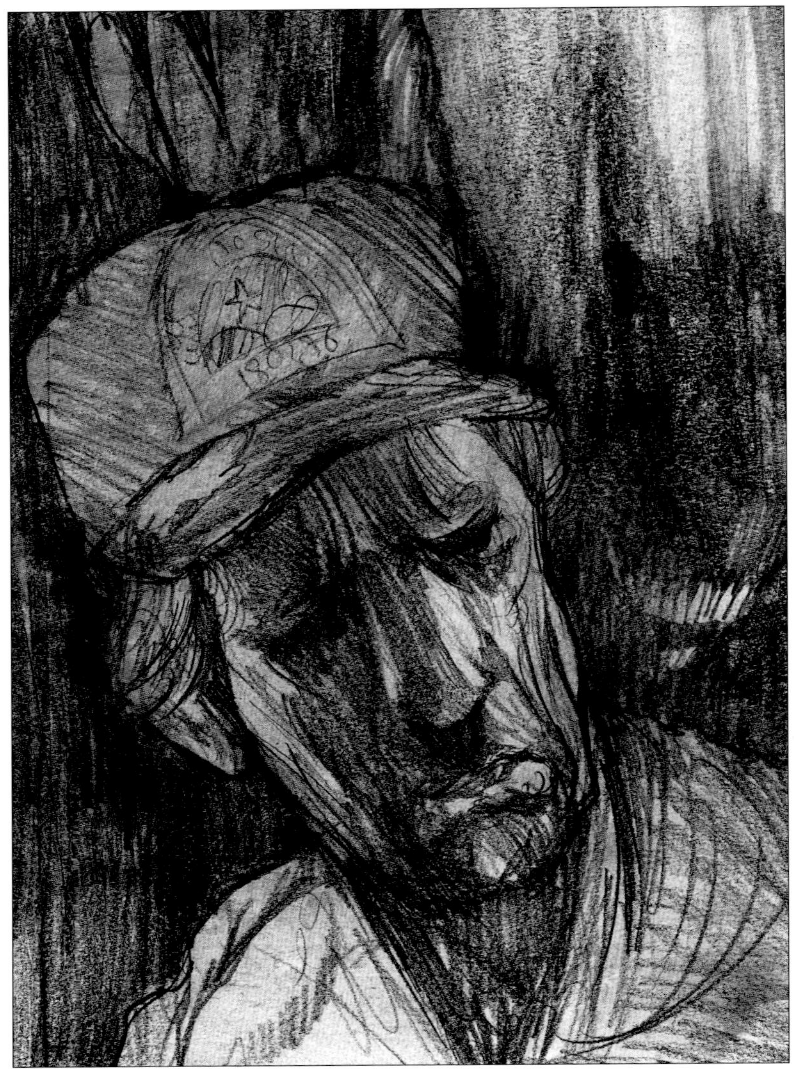

In the end I opted to illustrate one of my favourite scenes in the film, where Brett meets his unpleasant demise. I was thinking about *Alien* essentially being a haunted-house movie and I wanted to draw something that evoked that feeling of something in the darkness lurking behind. I also love the lines, shapes and textures of Harry Dean Stanton's face and wanted to try and capture that in an illustrative way.

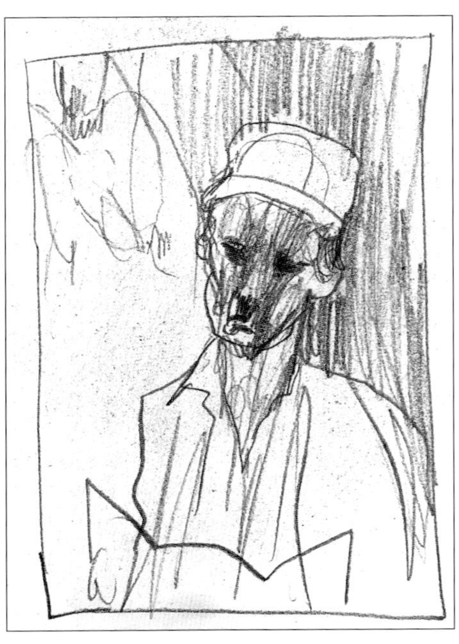

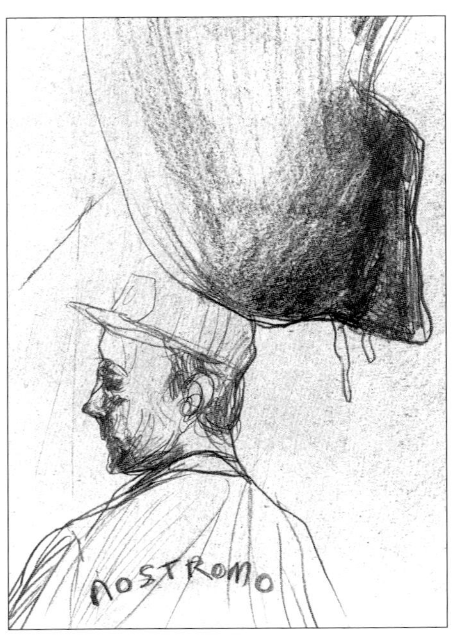

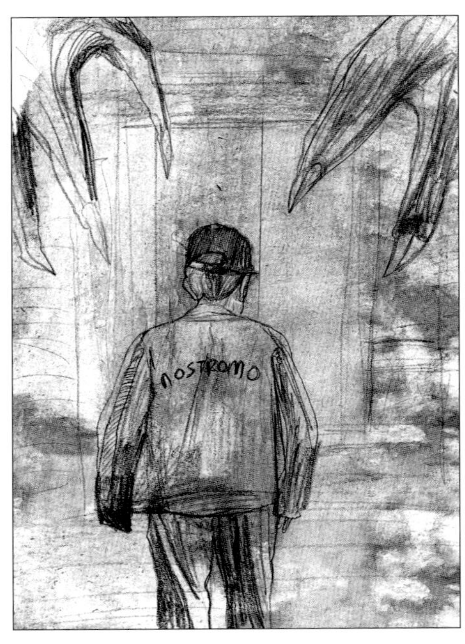

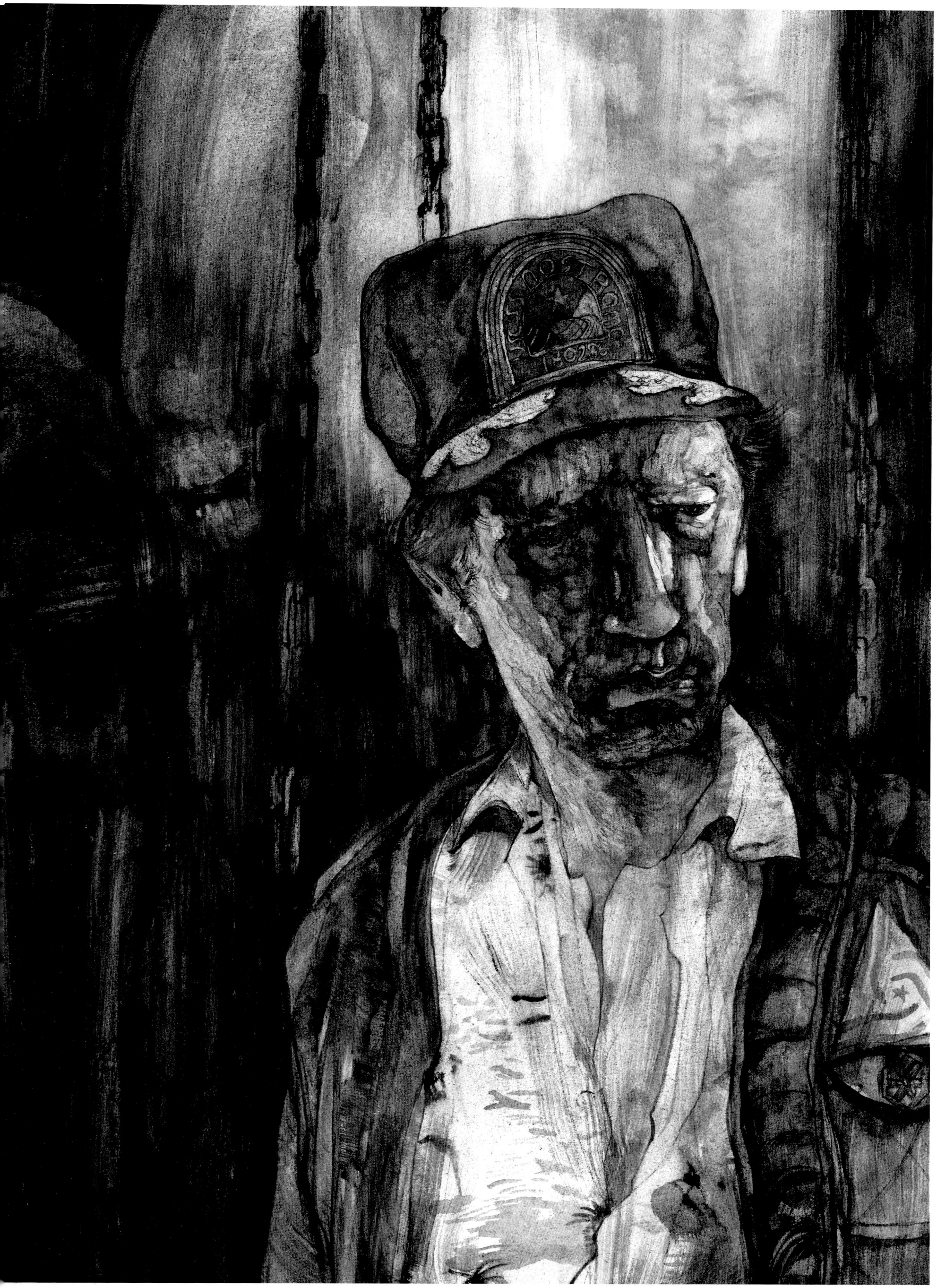
NOSTROMO
180286

RJ 'ARVALIS' PALMER

Big Chap Finds a Friend | digital | 39 x 55 cm

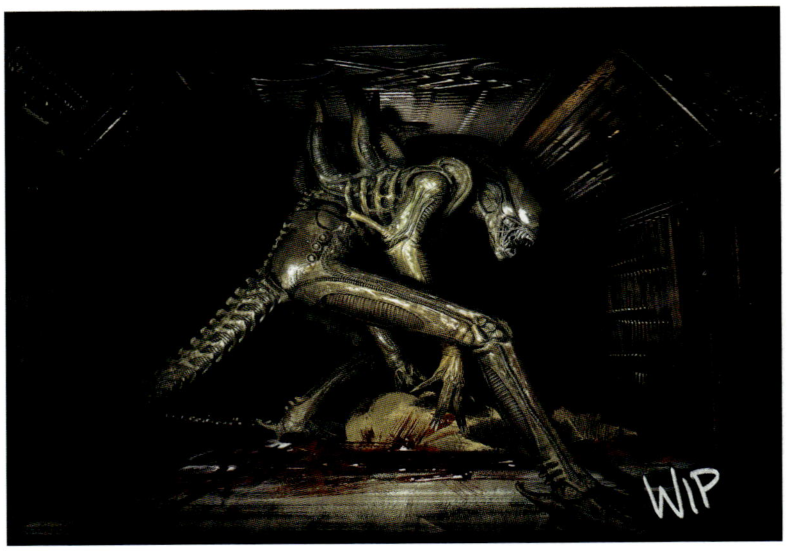

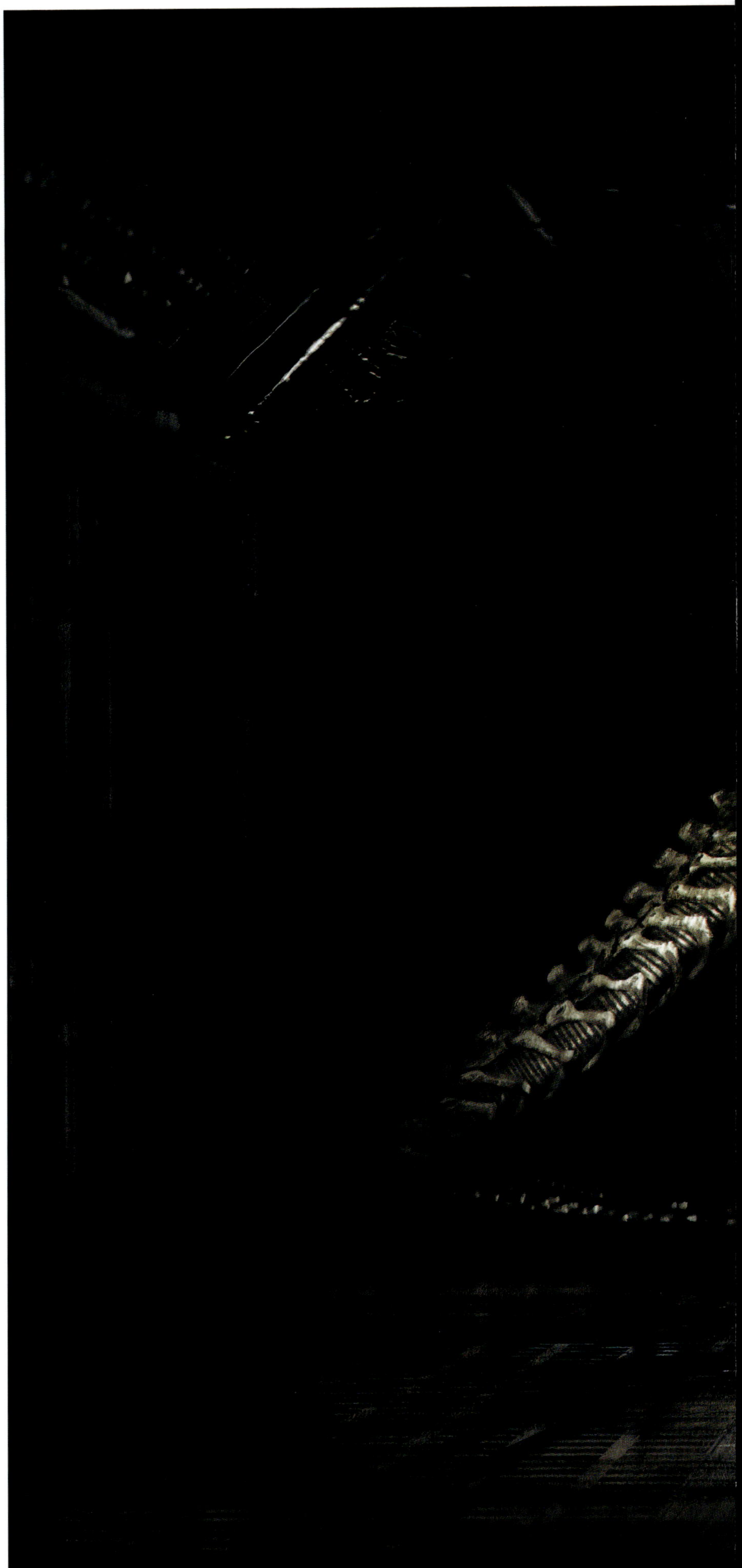

I was shown *Alien* at a very young age, probably too young, but it certainly made an impact. As a child I had all the toys and I've been drawing aliens as long as I can remember. I even have a distinct memory of seeing *Alien: Resurrection* on my eighth birthday at the cinema. So when I was asked to participate in this project, I jumped at the opportunity.

I once thought all Xenomorph designs were created equal. As I got older, my appreciation of the original alien design, the "Big Chap," far outstripped my interest in any subsequent designs. There is something so elegant about the oft-forgotten bio-mechanical design elements that were neglected in later iterations. These inorganic attributes make the thing so much more – for lack of a better word – *alien*.

There are a few elements I really wanted to hit on hard in my illustration. The fact that it was a man in a suit was important to me to convey. The creature "born" of a man, which moves like a man, makes it so much more unsettling to me. I've done a deep dive into H. R. Giger's work on creating the suit to really bring that extra level of care into my handling of Mr. Chap. A few interesting features of the original suit for you to look out for here: The heel spurs are actually mammal mandibles; the lips are slightly transparent, so you can see the teeth under them; the knuckles have what appear to be shirt buttons. And he's just really dang cool.

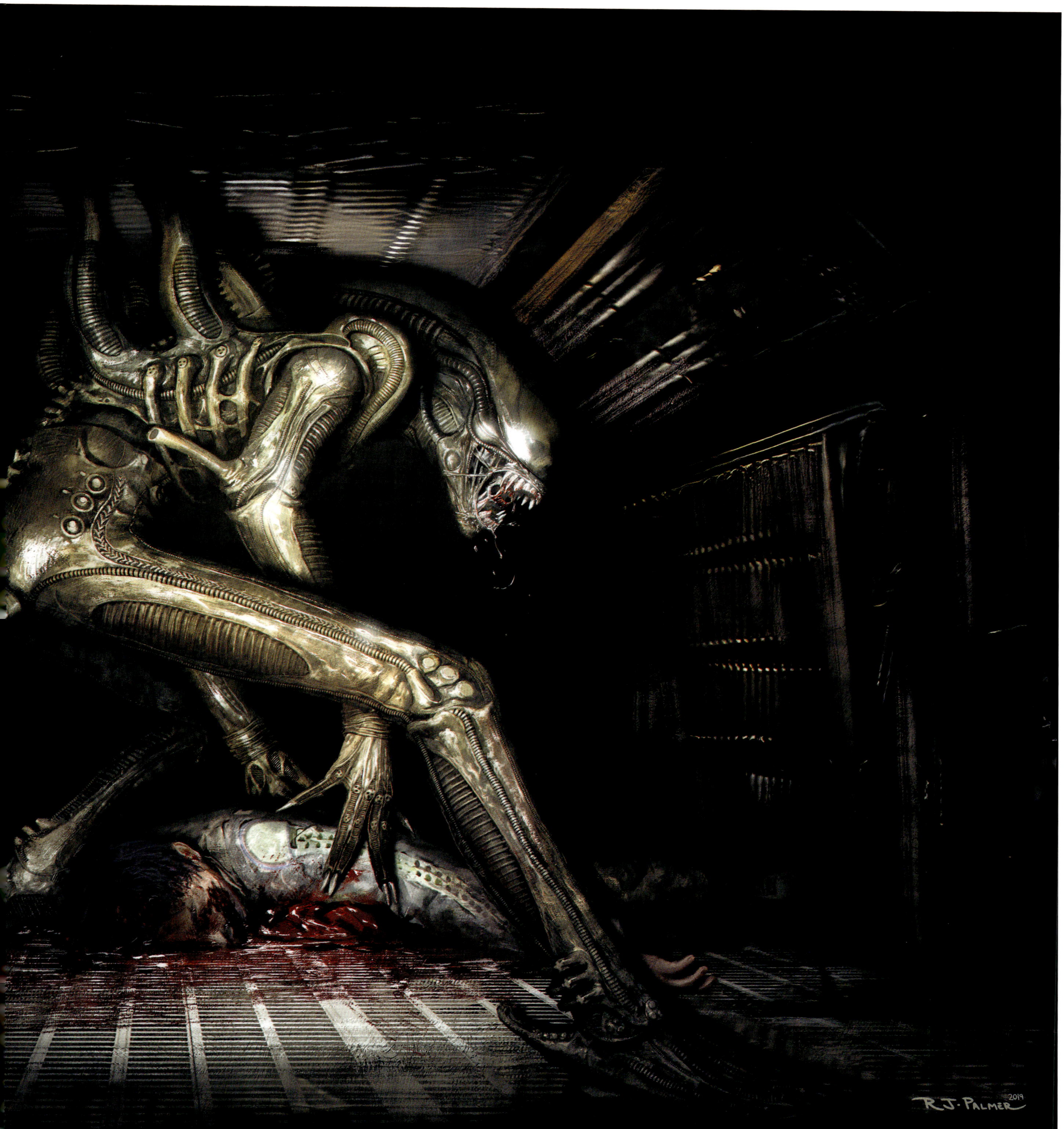
R.J. PALMER
2019

JUSTIN 'VBERKVLT' BARTLETT

Xeno Morph Born Again | digital | 43 x 43 cm

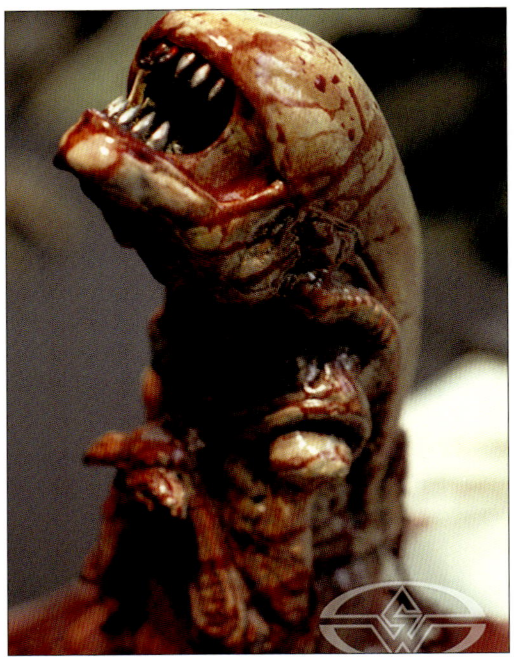

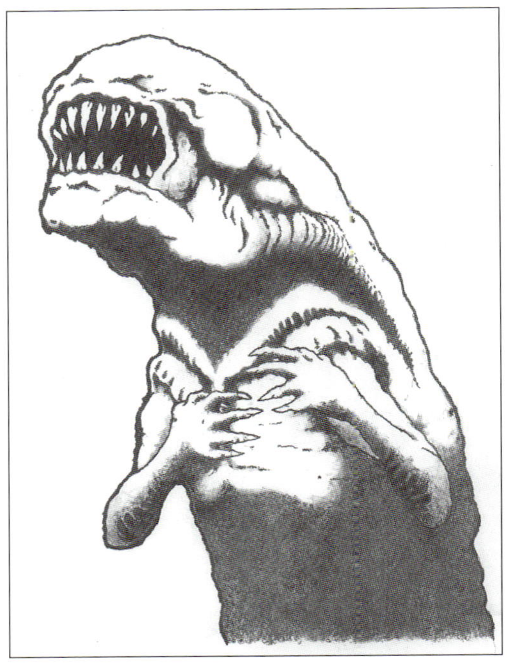

My first experience with the *Alien* franchise was the 1986 sequel that my father took me to see when I was nine years old. Granted, the film might have been a little age-inappropriate, but hey… it was the '80s!

By that time, watching science fiction and intense action films with my dad was pretty routine. Also, my grandmother and I watched horror movies together, as she was a fan of low-budget classics such as *The Stuff* and an avid Stephen King reader, too. Quite honestly, I think my dad really thought I could view the movie without being traumatized (too much), but perhaps the gritty realism and intensity was just a bit underestimated on his end.

I've often tried to piece together why *Aliens* simultaneously frightened me and drew me in. As a child, I was fascinated by insects and was quite knowledgeable about parasitic wasps and other odd insect life cycles. So, although I had witnessed Jason Voorhees, Michael Myers, and Freddy Krueger slash, impale, and decapitate dozens of victims on screen, the idea of humans serving as a host for a developing insect-like organism seemed one thousand times more realistic. After viewing the film with my dad and asking him if we could leave half way through, we met up with my mother for lunch. As they love to recall, I was as pale as a ghost – which says a lot, since I was pretty fair skinned and red-headed!

Not too long after viewing the James Cameron sequel, I saw the 1979 original *Alien* on VHS and the slower atmospheric doom further solidified my love of the franchise. Whereas the sequel was my favorite as a kid – possibly due to Hudson's one-liners – the original became my preferred instalment as I grew older.

By the time *Alien*^{3} was released (which I love too!), I had collected, traded, and "acquired" dozens of Dark Horse published comics and *Alien* action figures produced by Kenner. Those years also were a spawning ground for a passion for heavy music, which is why I felt it more than appropriate to combine my love of two British franchises – one created by Ridley Scott and the other by a group of long-haired Birmingham exports.

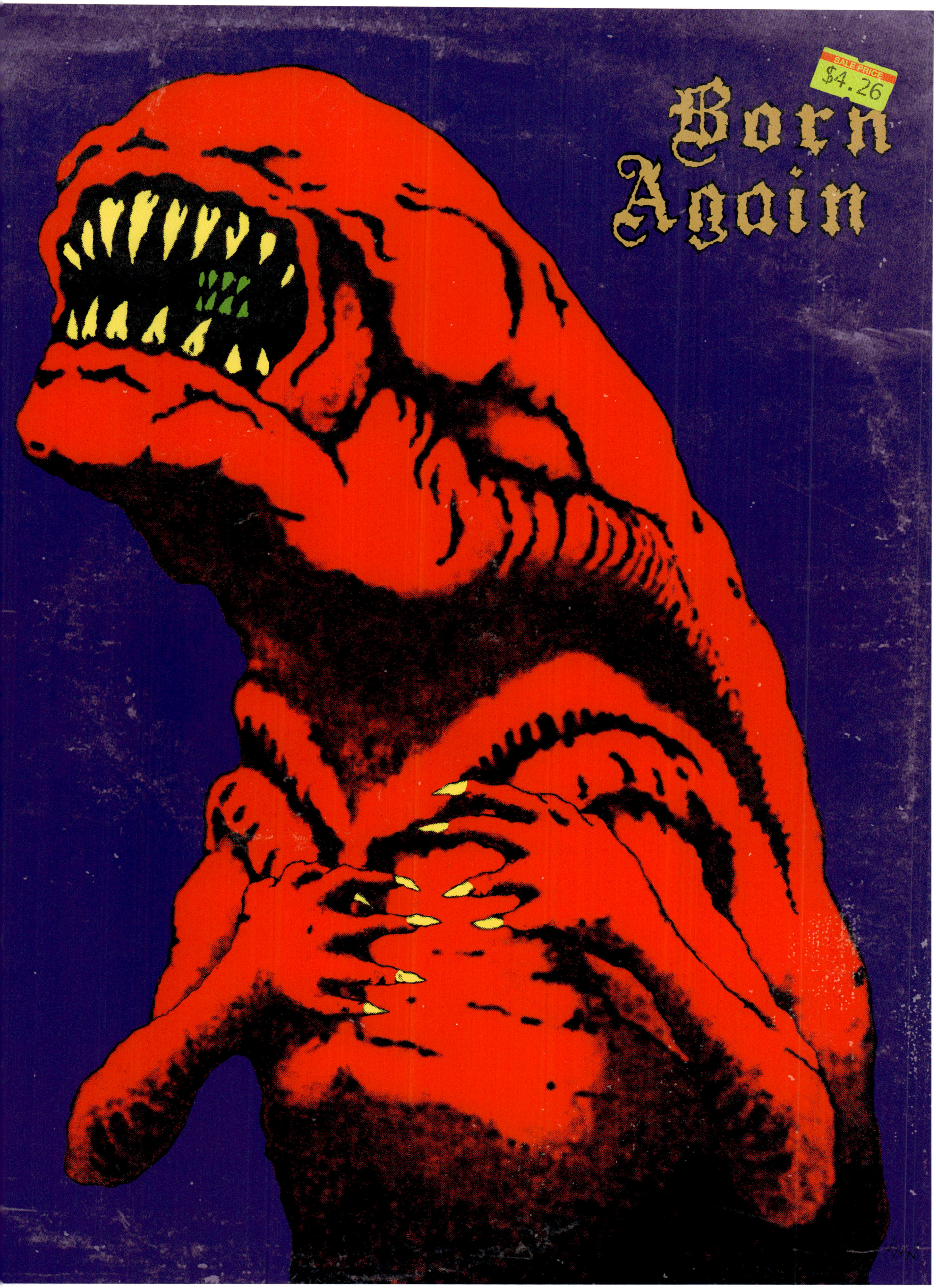
Born
Again
SALE PRICE
$4.26

CAROLYN CRAGGS

Human Meets Alien | ink, gouache and coloured pencils on paper | 36.5 x 26cm

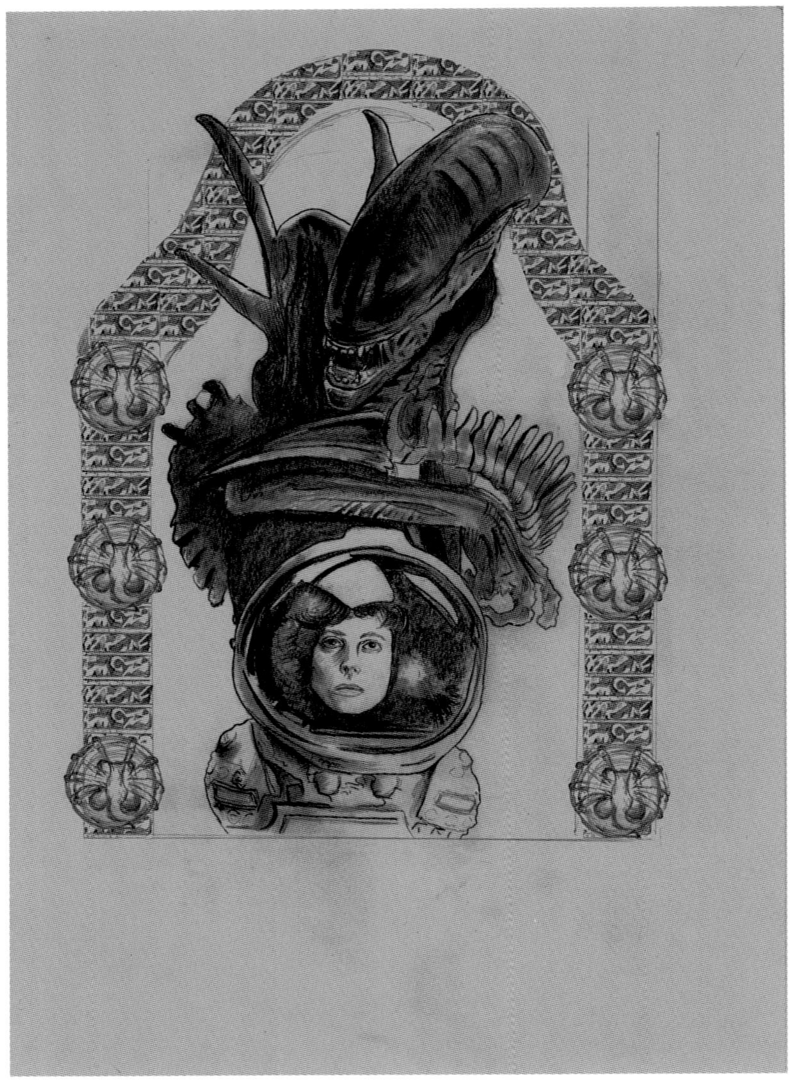

Growing up with a childhood dominated by 1970s and 1980s cinema and TV shows meant (in my opinion) that I was lucky to see the birth of franchises like *Alien* gain popularity. By the time I saw *Alien* on VHS, it was already ten years old and there were few female heroines at that time really for kids like me. Aside from Princess Leia, Ripley was the other standout female role model in a science fiction world.

Ripley's vulnerability as a human was always a quality I enjoyed watching Sigourney Weaver play out. She was just trying to do her job and she ended up having to form an understanding of the alien to survive. I wanted that connection between them in the juxtaposition of those characters in my piece.

I used the dark colours favoured in the movie to create suspense to influence the viewer's perception of Ripley being in danger in the famous end scene. The alien is made up of layers of airbrushed ink, gouache acrylic and coloured pencil. H. R. Giger's designs were so detailed, and I wanted to show that somehow without losing the focus of the message.

My first draft of this piece was to feature a Giger border, but I felt it distracted too much from the central elements, so I scrapped that idea.

I wanted to convey to the viewer of my artwork the feeling of anxious excitement and concern for Ripley in the end scene. She's so close to the alien and you just hope she'll be okay, which merges that element of realism into a science fiction world where human meets alien.

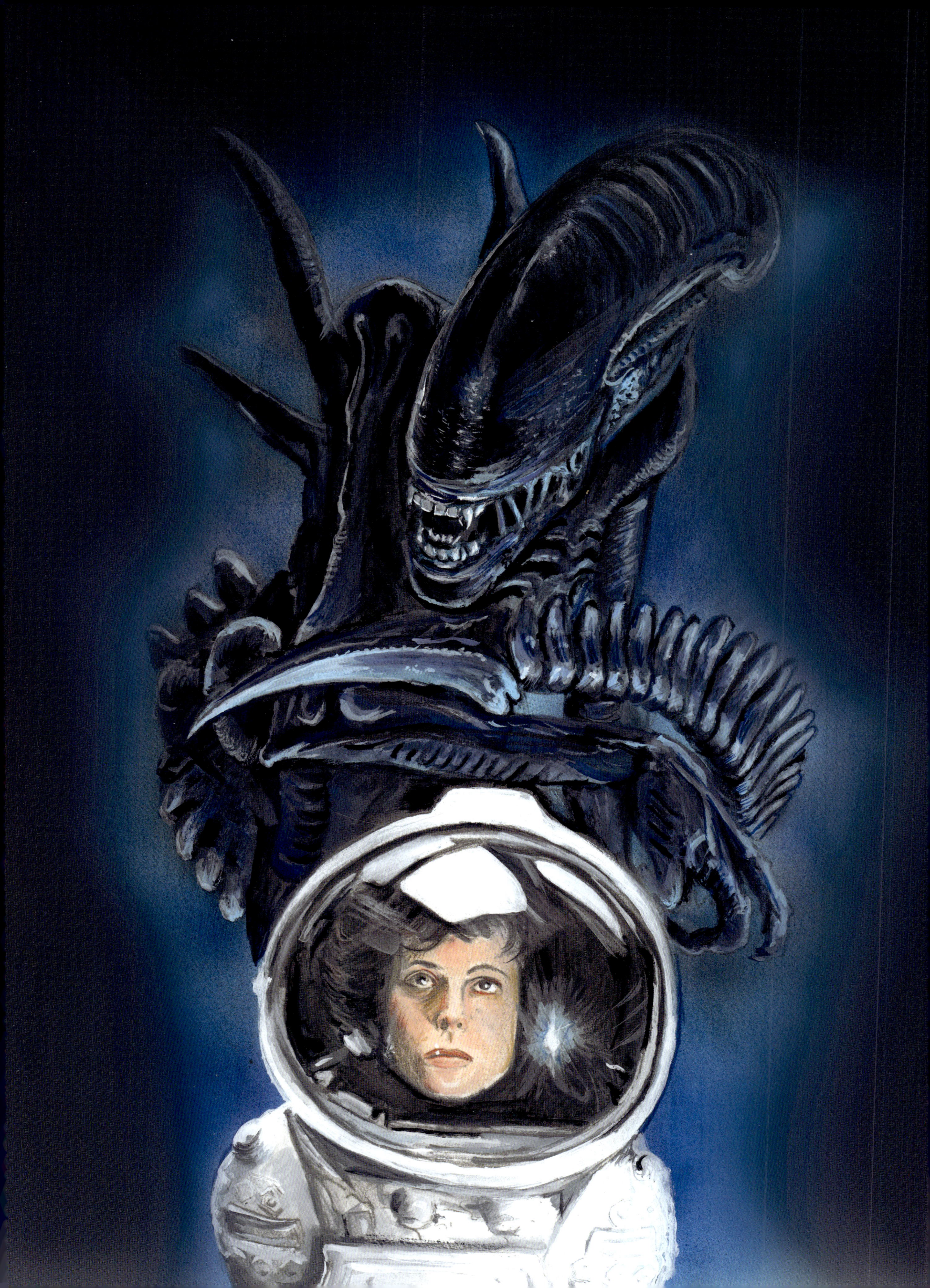

MARTA ALVIM

Xenobed & Xenotypes | ink on paper | 21 x 30 cm & 60 x 45 cm

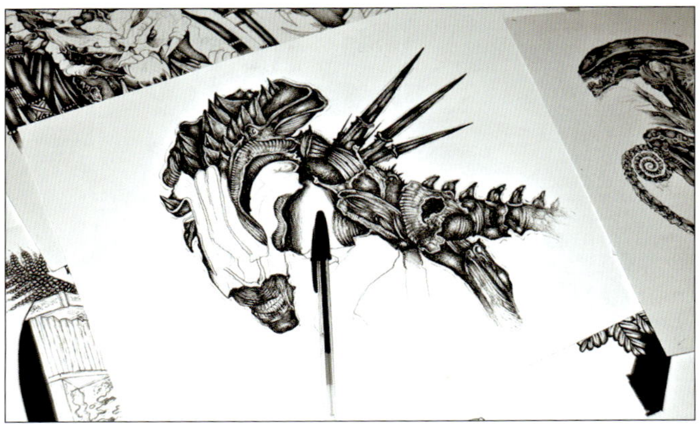

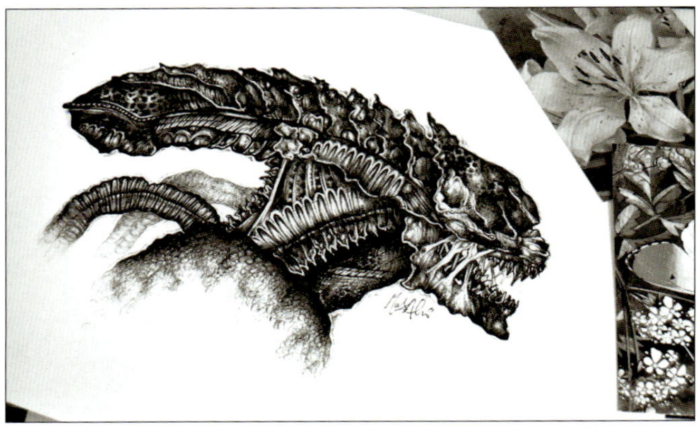

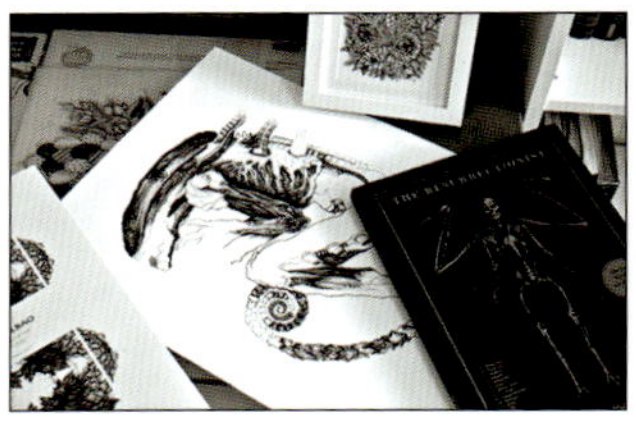

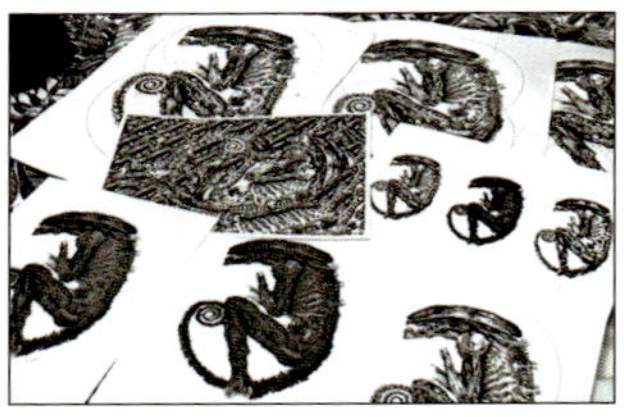

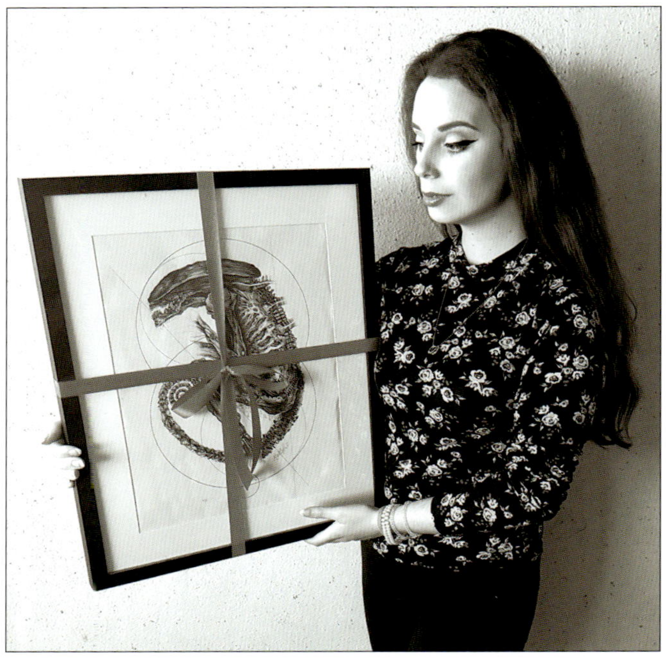

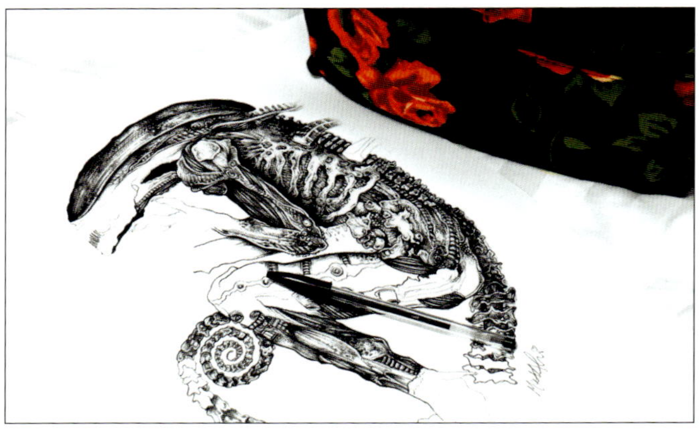

Alien is not just an incredible masterpiece, but the start of a whole new kind of cinematography.

Alien means creation, science and art to me. I see it as a perfect balance between horror and reality, as well as a very smart and peculiar way of imagining what our future could be like and which organisms may live beyond our planet. The raw and realistic emotions of the characters in the film towards finding such a different and destructive being is what makes the story so believable and iconic.

Xenomorphs were created with so much attention to detail that they automatically grab anyone's attention, especially mine, being a fan of fictional creatures. This franchise makes me question myself as a living being and inspires me to study these creatures, challenging me, as an illustrator, to create something incredibly intricate to the eye.

As a scientific illustrator, the looks and complex anatomy of Xenomorphs have had me obsessed since the first time I watched the films. Creatures featured in the franchise are my absolute favourite things to draw. I like to capture their complicated physiognomy with something as simple as a biro and create a living species out of a blank sheet of paper.

My illustrative pieces for *Alien*'s 40th anniversary focus on the 'beautifully grotesque' – which is how I would describe the film – and cosmic mathematics. A piece of art. A nasty piece of art.

Although I'm aware of the danger, I would very much like to own a pet Xenomorph.

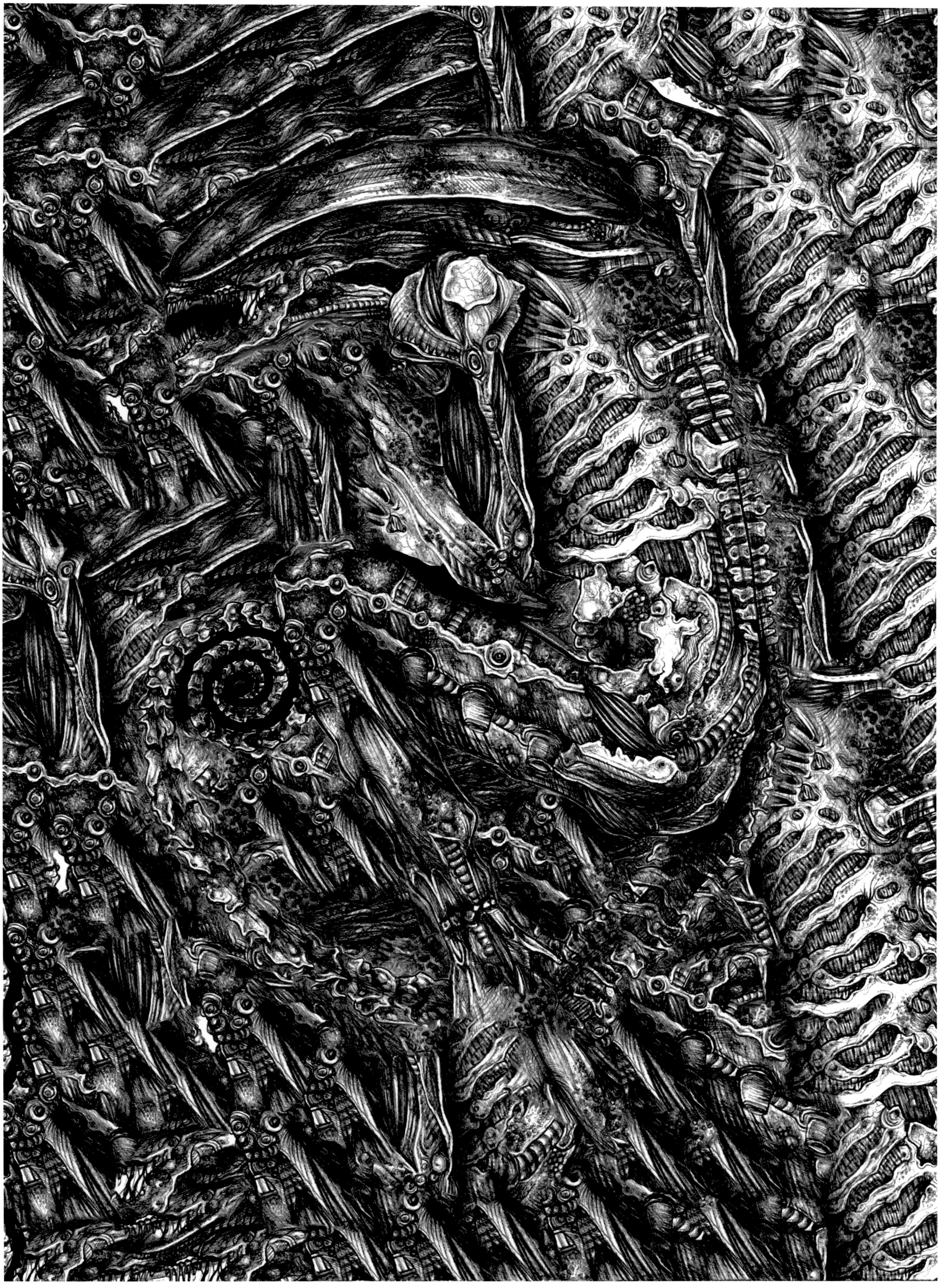

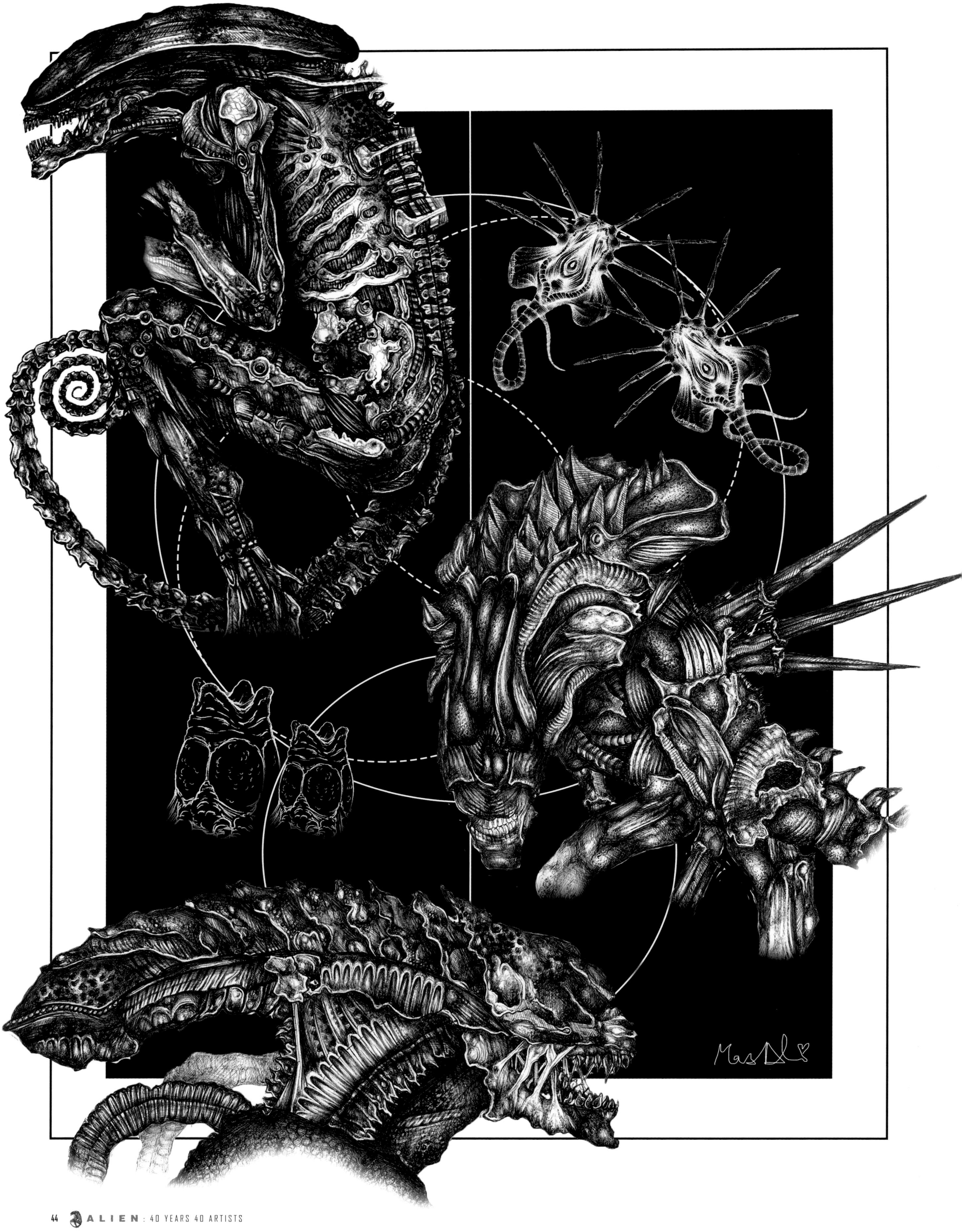

JUAN ORTIZ

Alien & Obcy | digital and illustration | 43 x 27 cm

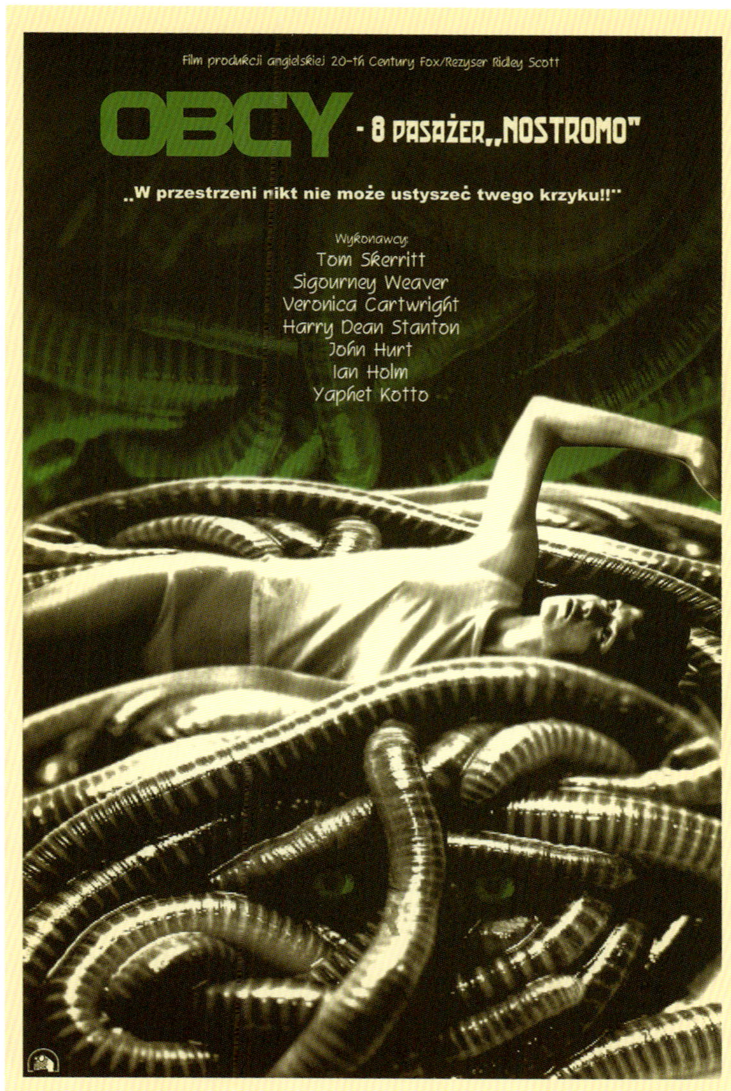

I was sixteen when *Alien* premiered. I can remember standing in line, on a rainy evening, for two hours to buy my ticket. I even purchased my *Alien* program book and picked up my free 'You Are My Lucky Star' button on my way into the theater. Both of which I still own. Later, I would devour whatever I could find on H. R. Giger's work.

Recently, I became a fan of Polish movie posters. So when I was asked to contribute a piece of art for this book, I knew that it would be the perfect opportunity to try my hand at creating one of my own. The three ideas I submitted are Polish-inspired posters in what I consider my 'style': Few elements and limited color. Cropping is something that I enjoy doing as well. And, in the case of the final *Obcy* poster, was necessary, in order to incorporate the helmet within the title. The eye within the helmet, I hope, will add a bit of creepiness to it.

What I didn't want was to show the actual alien from the film. That also is something that most Polish posters were known for, since often the designer had not seen the movie prior to designing the poster.

Alien would have played as well today as it did forty years ago. Maybe more so, when you juxtapose today's climate in Hollywood and in other workplaces. The Xenomorph, with its elongated head, clearly a phallic symbol, is using violence to dominate, until it comes up against a strong-willed, independent woman. I'm sure the filmmakers knew what they were saying, but it may have been nice to continue the conversation within the sequels.

Science fiction has always been a vehicle for social commentary – and *Alien* is no exception.

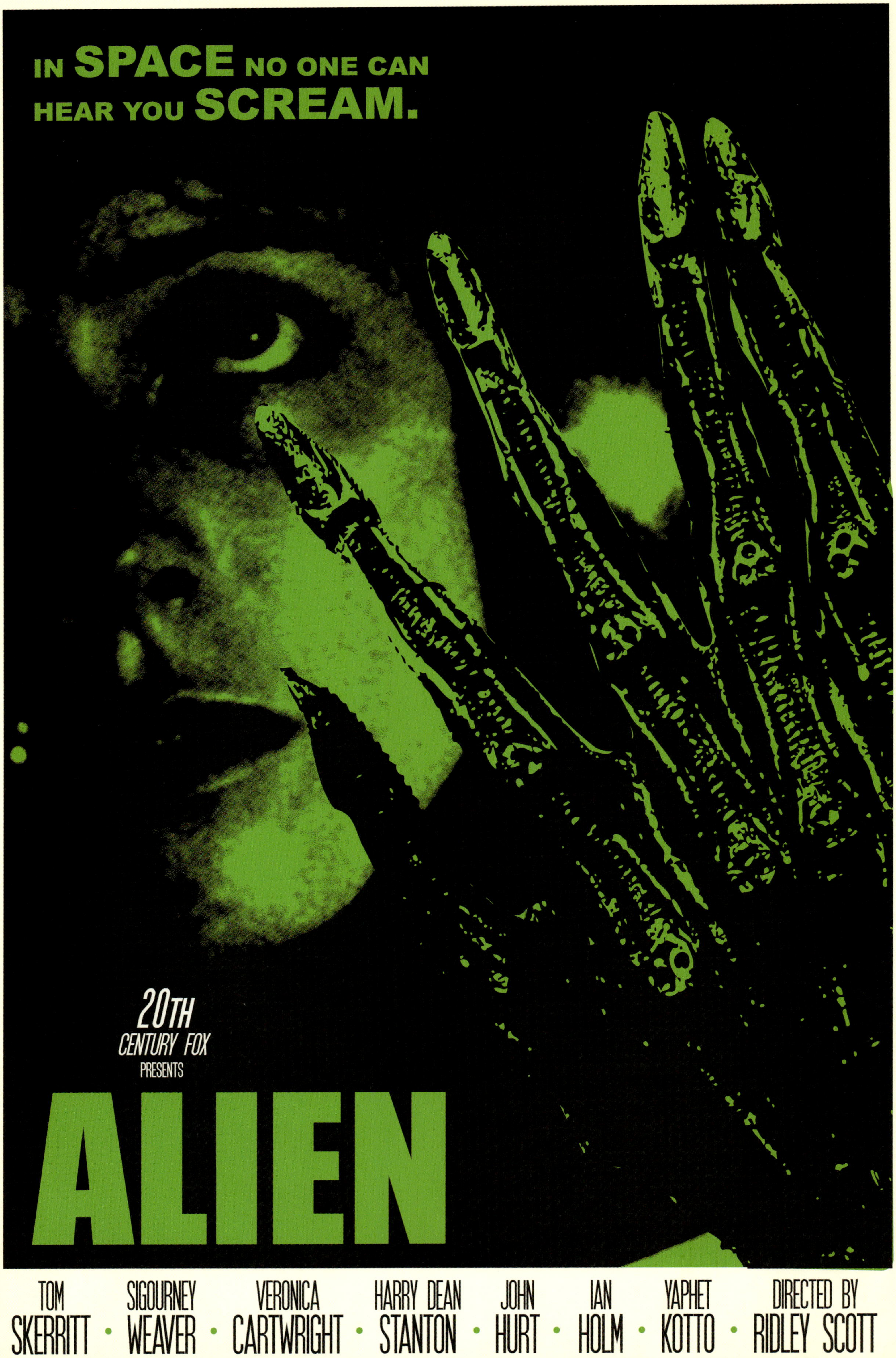
IN SPACE NO ONE CAN
HEAR YOU SCREAM.
20TH
CENTURY FOX
PRESENTS
ALIEN
TOM SKERRITT • SIGOURNEY WEAVER • VERONICA CARTWRIGHT • HARRY DEAN STANTON • JOHN HURT • IAN HOLM • YAPHET KOTTO • DIRECTED BY RIDLEY SCOTT

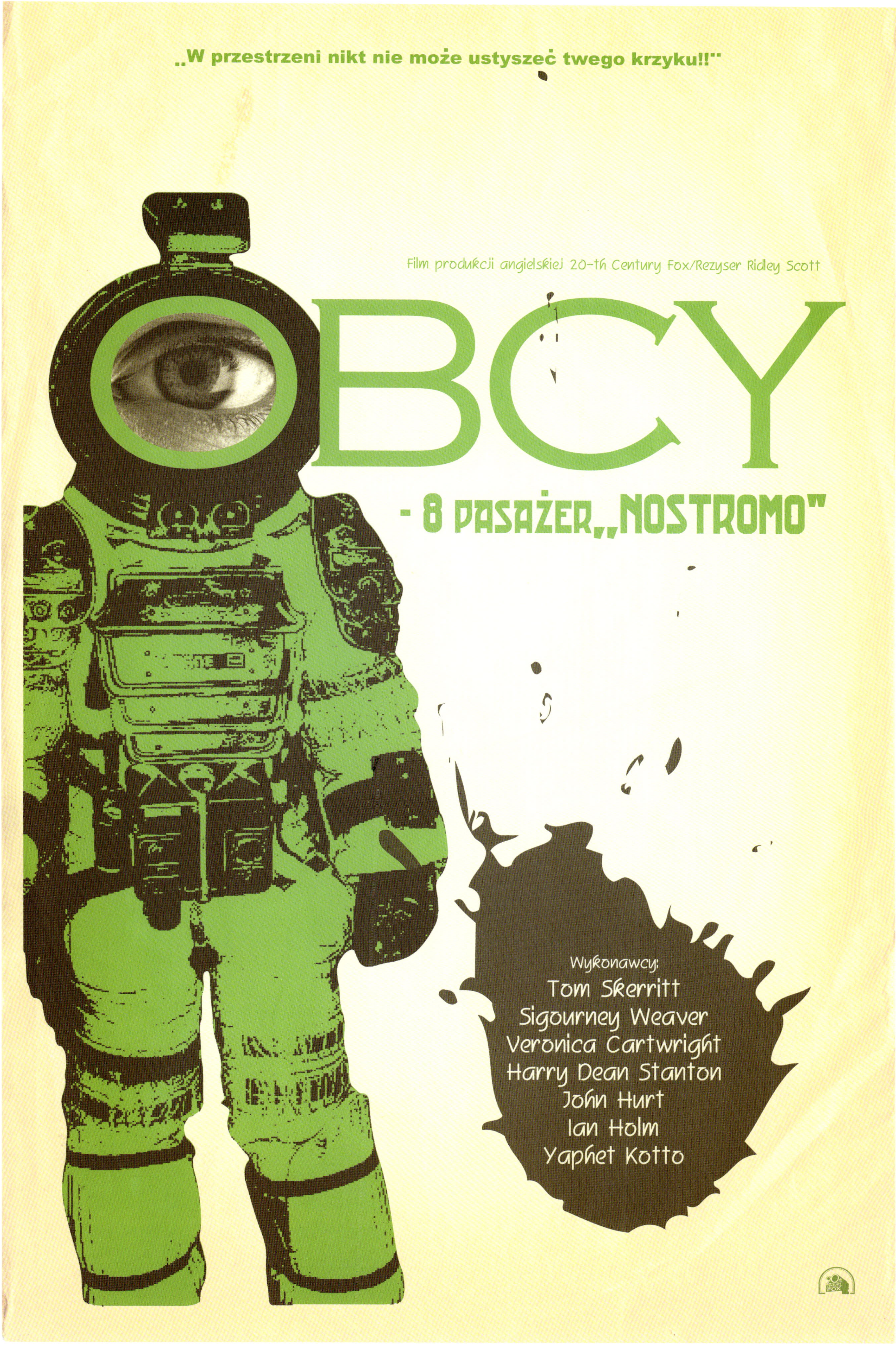
„W przestrzeni nikt nie może ustyszeć twego krzyku!!"
Film produkcji angielskiej 20-th Century Fox/Rezyser Ridley Scott
OBCY
- 8 PASAŻER „NOSTROMO"
Wykonawcy:
Tom Skerritt
Sigourney Weaver
Veronica Cartwright
Harry Dean Stanton
John Hurt
Ian Holm
Yaphet Kotto

JACQUELINE GALLAGHER

You Are My Lucky Star | acrylic paint on panel | 50 x 40 cm

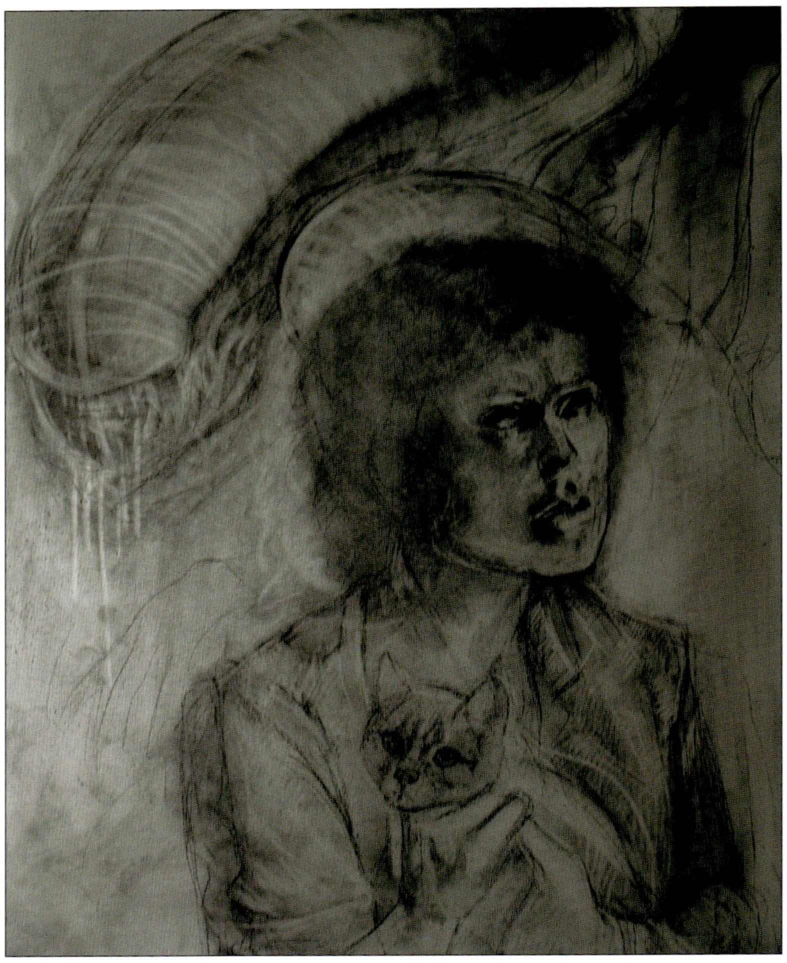

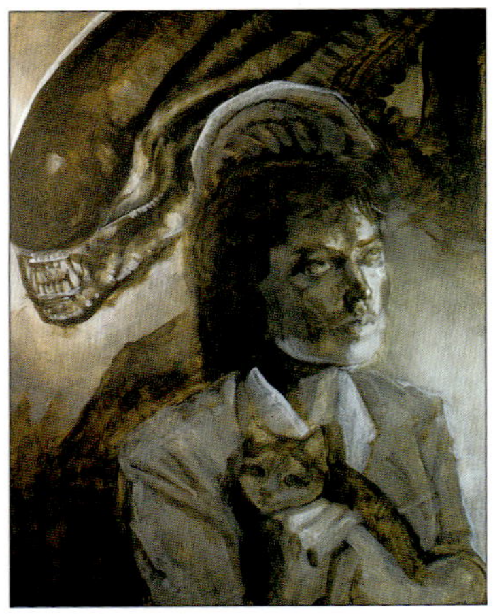

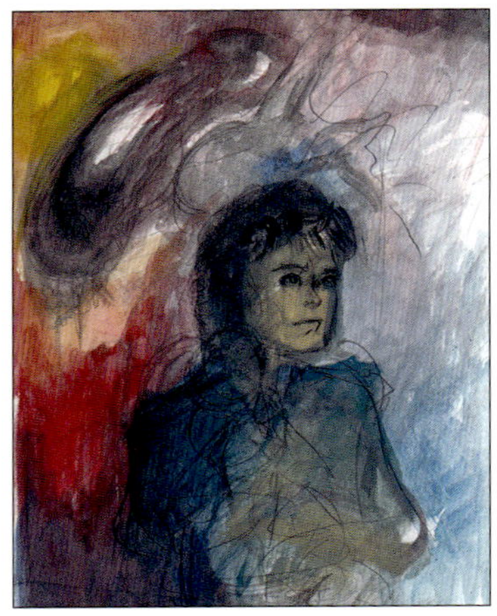

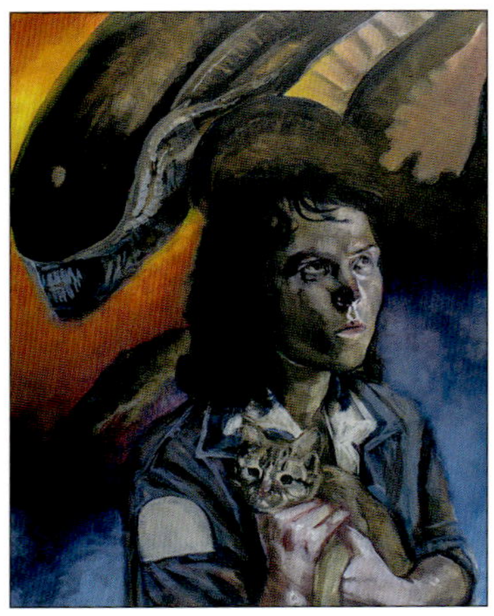

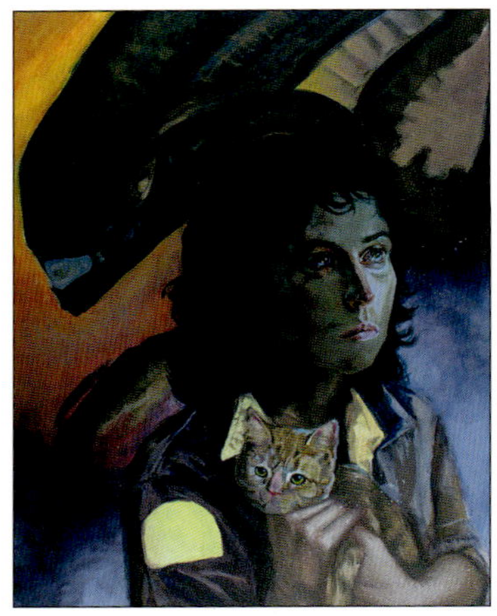

I saw *Alien* for the first time at a very young age, as I watched a lot of horror movies growing up. In my household we didn't so much watch "family movies" as we watched pretty much all movies as a family. My parents weren't too concerned with censorship for me or my siblings, but they did give us an army blanket they dubbed a "hidey sheet" to duck under if we got too scared. We loved it. The Xenomorph was one of the first movie monsters that stuck with me and to this day it is still probably my favorite. H. R. Giger's stealthy, slick, oddly industrial creature with gleaming silver teeth didn't feel familiar to me in any way; it was like nothing I had ever seen and it was terrifying.

While it would be easy for such a shockingly scary creature to completely steal the show, especially for a seven-ish year old, Jonesy also struck a chord with me. I have always loved animals and am usually much more concerned for their well-being in a movie than I am with their human costars'. Ripley's concern over Jonesy throughout the film really made me identify and care for her, too, which made the whole movie even more frightening. As I got a little older I started to really appreciate Ripley's character; I started to realize what a badass she was! Here was a woman in a horror movie who wasn't there just to be ogled and then slashed up. She was cool-headed, tough, and determined, and she fought back through her palpable fear.

When I was asked to contribute a commemorative piece based on the film, I knew right away I wanted to center on the two survivors of the USCSS *Nostromo*, the unbeatable duo of Ripley and Jonesy. Between the intensely subtle acting ability of Sigourney Weaver and the creeping of Ridley Scott's direction, a woman and her cat somehow rival the on-screen presence of this perfect killing machine.

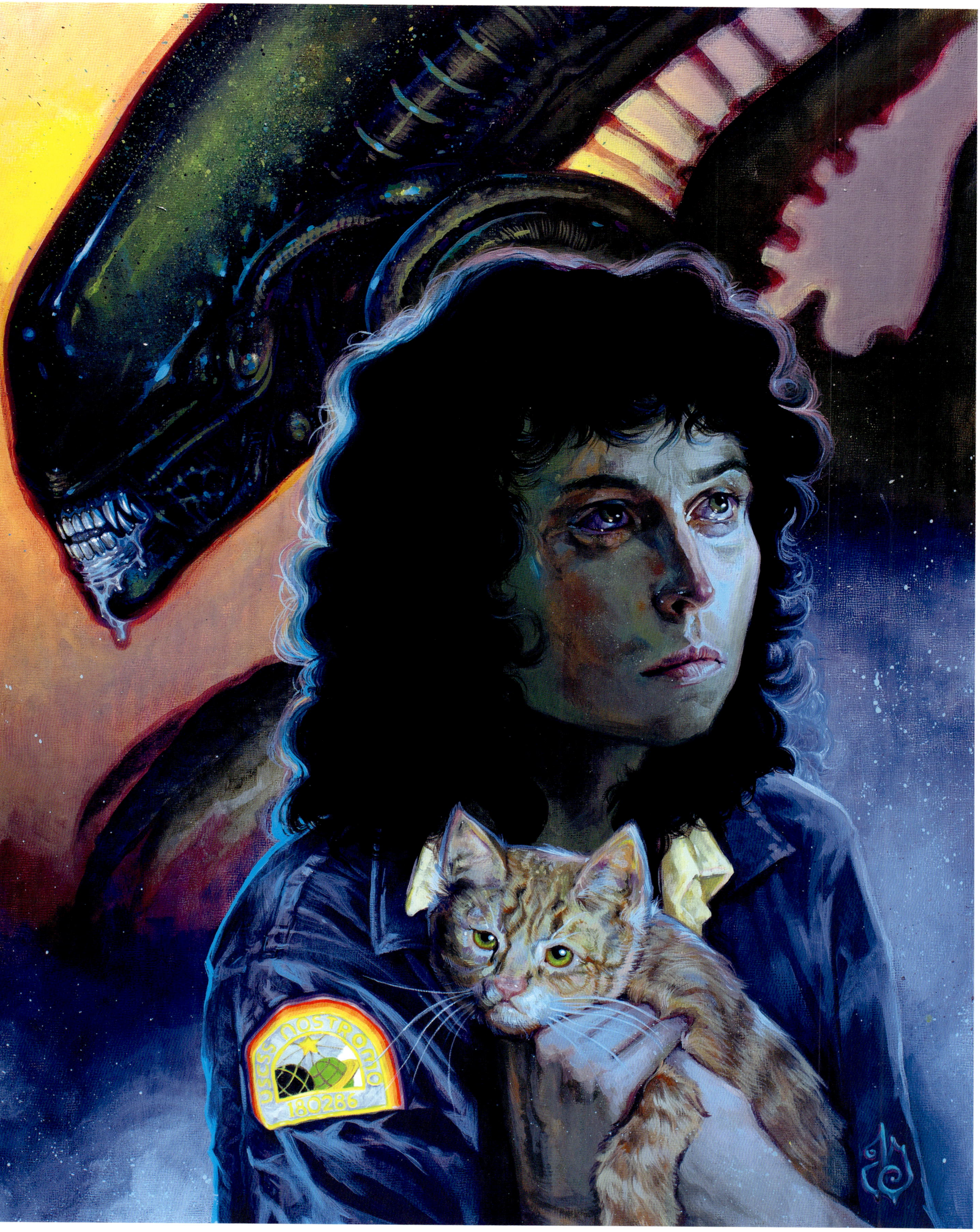
USCSS NOSTROMO
180286

NATHAN J. ANDERSON

Derelict Trek | digital | 60 x 45 cm

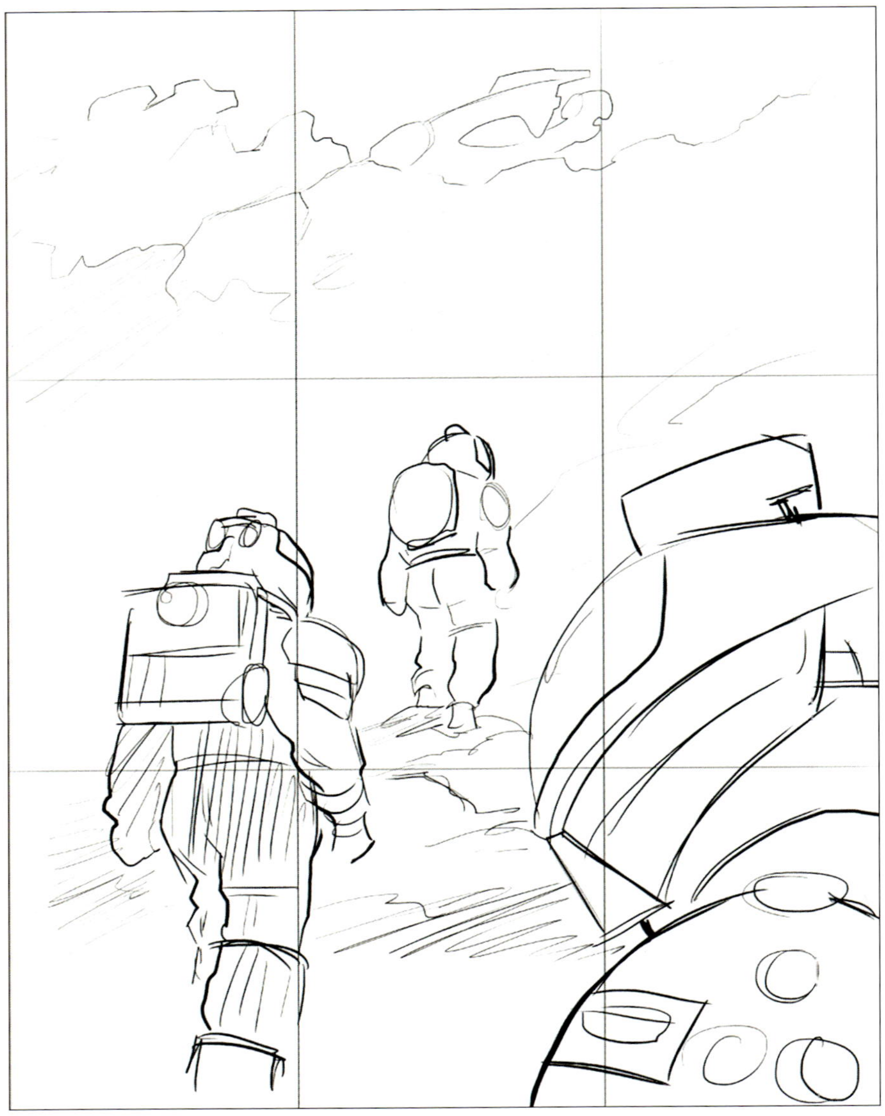

A *lien* is one of those films that I'm inclined to say is nearly perfect. Not only is it truly imaginative and groundbreaking in its respective genres of science fiction and horror, but the level of filmmaking and writing is top-notch, and its status as a tried and true classic is wholly deserved. As an illustrator, part of what makes me love *Alien* so much is admiring how much artistry and craft was put into it, and a lot of that is due to how familiar I am with the work of the concept team, consisting of greats like Jean 'Moebius' Giraud, Ron Cobb, Chris Foss and, of course, the late H. R. Giger. I had not yet been born when *Alien* was first released in theaters, but I can imagine how shocking it was to those that were, and how it became a genre-defining hit almost instantly.

As for my piece, I made a guess that a lot of the contributing artists may do work centering around the alien itself, and with that in mind, I wanted to depict a lesser-represented scene that happens to be among my favorite moments in the film: the crew's perilous, fog-enveloped trek to the derelict alien spacecraft. The dreary and hostile, almost gothic atmosphere in the scene is a visual that has really stuck with me all these years, and with it preceding the crew's discovery of the giant pilot's corpse and its cargo, is one that the film simply cannot do without.

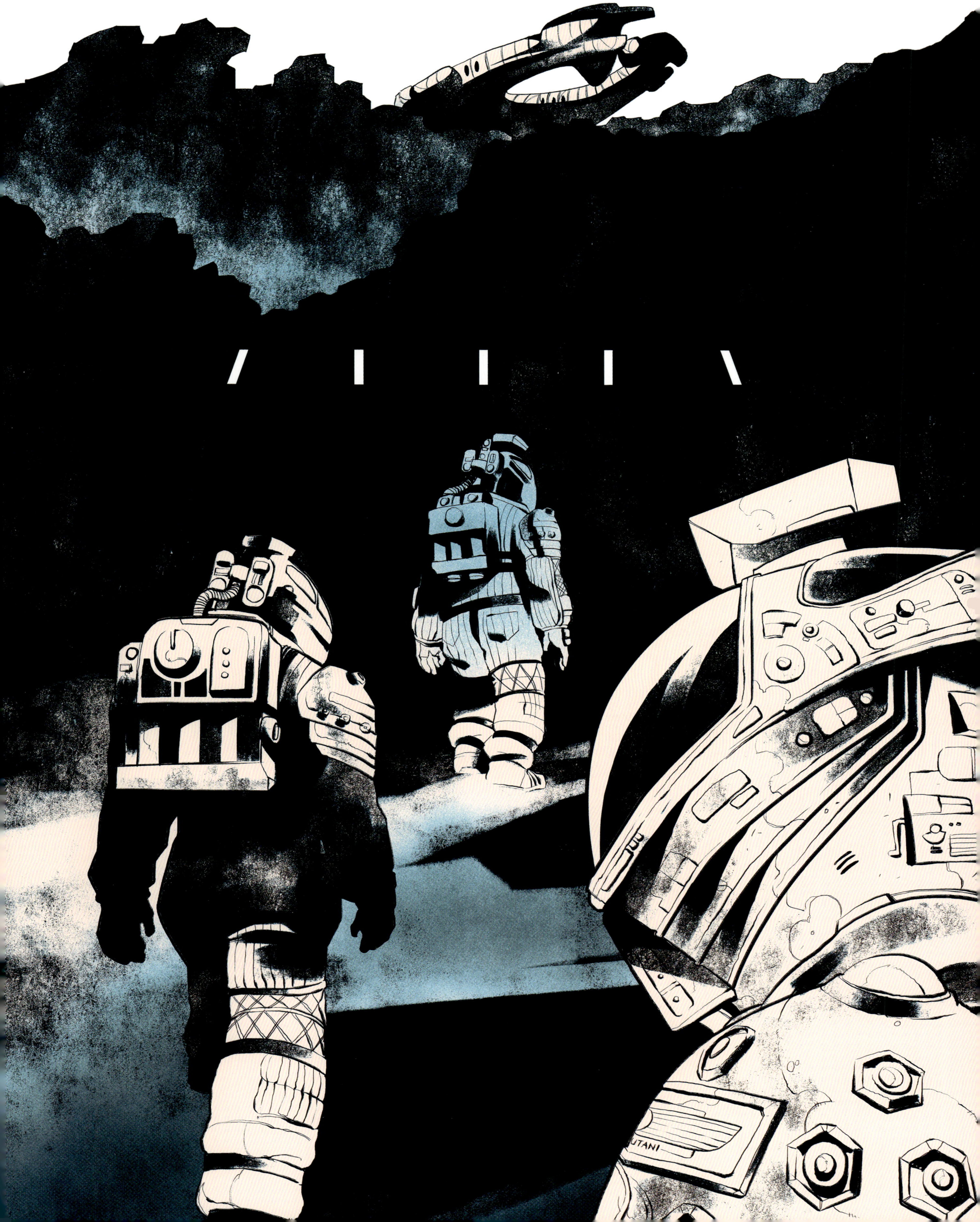
UTANI

CORIN HARDY

ALIEN | ink on paper | 23 x 28.75 cm

Alien means so much to me on so many levels.

I saw it way too young, about aged 8 or 9, I think, and was beyond petrified. It's probably the first film that made me feel sick with utter dread. But this is not attributed to it simply being a horror film or a scary movie.

I was staying at a friend's and his father was the only person I knew who had a VHS player. We watched this video with a black cover with a green egg on the front. That was all we knew back then. "In space no one can hear you scream" – that was a great tag line. Felt scary just thinking about it. Like drowning in space or something. Midway in, probably after 'John Hurt,' I felt so disturbed I took myself off to bed, telling his mum I felt ill. As I lay in a bunk bed surrounded by darkness, the glow-in-the-dark stickers started turning the ceiling at my friend's into an endless galaxy… But all I could see, as I lay shivering with fear, was the black spaces between the stars that surely were inhabited by… that *thing*. What was that *thing*??

It was many years until I finally had the courage to watch the film again. But aside from the obvious visceral terror, I think the main thing that had got to me was that feeling of guilt; of knowing that they shouldn't be messing with stuff on that other planet, they should just leave it alone… They shouldn't be bringing that *thing* back on board (but they had no choice, since it wrapped itself around their crew member, but still….). And the kicker was that brilliant but brief moment of respite, when it seems everything is going to be alright again, when they sit around the table for dinner and they're all pleased that John Hurt seems to have recovered, and my god you want him to be okay and then he starts coughing...

Alien was my first real introduction to pure 'horror,' to 'body-horror,' and to a new level of intricate special effects and flawless, elegant, nightmarish and original creature design. But what I couldn't know then was the reason it had terrified me so much was because of how *real* it all felt; how this balance between something grounded, real, relatable and functional was combined with this devastatingly hellish creation and a believable creature biology that would feel just as at home on a BBC nature documentary: the egg > the facehugger > the thing that grows inside you > the birth > and the black creature with the acid blood that stalks you until you die. *Alien* is *perfect*.

What I gained throughout my later life, watching *Alien* at different stages as an aspiring filmmaker, was how incredibly seriously the crafting of this whole world had been taken, imaginatively in its inception by Dan O'Bannon (and Ronald Shusett/Walter Hill), conceptually and creatively by Ridley Scott and his crew, and in the details and design of the monster by the inimitable H. R. Giger. Such a powerful, unique and inspiring combination.

Alien is such a special sci-fi horror movie with a rock-solid cast and a perfect monster. Every time I think about it I marvel that it was created and looks the way it does. It holds up every time.

Here's to A L I E N . I love you.

(*Please note, my sketch was drawn from memory after a couple of G&Ts on a late-night flight back from Los Angeles to London whilst thinking about *Alien* and this anniversary book.)

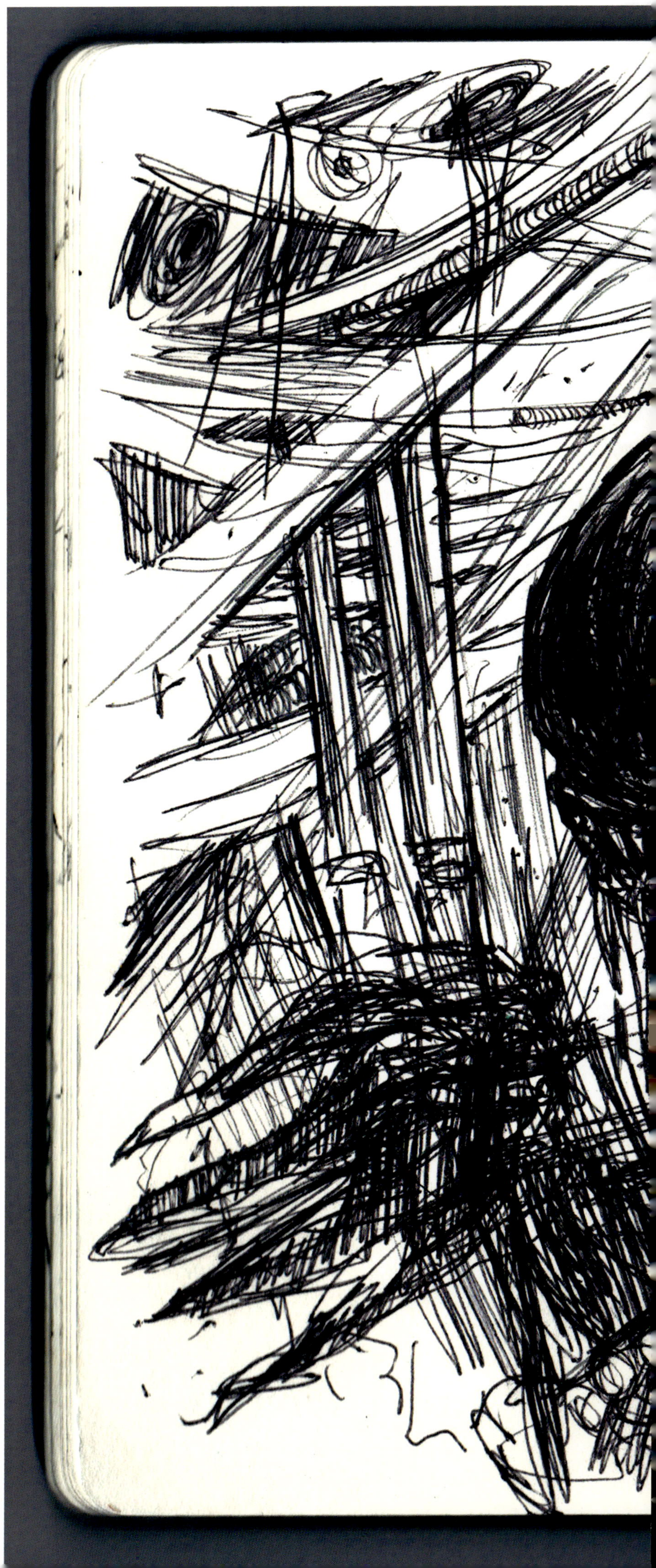

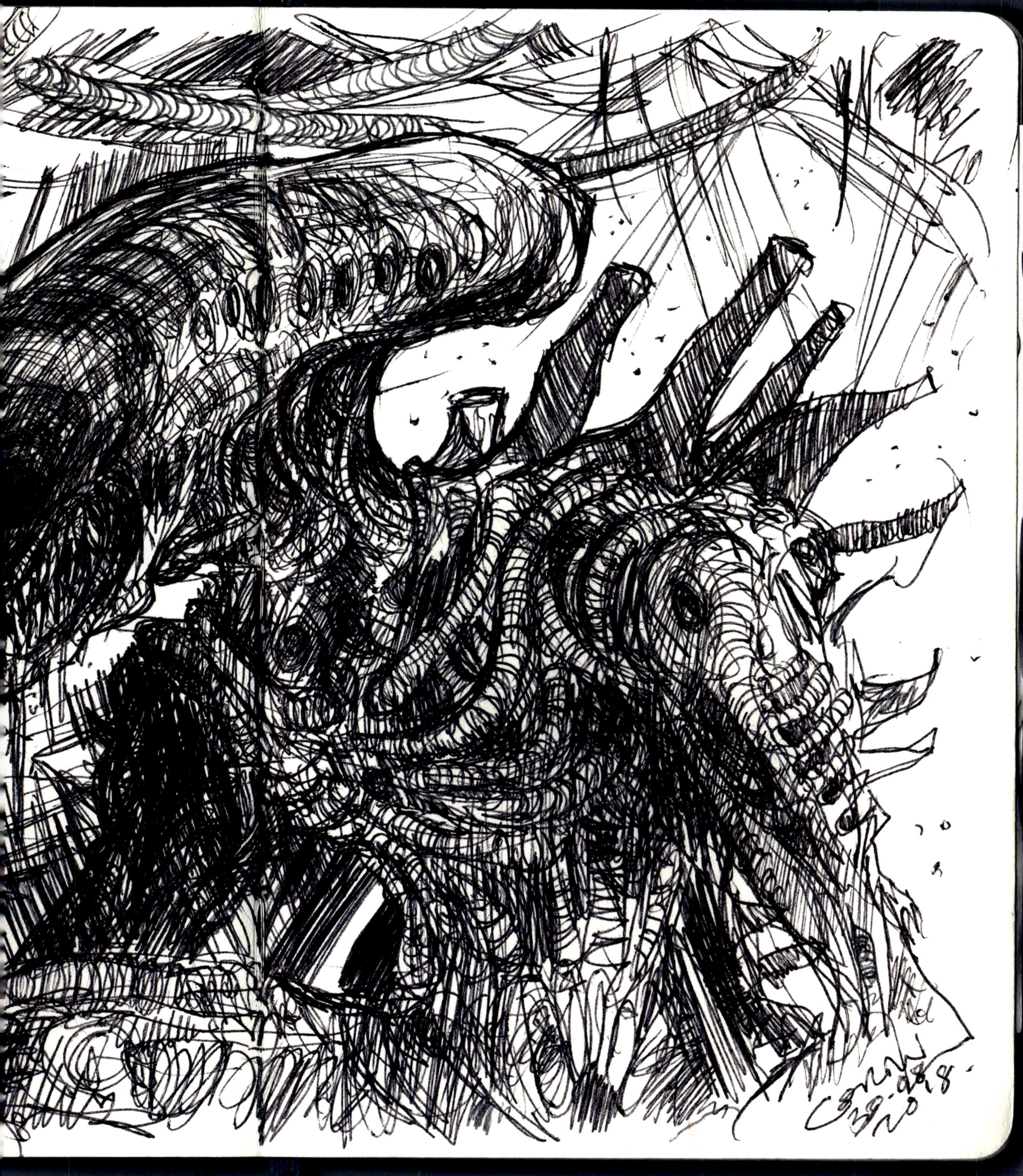

MARTA LECH

Alien 1 | pigment on black paper | 36.5 x 26 cm

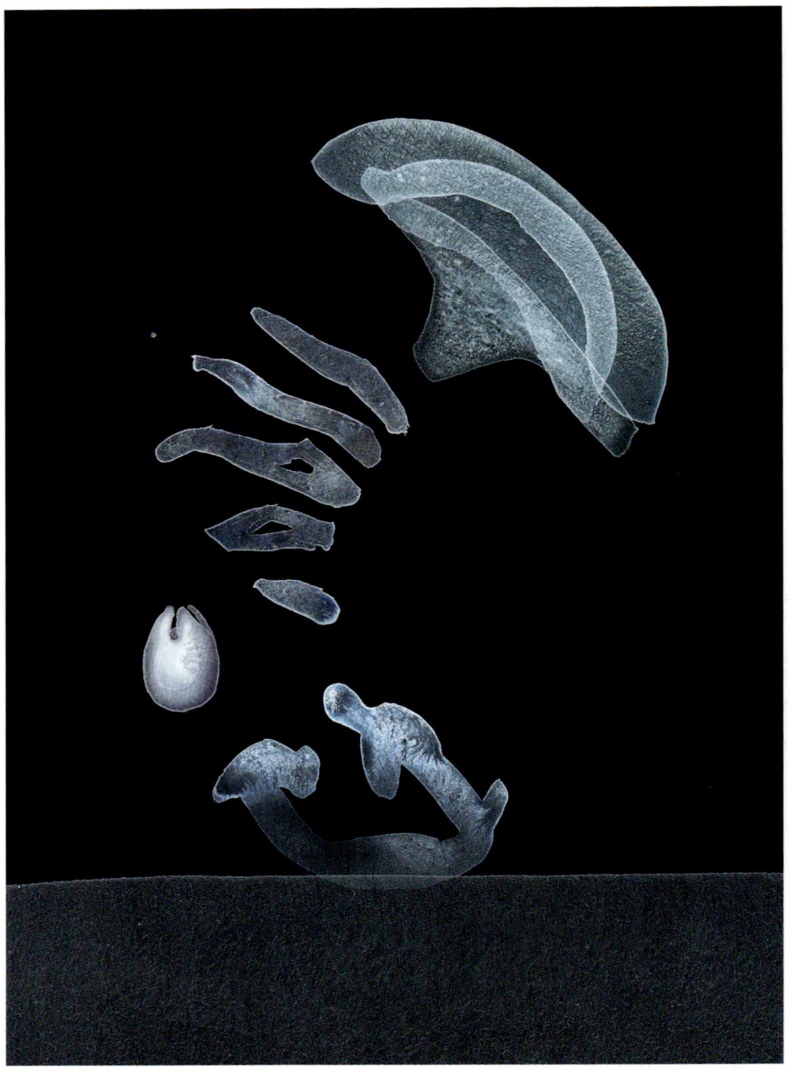

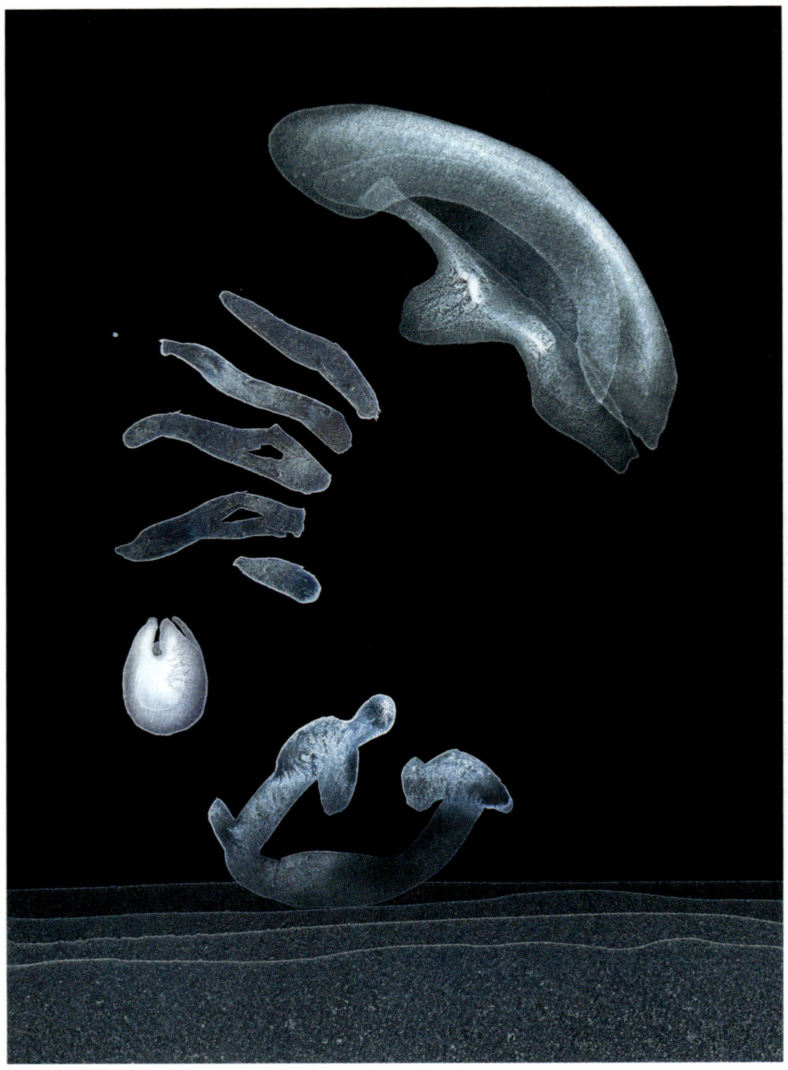

As a printmaker and a painter, I concentrate on my original artworks and design projects on a daily basis, but occasionally I also take on commission projects, such as book and CD covers, illustrations and animation design. Having a settled subject is a very enjoyable and interesting type of work for me. While working on the *Alien* theme I first selected all the elements from the movie that relate to the emergence of an alien form of life. At the beginning, sketches included a wide range of white shapes on a black background. In the final project, some of them, such as the Derelict space ship, an egg and a characteristic elongated head suspended over the horizon, shaped the body of the alien. The simple and dark image resembles a floating, mysterious, sinister ghost, as well as an X-ray picture of an organism subjected to scientific examination.

The technique that I applied helped me to create an ambience of horror that is part of the appearance of an unknown creature. I used a method of painting based on using bright pigment on black paper. I have been working and experimenting with this technique for years, but even though I am able to foresee its possibilities and limits to some degree, the final effect always surprises me. Transparent and overlapping layers of ink form a complex of soft outlines and suggest an extraterrestrial context. They seemed perfectly to illustrate both the futuristic and organic features of H. R. Giger's alien, without the literal, realistic portrayal of the elements or shots from the movie.

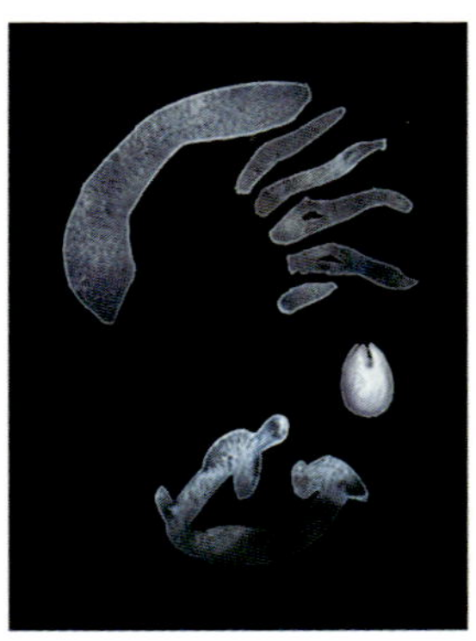

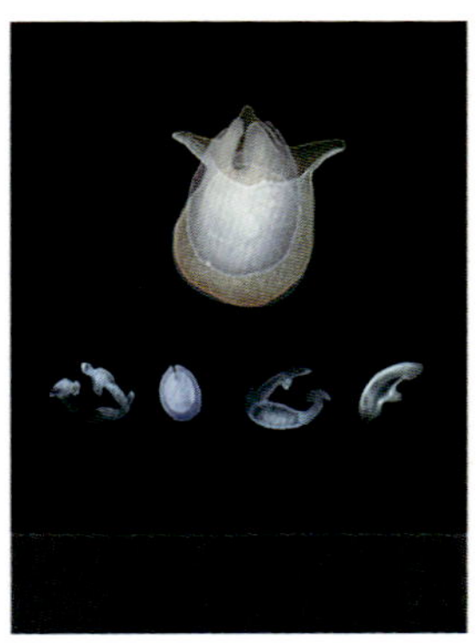

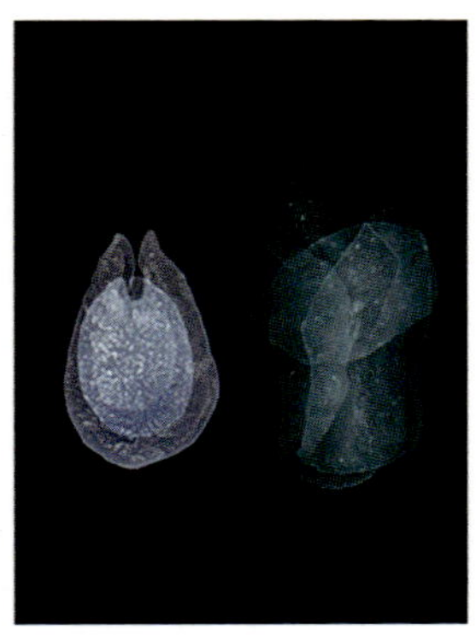

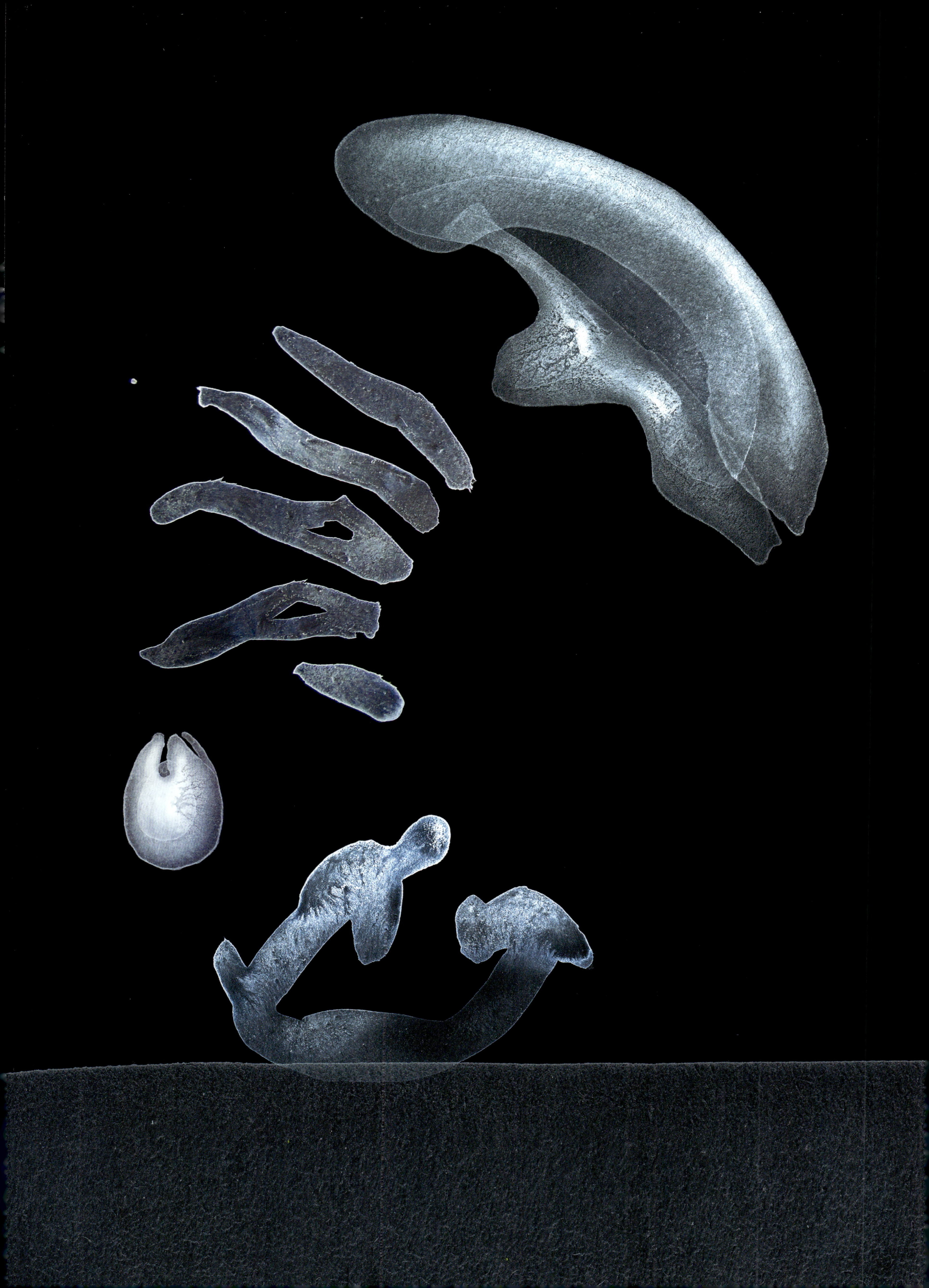

M.J. ERICKSON

What Is Special Order 937? | digital | 73 x 52 cm

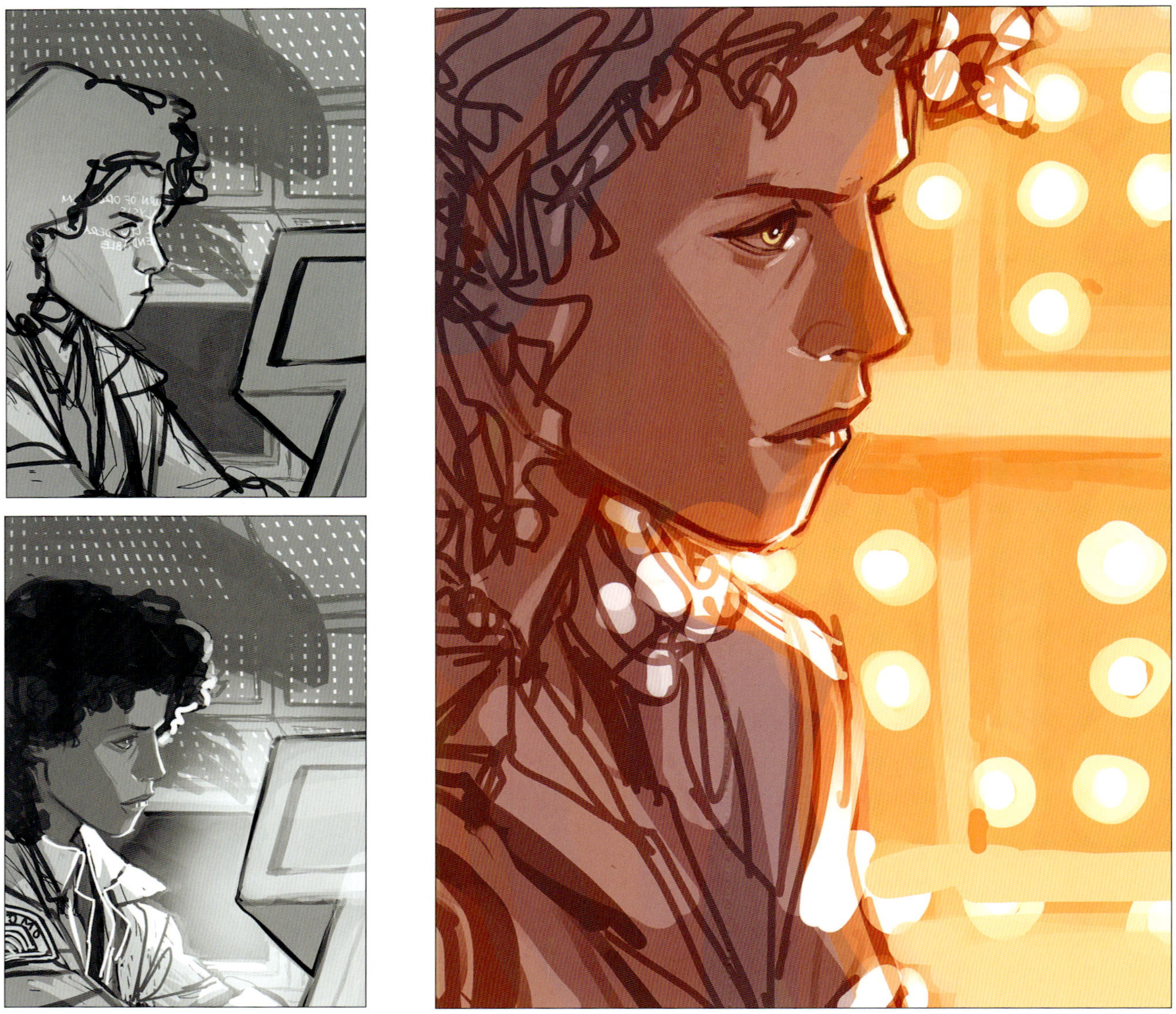

The first *Alien* is one of my all-time favorite films. Initially I just knew it was cool and made me want to draw aliens, then as I got older I learned to appreciate how incredibly visual every element of the story is. I also love how it uses uniquely sci-fi elements to tap into very primal, intimate fears. On a more personal level, Ripley has always been one of my favorite characters. She's intelligent, brave in spite of her fear and fiercely protective. She also doesn't seem to care much about being liked, which was pretty aspirational for a self-conscious teenage girl.

It's difficult to take a screenshot of the film that isn't inspiring. The sets, framing and lighting are all striking, but for this illustration I went with one of my favorite scenes – Ripley querying Mother. The room design for the computer core is iconic, and I love the way Mother's grim replies reflect off of Ripley's face.

For me, *Alien*'s always been about Ripley versus both the Xenomorph and this sprawling, immoral scientific advancement, so I wanted to fit them both in to my illustration. Having the shadow of the Xenomorph melting into Mother's lights looks cool, but it also really emphasizes the company's role as the instigating agent behind the monster.

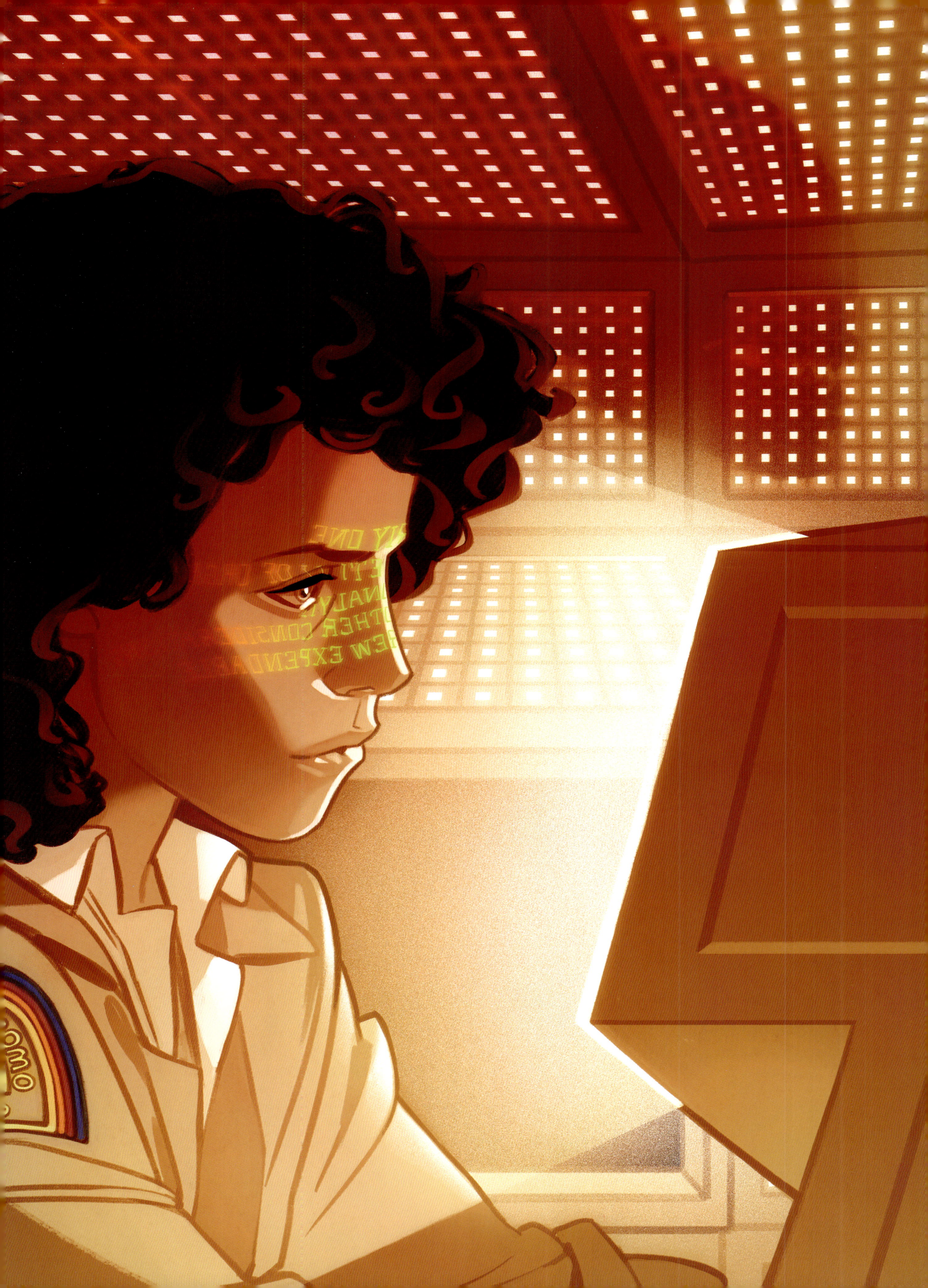

ANSON AGUIRRE FIRTH

Alien | ink on paper | 40 x 30 cm

My first contact with the *Alien* franchise was at eight years old. I remember distinctly being gathered around my grandmother's old television set with my brothers and older cousins. *Aliens* was being shown on prime-time TV on a Saturday night in November 1997.

The title card emerged and, oh boy, we were in for a crazy ride. From its slow, mysterious and excellent character-building intro to its incredible set designs, action sequences and amazing creatures, I immediately fell in love with the movie. I was particularly drawn to the incredible animatronics on the alien queen and its perfectly polished design created by Stan Winston and his team. After we finished watching the movie, we moved out to the garden, assumed the role of soldiers and started hunting down imaginary alien warriors.

Soon after, I found out there was the original *Alien* movie from 1979. I went with my mom and rented it from our local Blockbuster. I believe I watched it every night until we had to take it back the following week. Then, one of my older cousins invited us to play his recently purchased *Alien*^{3} game for Super Nintendo, where we needed to save hopeless prisoners from being eaten by Xenomorphs and obliterate the Xenomorph species once and for all. From that moment on, my passion for *Alien* and space horror was born.

One of the aspects I kept enjoying about the movie was the aesthetics of the creatures: mysterious, scary, fierce and intimidating. Soon enough I found out about H. R. Giger and purchased my first Giger art book. As I flipped through the pages I found myself falling in love with his work more and more. It was daring, overtly explicit and a world of its own. His studies of biomechanics and work on *Alien* was exquisite. That inspired me to start drawing my first Xenomorphs and I haven't stopped since.

In commemoration of *Alien* reaching its 40th anniversary, I was kindly asked to create an intimate work that portrayed my relationship to the franchise. I knew right away what I wanted to do: celebrate the incredible Xenomorph design. This work is both an exploration of this subject as well as a character study of the alien life cycle and its social hierarchy, and how carefully they are linked to each other, by mimicking the ones we find in insects nowadays.

This work is also both a celebration of the franchise as well as a tribute to Giger and Ridley Scott, as they have given us (together with the amazing animatronics from Stan Winston) the best sci-fi movie made, as well as the best sequel ever made.

Game over man! Enjoy.

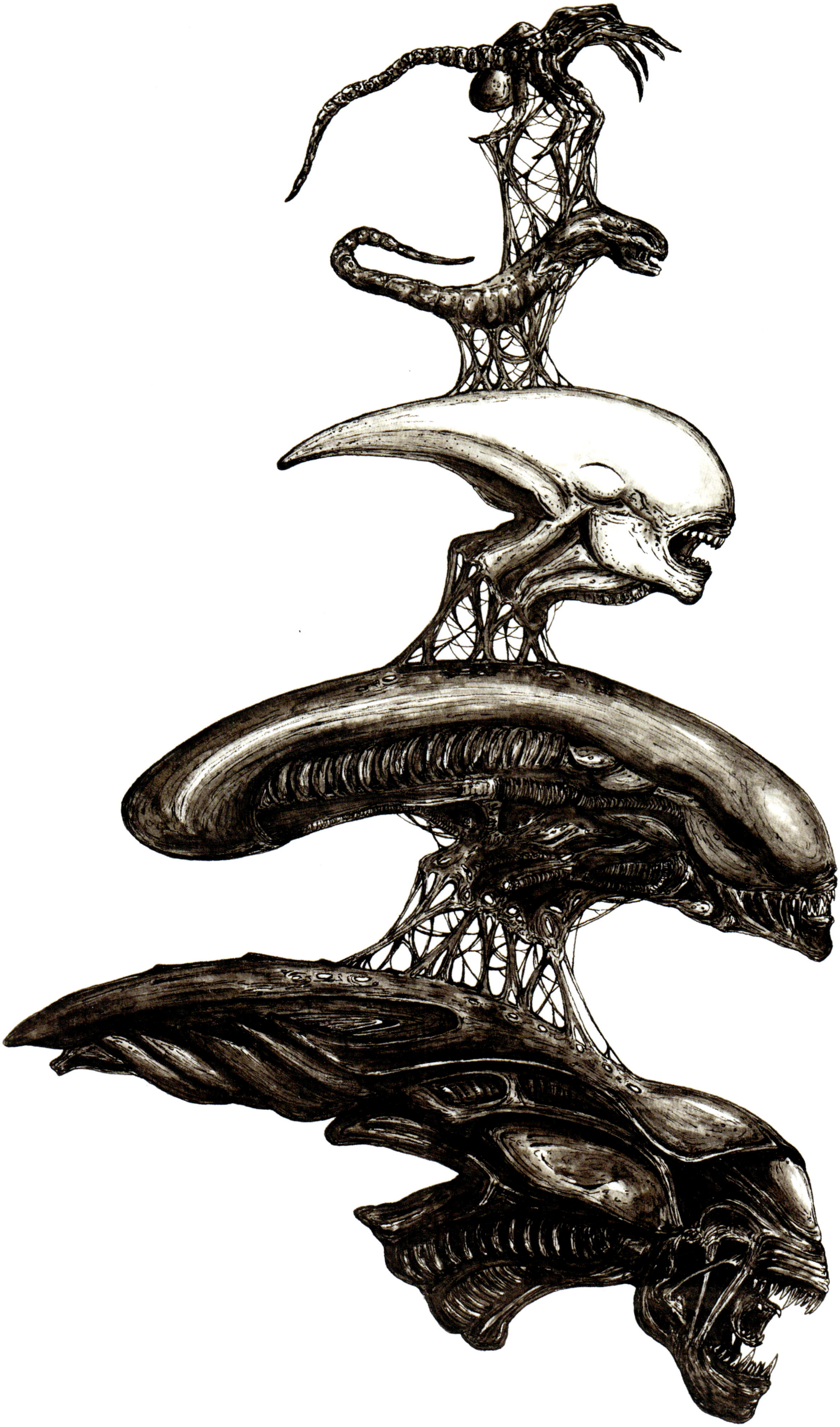

GONZALO 'GENZOMAN' ORDÓÑEZ ARIAS

Biological/Industrial | digital | 45 x 32 cm

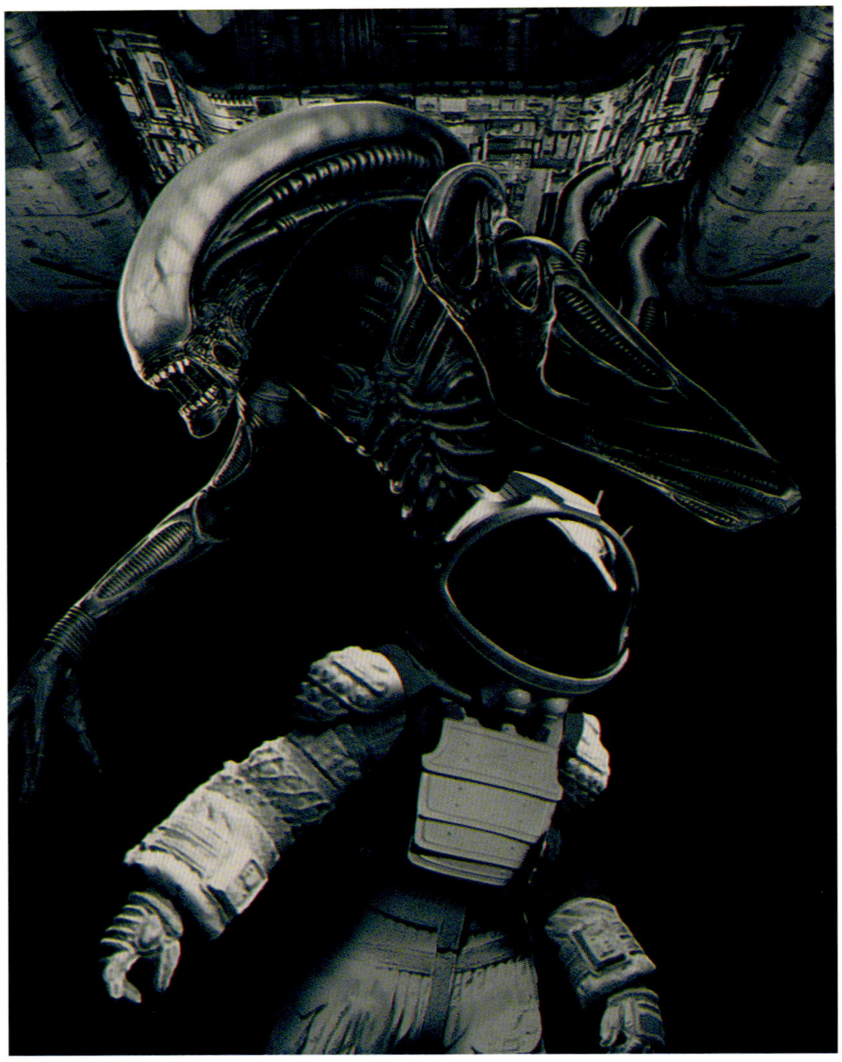

I love the *Alien* franchise. My father took me to see the first movie when I was a little child (apparently he thought it was another space adventure in a galaxy far, far away). This happy accident made me fall in love with horror and sci-fi movies at a very young age. It was not just about the creature, I was obsessed with the world of the film. The mysterious music of Jerry Goldsmith. The realistic and scientific tone that made it feel closer to a documentary than to a fictional movie. The contrast between the surreal biological horror of the surface of LV-426 and the Derelict of H. R. Giger, and the industrial chaos of the *Nostromo* and the impressive mechanical designs of Ron Cobb and Chris Foss. Everything in it had a detailed, baroque and grim atmosphere.

Based on this, I tried to create an illustration that was a tribute to the style of H. R. Giger and the designs of Cobb and Foss; an amalgam of both elements of the film, the alien and the industrial.

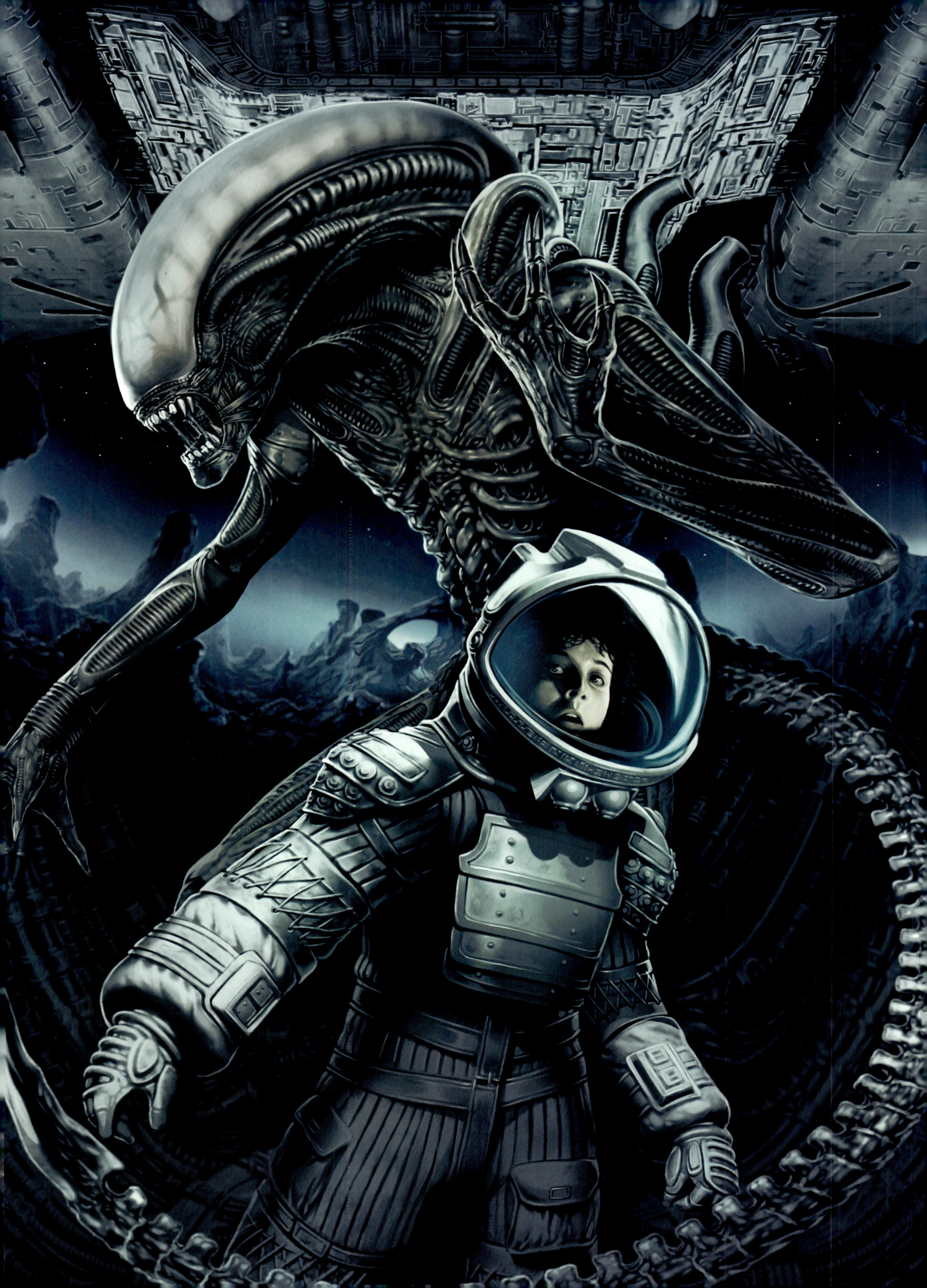

TIM CLINARD

ALIEN | digital | 48 x 33 cm

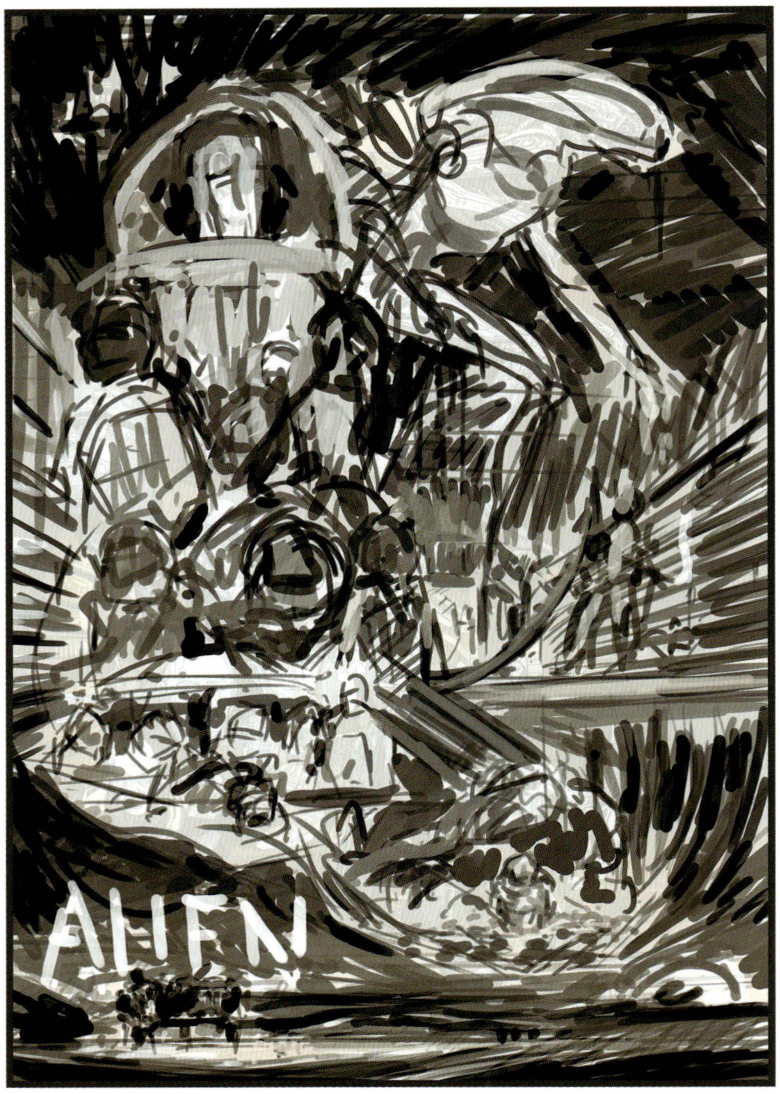

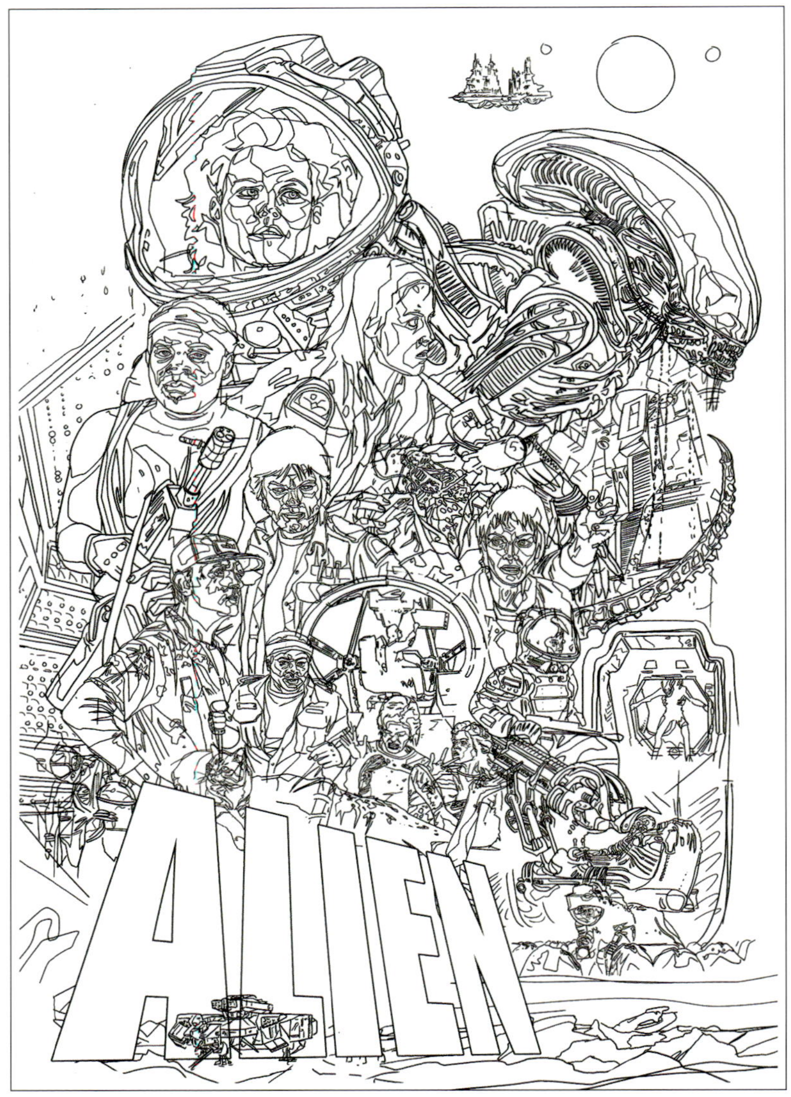

Alien is among my favorite films of all time. On first viewing, Ridley Scott's vision was like nothing I had seen before and continues to resonate with me today. As a visual person, I can appreciate deeply the masterful skill and passion those creative people possessed to construct such a beautiful, believable world. Their skill was only matched by a terrifying story and a stellar cast of actors to bring it all to life.

When I approach any piece I challenge myself to answer: Who, what, where, and when? This movie is special and I wanted to look at this poster and remember as much as I could about the film. A single image that would attempt to convey a lot of the major elements of the movie. I aimed to achieve this by compiling all the characters and as many poignant moments as I could fit on the page. When communicating the story I utilize scale and composition in an effort to draw the viewer through the piece, allowing them to experience the film as if they were watching it again for the hundredth time. From landing on the surface of LV-426, to Kane encountering the eggs in the belly of the derelict, the famous chestburster scene, Ash's demise, Ripley's iconic flamethrower, and ultimately her donning the space suit, facing the beast, and ejecting the Xenomorph into outer space.

I thoroughly enjoyed making this piece and I truly hope all the *Alien* fans out there can enjoy it too.

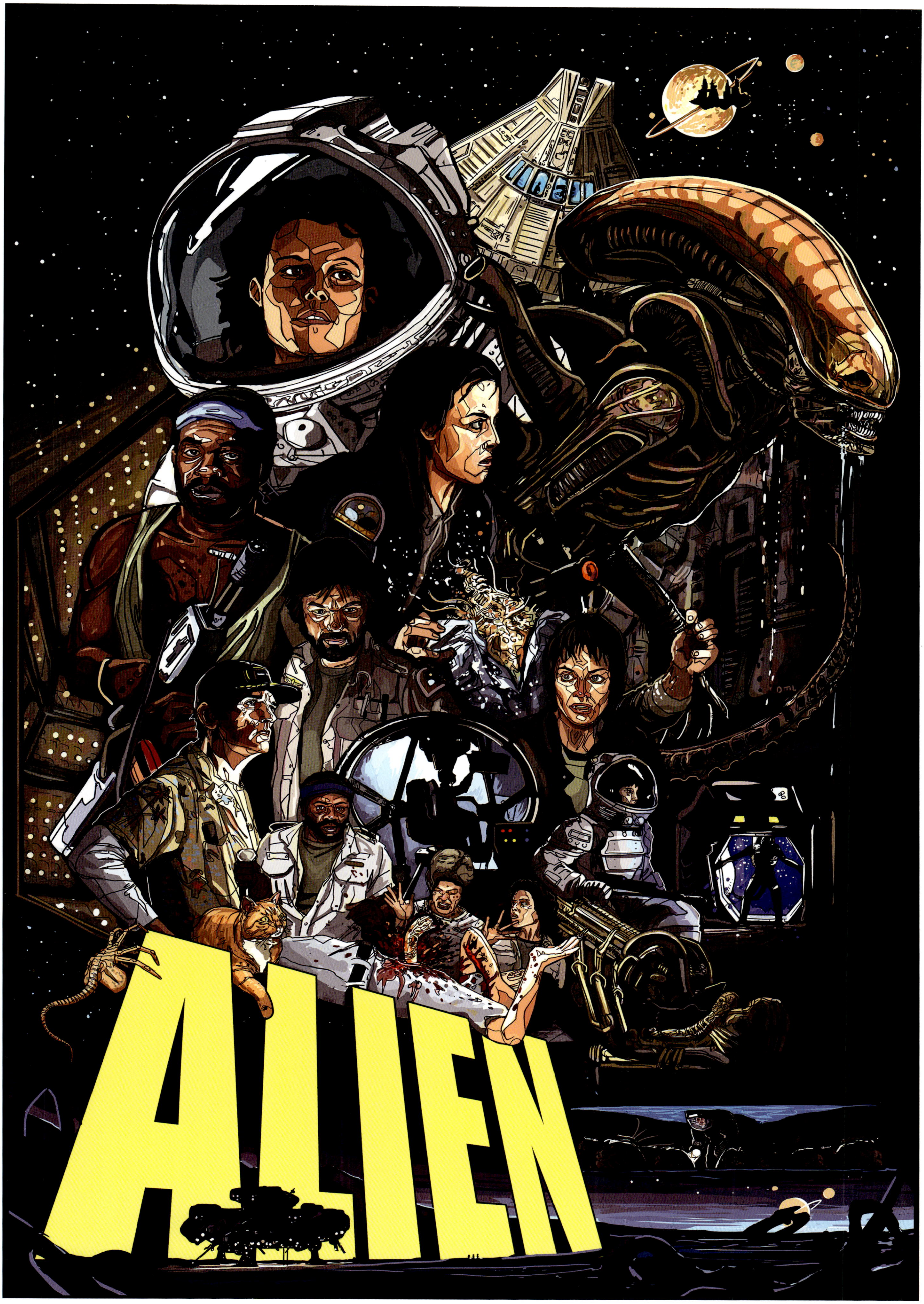
ALIEN

CHRIS 'ZHOURULES' SHEHAN

Xenomorph | pencil and ink on paper | 43 x 28 cm

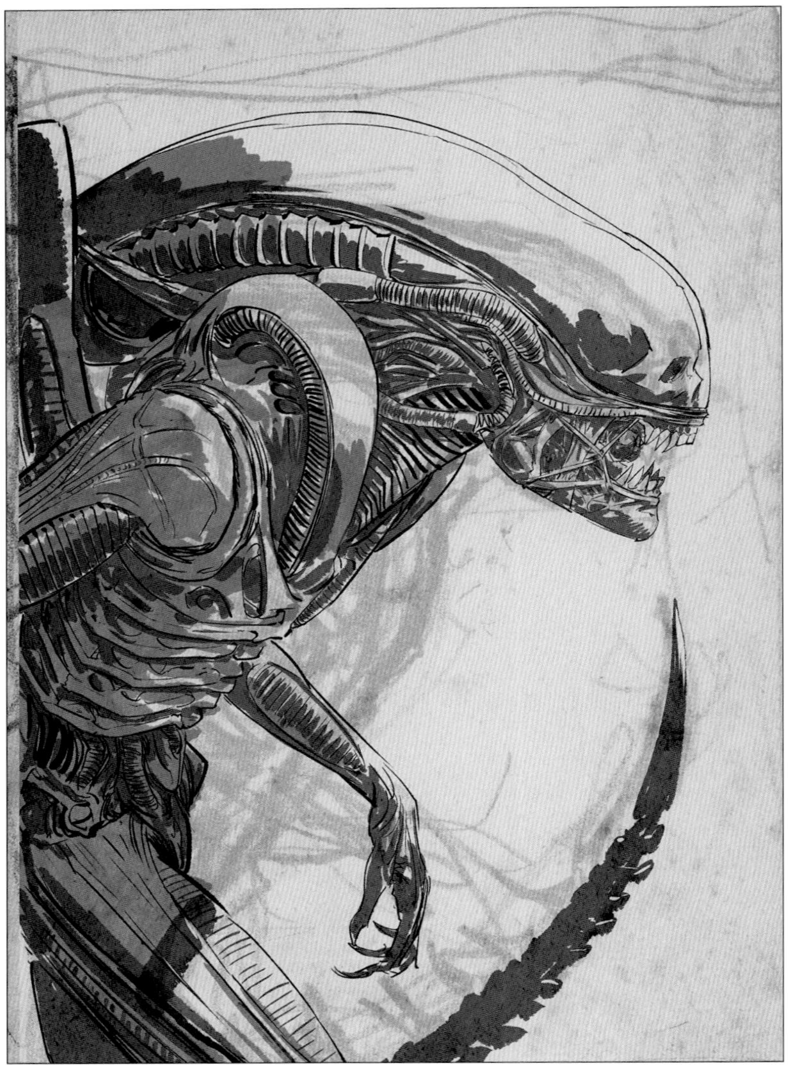

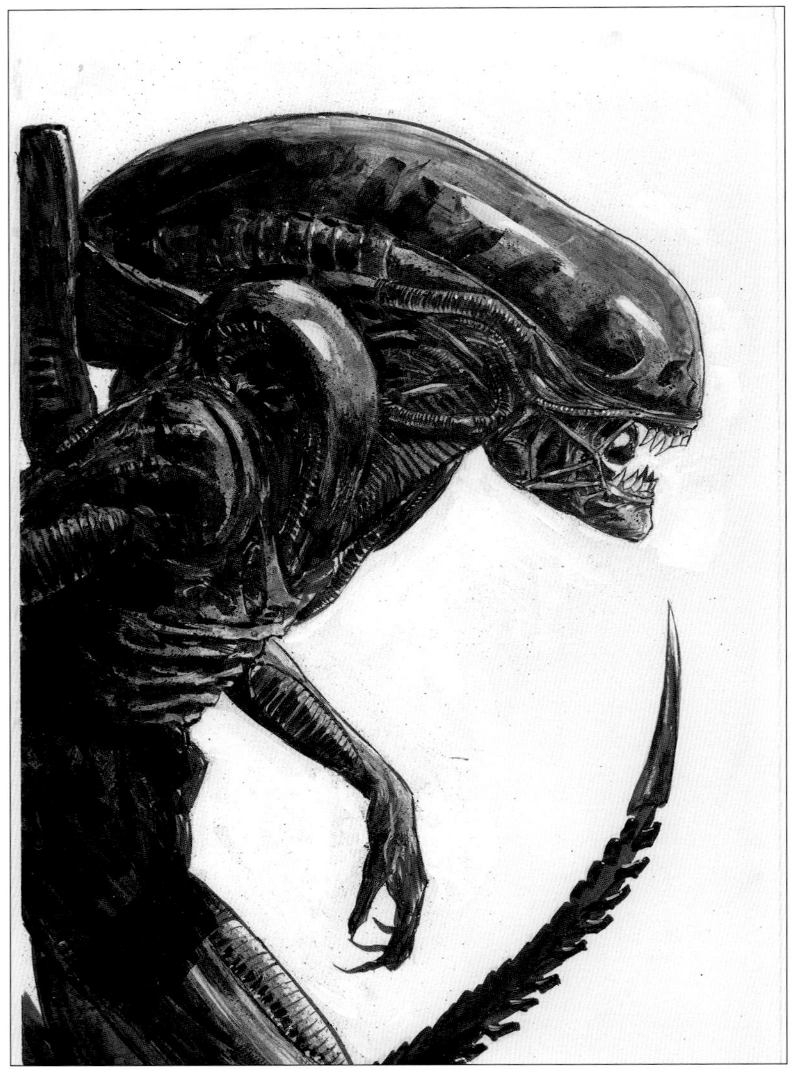

I was born in 1990, quite a while after the first *Alien* came out. But there's no doubt that the classic Xenomorph has been a very big part of pop culture since its inception. I grew up with friends who had the toys, seeing *Alien* and Xenomorph references in parody, but I was never allowed to watch movies like that as a child. But I grew up loving sci-fi because of *Star Wars*. I grew up appreciating practical effects without even realizing it. I also got to witness the early days of CGI. There was magic in older films that was lost along the way, but has been making an amazing comeback as technology improves. That being said, I'll never forget when I finally decided to watch *Alien*. I was in my early twenties, so I was able to see the film without nostalgia goggles. And I was at an age where I could appreciate cinematography, practical effects, and all of the work that goes into masterful filmmaking.

While I'm incredibly late to the party, *Alien* immediately became one of my top favorite movies of all time. It means a lot to me as an artist, as a storyteller, and as someone who appreciates sci-fi and being transported while watching a movie. I rarely, if at all, see films that come along to rival the first *Alien*. I spent an entire month literally studying and sketching shots from the movie just to learn from it. 1979's *Alien* is a piece of art. So what better way to appreciate art than with my own art.

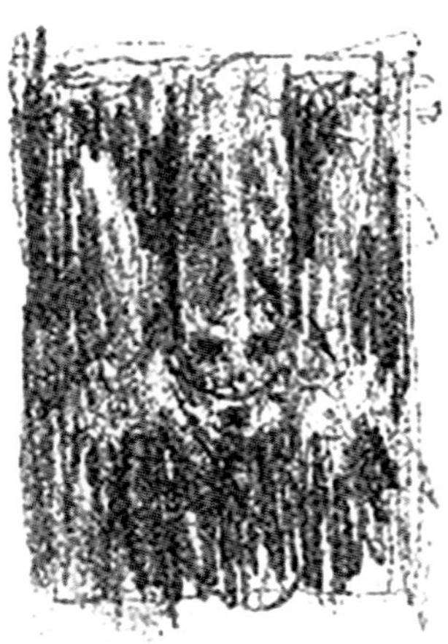

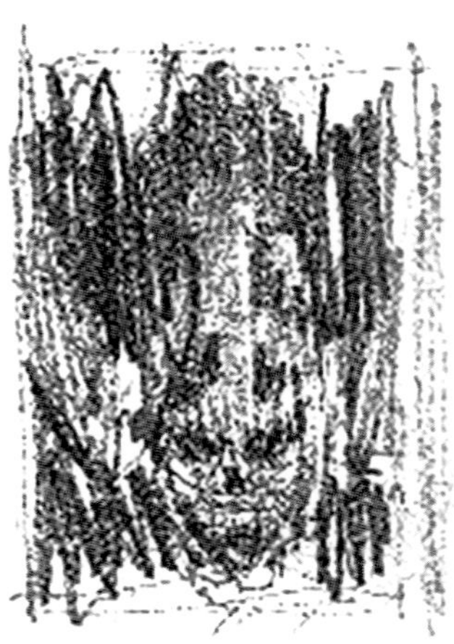

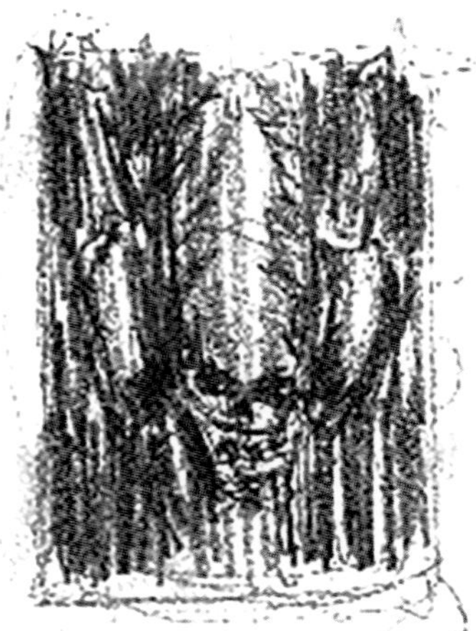

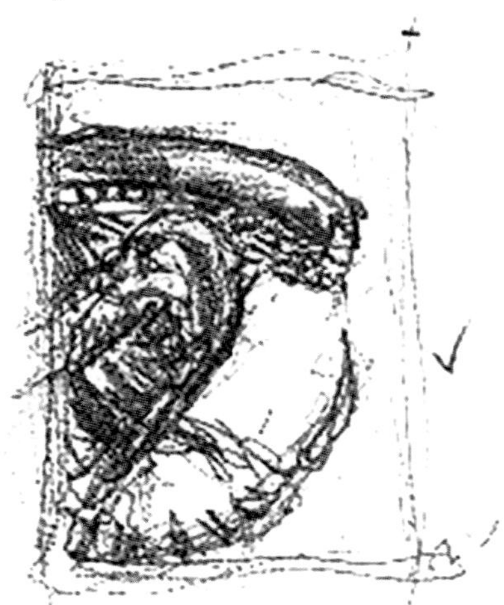

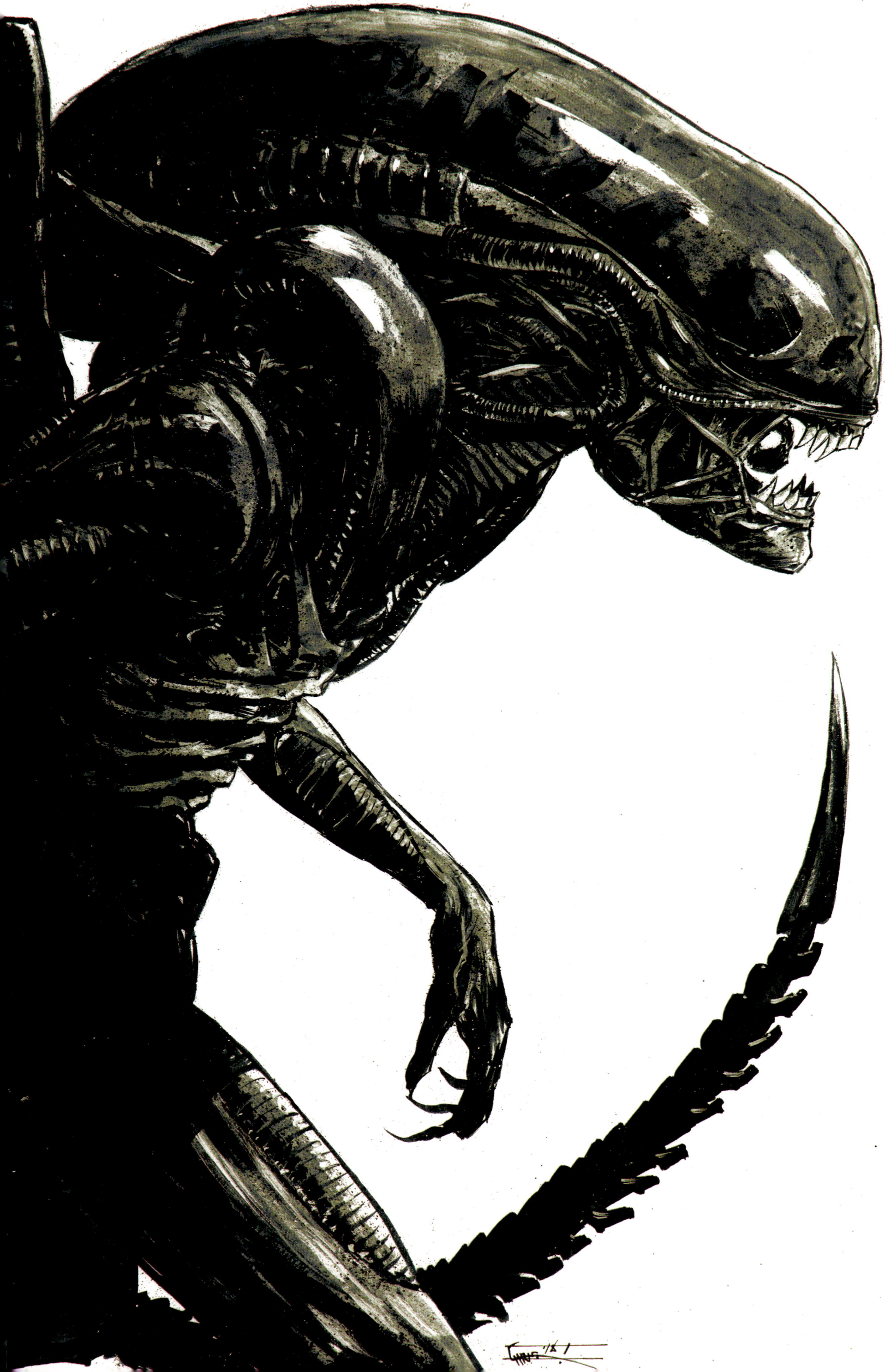

KATHERINE KUEHNE

ALIEN | digital | 39 x 28 cm

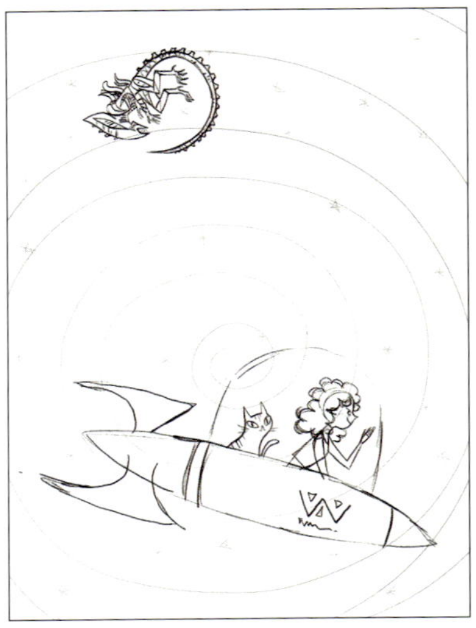

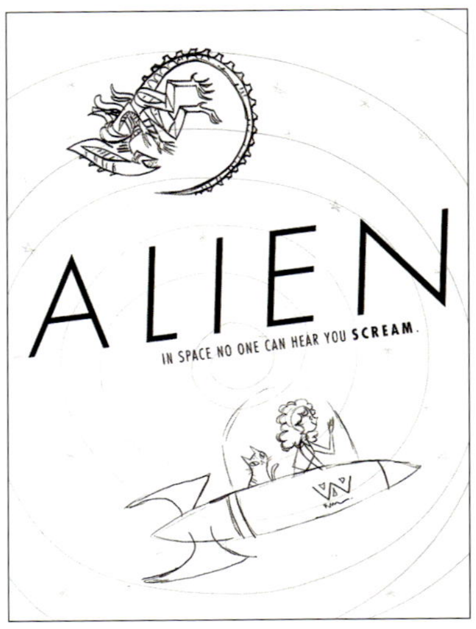

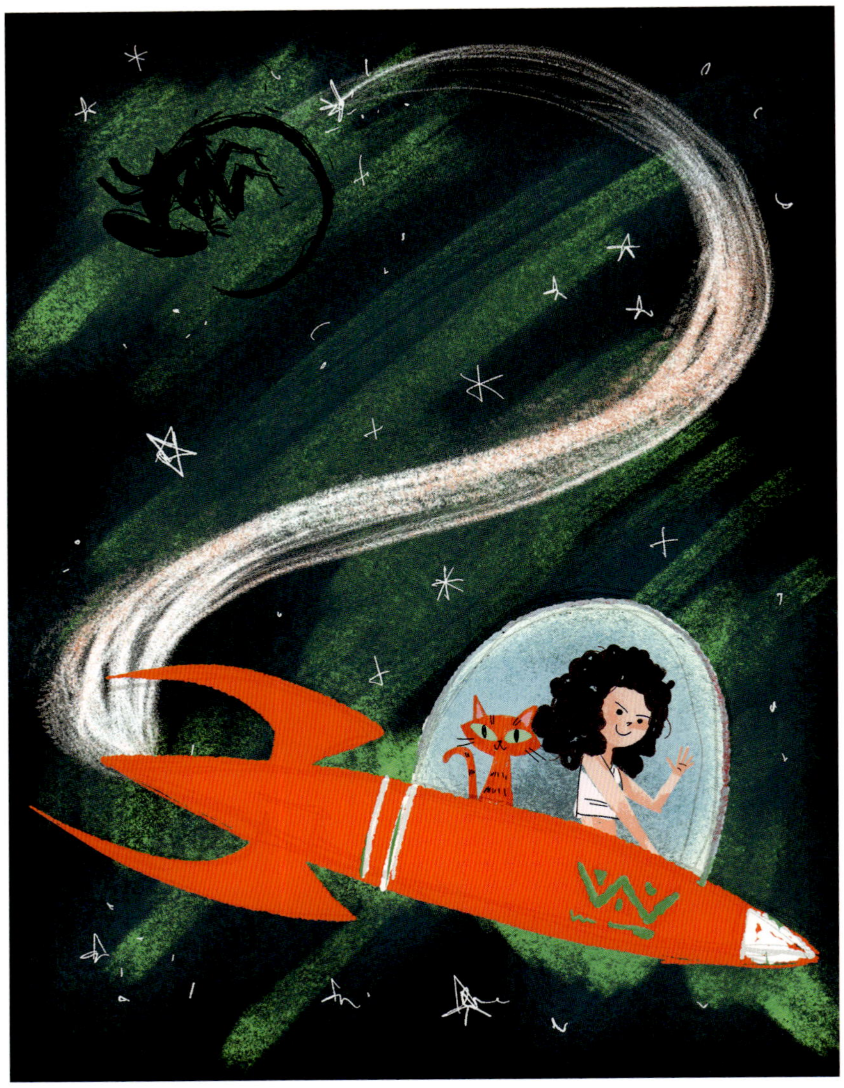

Alien is such a special movie to me. While I am a big sci-fi fan, I am kind of a chicken when it comes to all things horror. I was unwilling to even give this movie a chance for a long time, until a friend finally forced me to sit through all of it. Wow, was I grateful he did, though! It still scares me every time I watch it – Jones surviving is always my biggest concern! But it's the reason I'm now willing to even give any other horror movie a chance. Because who knows what else I had been missing out on all these years? So thank you *Alien* for broadening my movie horizons a little more.

Since *Alien* is a horror movie, though, this means it lends itself best to dark, spooky art. But the moment I was asked to do this illustration I knew I wanted to do something a little more lighthearted with it. My own personal style is a bit whimsical and that's the kind of art I'm drawn to most myself. So I wanted to make this illustration for all the other *Alien* fans like me out there that enjoy a little silliness in their art. I hope that whoever is reading this now will appreciate this illustration just as much as I enjoyed making it.

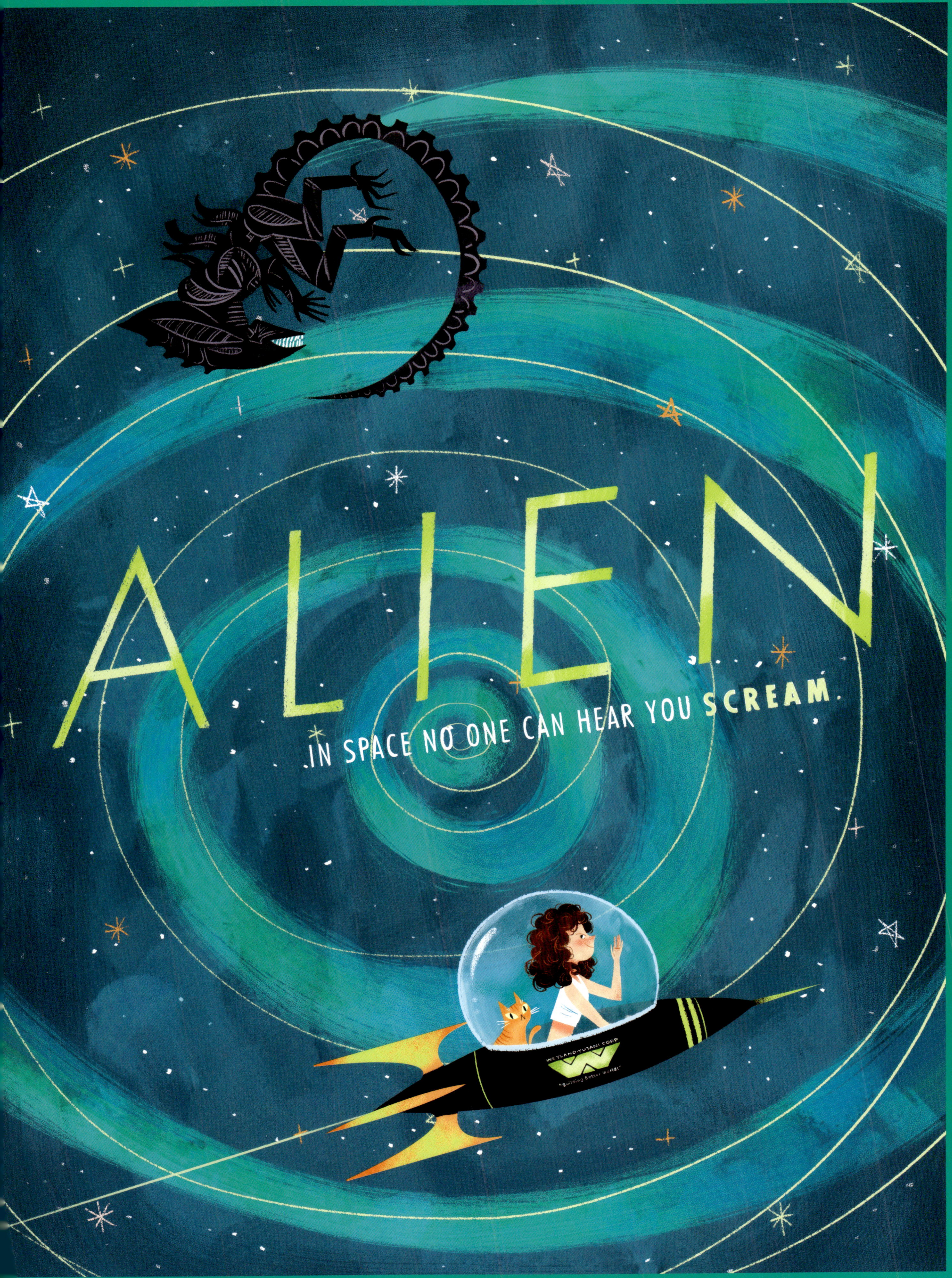
ALIEN
IN SPACE NO ONE CAN HEAR YOU SCREAM
WEYLAND-YUTANI CORP
"Building Better Worlds"

RUSSELL WALKS

Get Paid to Sleep & Let's Head Off-World! | digital and illustration | 36 x 26 cm

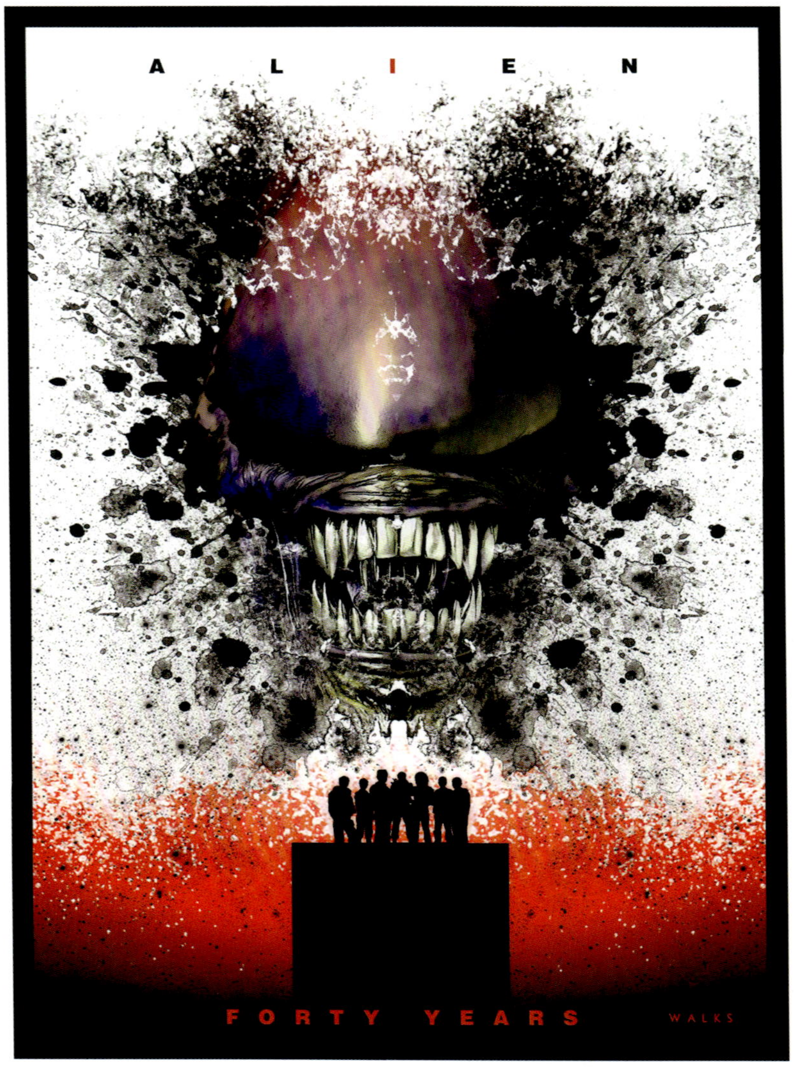

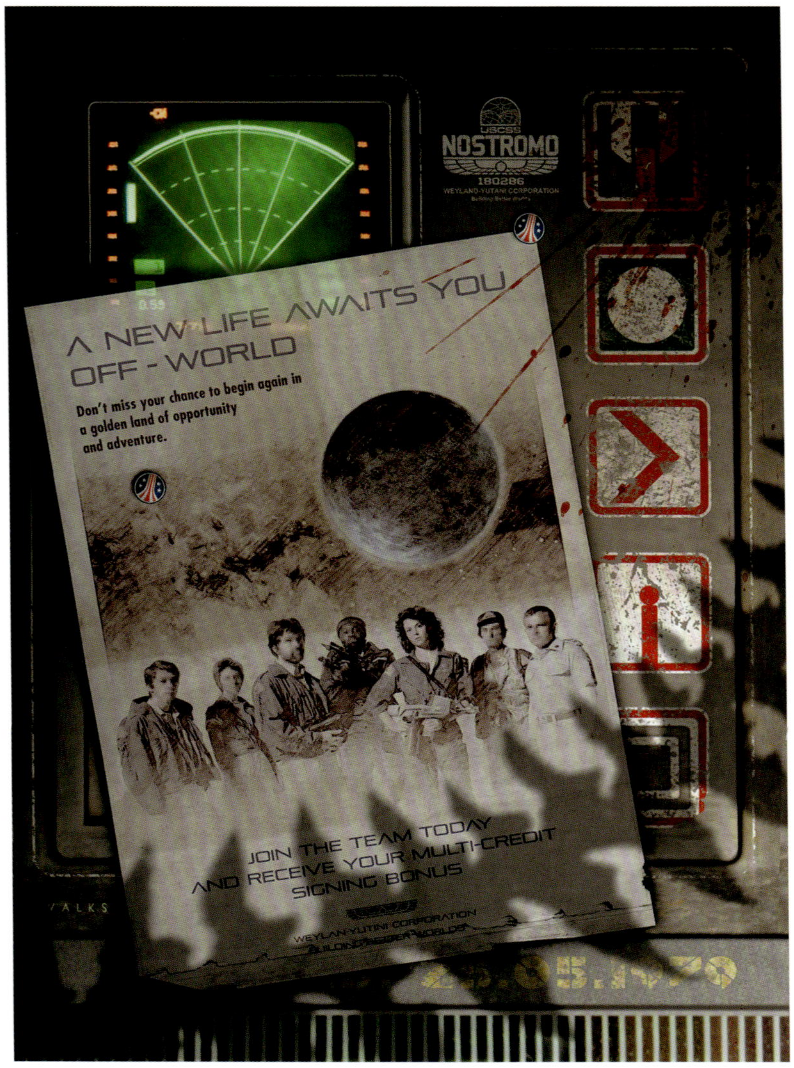

I've always thought of *Star Wars* (which I love unconditionally) as something sort of like comfort food – hot salty french fries, maybe, or chocolate ice cream. It's always there for me, and it never fails to make me feel better – a little more optimistic about life, I guess, and about the universe in general. *Alien*, on the other hand, is like that spicy taco you eat after midnight, knowing the whole time – even as you add salsa verde – that you'll still be awake and uncomfortable at three or four in the morning.

On its surface, *Alien* is about shadows and darkness and the things that hide in the spaces we can't see. You could argue that's also what *Alien* is about on the layers below the surface – that it's about corporate greed, and the idea that the real evil in *Alien* isn't the creature itself, but is, instead, the company, Weyland-Yutani, that values profit over life. That idea, and the idea that maybe things aren't so different right here on Earth, adds a level of discomfort that, like the heat from that super-spicy taco, lingers.

For me, though, that's just the seasoning. The reason I keep returning to *Alien* is because Ripley's struggle to survive, even in the face of overwhelming, ever-increasing odds, resonates with me. Ripley's dedication to life is, for me, the meat of the movie, and is why I love *Alien* as much as I do. It's the reason I watch, alone in the darkness, long after midnight, even though I know there's a good chance I'll still be awake when the sun rises.

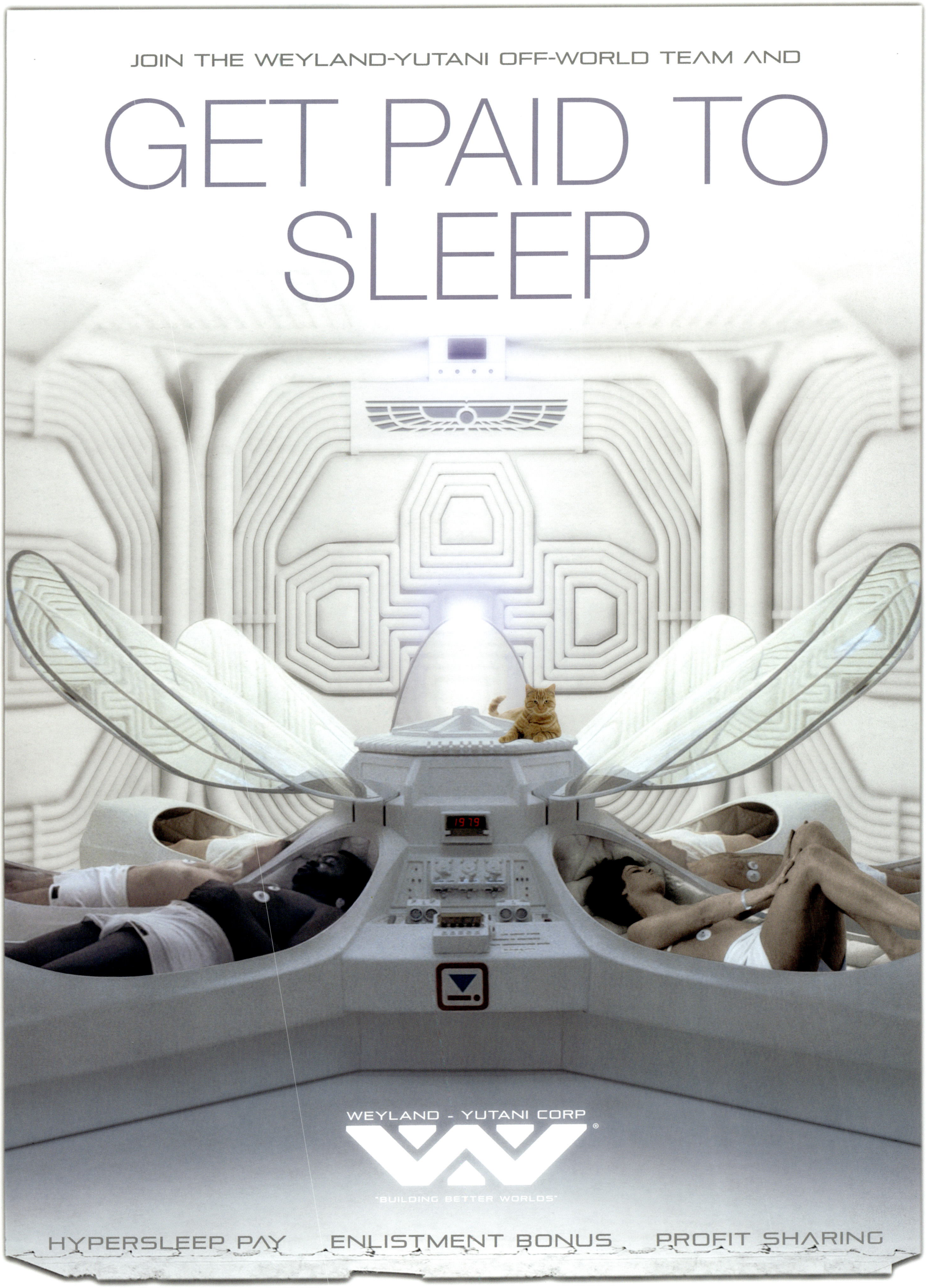
JOIN THE WEYLAND-YUTANI OFF-WORLD TEAM AND
GET PAID TO SLEEP
WEYLAND - YUTANI CORP
"BUILDING BETTER WORLDS"
HYPERSLEEP PAY
ENLISTMENT BONUS
PROFIT SHARING

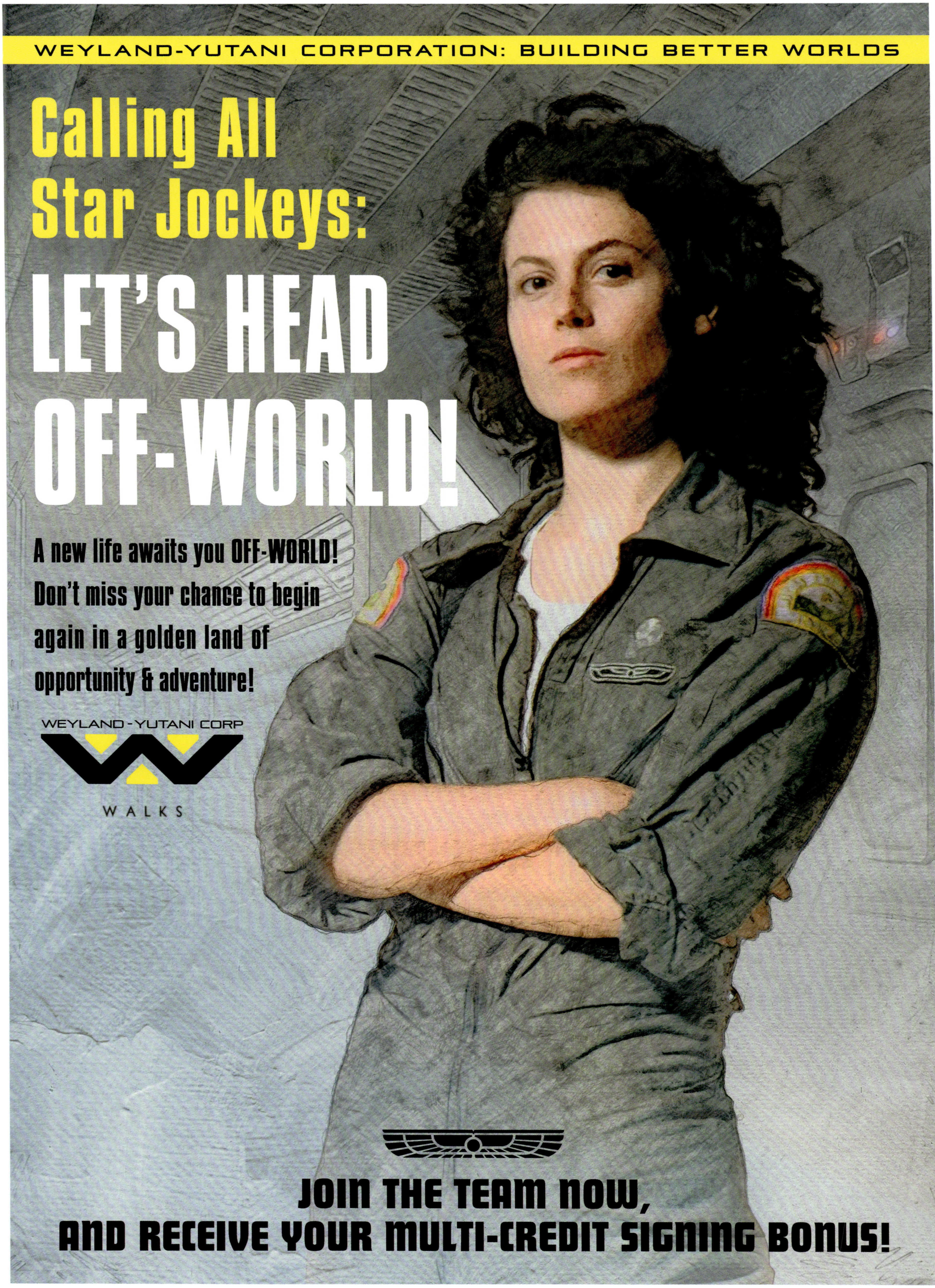
WEYLAND-YUTANI CORPORATION: BUILDING BETTER WORLDS
Calling All Star Jockeys:
LET'S HEAD OFF-WORLD!
A new life awaits you OFF-WORLD! Don't miss your chance to begin again in a golden land of opportunity & adventure!
WEYLAND-YUTANI CORP
WALKS
JOIN THE TEAM NOW,
AND RECEIVE YOUR MULTI-CREDIT SIGNING BONUS!

DENIS VILLENEUVE, SAM HUDECKI, TANYA LAPOINTE

Knossos 1700 BC | concept by Denis Villeneuve, illustration by Sam Hudecki, text by Tanya Lapointe | 49 x 71 cm

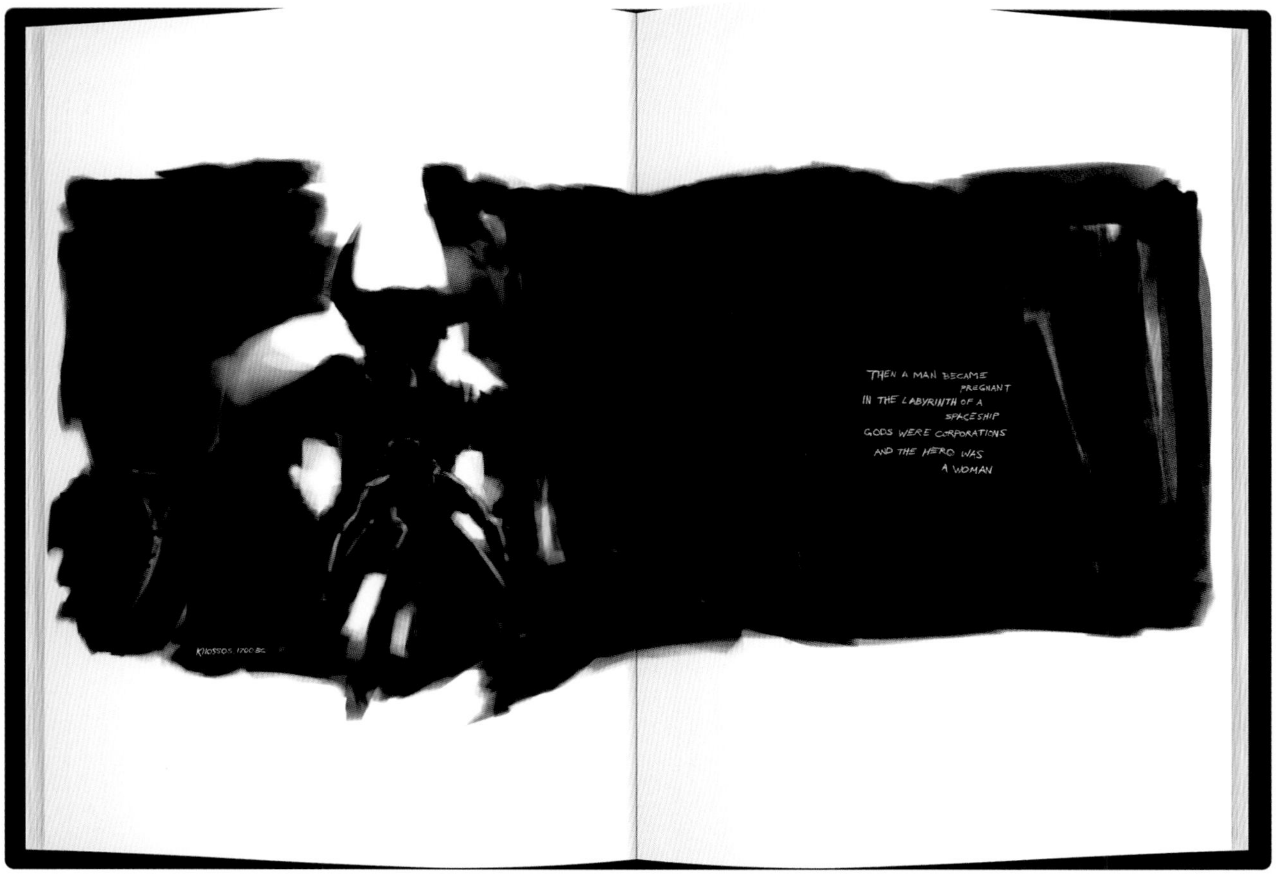

That "the hero was a woman" resonates with me. I think we should all aspire to be heroes, no matter how big or small our actions.

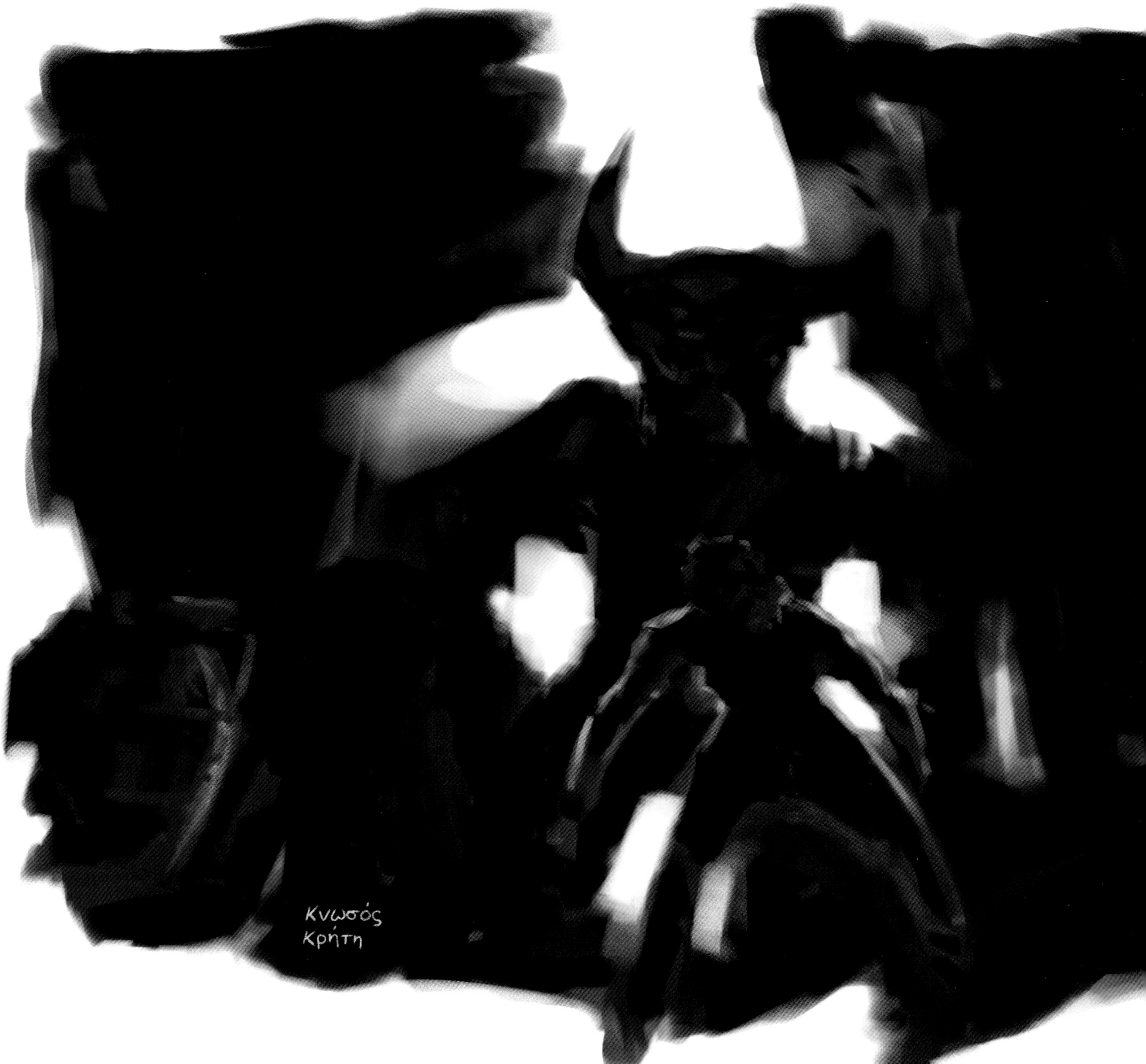
Κνωσός
Κρήτη

THEN A MAN BECAME
PREGNANT
IN THE LABYRINTH OF A
SPACESHIP
GODS WERE CORPORATIONS
AND THE HERO WAS
A WOMAN

TRISTAN 'T-REX' JONES

Lambert's Scream | illustration by Tristan Jones, colours by Simon Gough | 31 x 21 cm

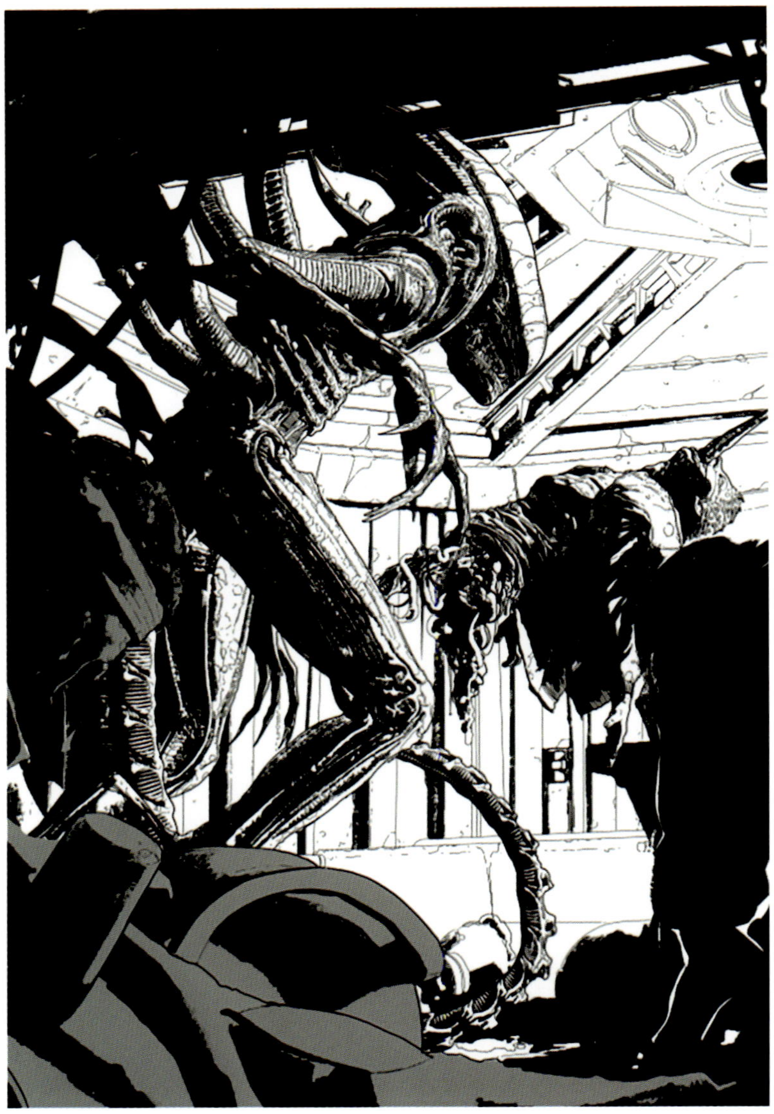

Everything about *Alien* is utter perfection to me. The storytelling – both scripted and visual – the design, the sound. How it's informed my own sense of storytelling, both visually and narratively, cannot be overstated, and the text itself cannot be over-studied. The attention to detail – cutting to the core of what's pertinent without being bogged down in theatrics – is incredible and something I've always strived for in my own work, whether it's written or drawn, which is why working on the *Alien* comics for Dark Horse has literally been a dream come true. Dark Horse's original stories were also the first comics I bought month to month on my own, ushering in my exposure to the greats, like Doug Mahnke, Kelley Jones, Steve Bisley, Richard Corben and, perhaps two of my own biggest influence personally, Mike Mignola and Kilian Plunkett. I could retire from comics tomorrow and be happy having worked on what I have… (But I won't, because I have more aliens to draw!)

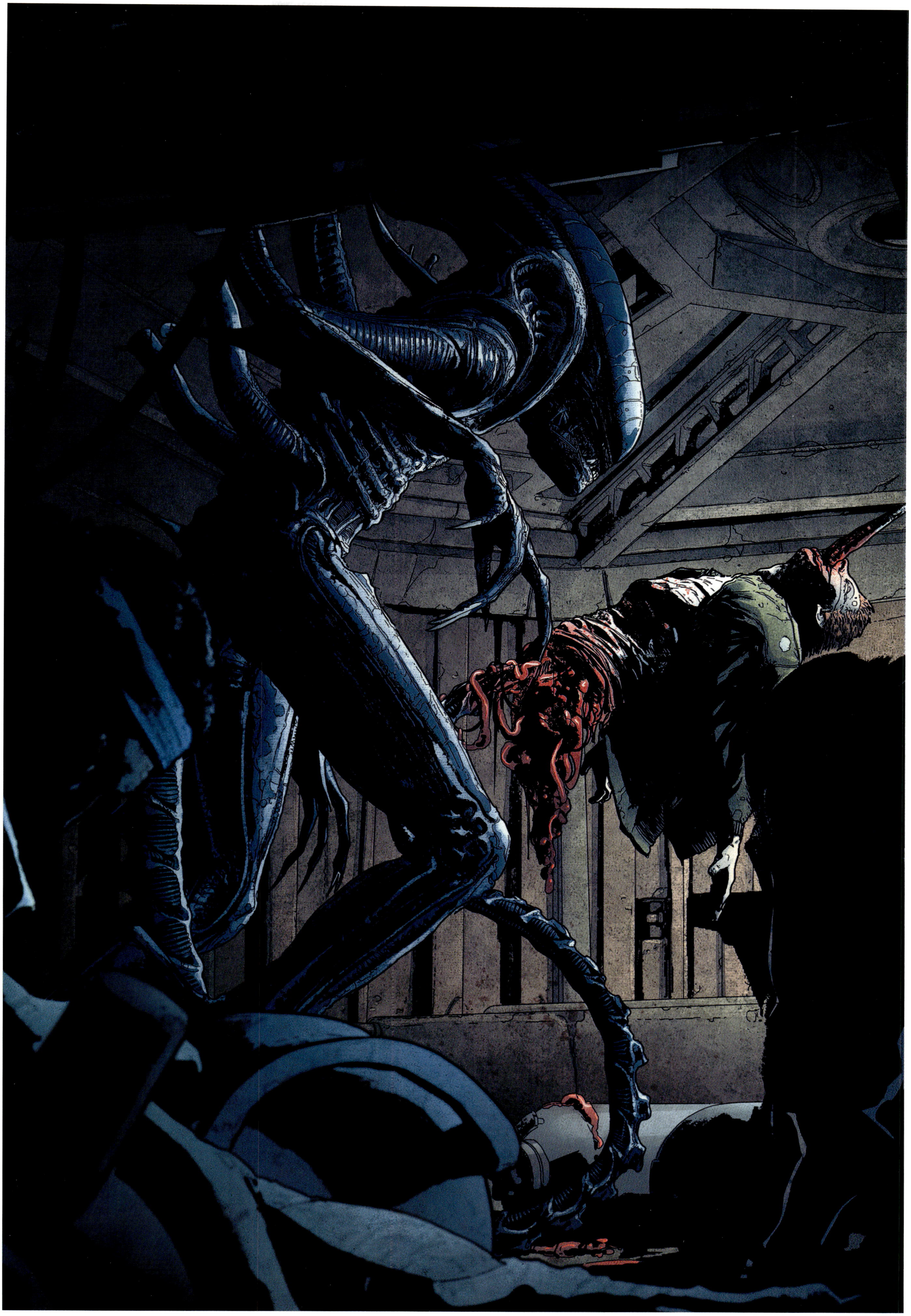

RORY LUCEY

Good Boy | digital | 73 x 52 cm

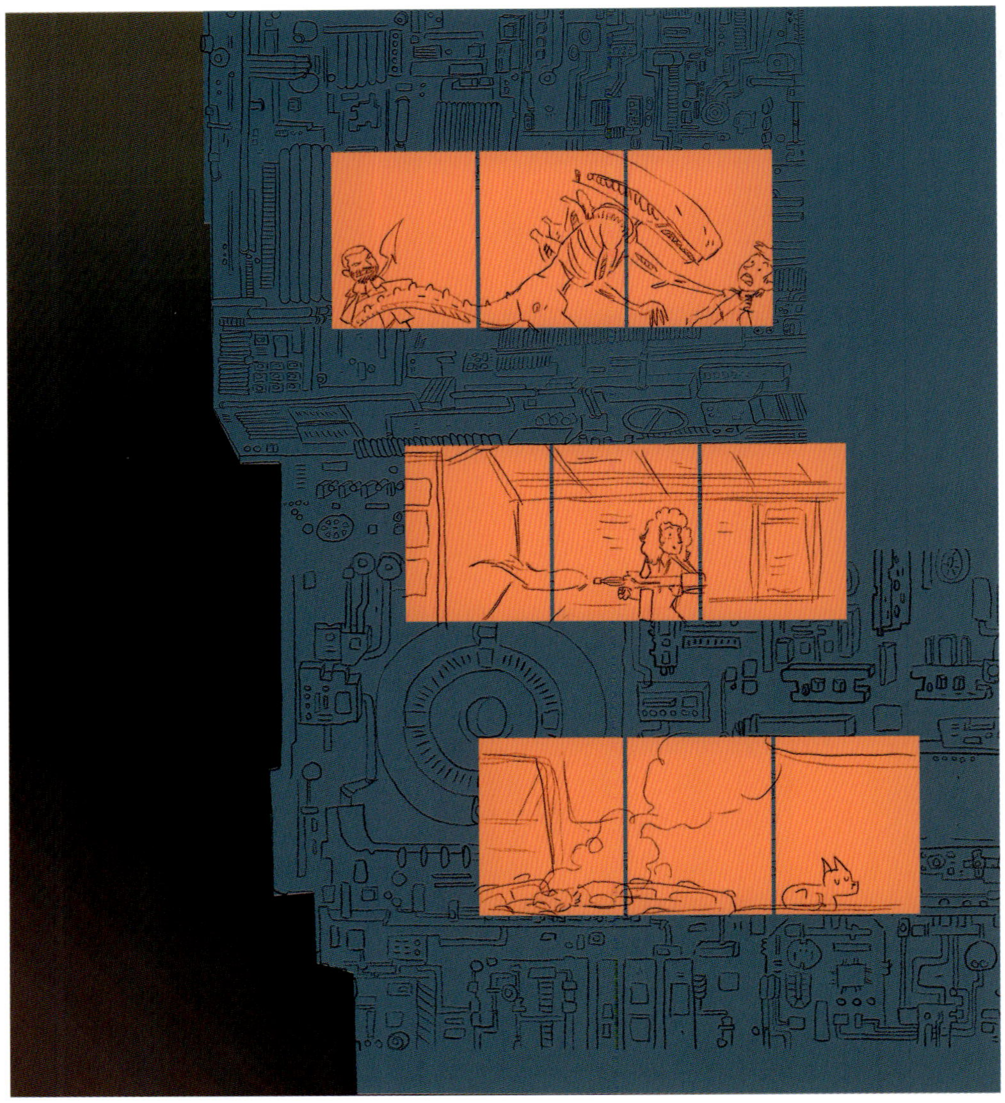

I could write at length about the moments and details of *Alien* that I love – the hidden fury of Ripley patiently telling Ash he broke the chain of command, the way John Hurt eats spaghetti before he dies, that Ridley Scott put his kids into space suits to get the scale right when they're on the moon of LV-426. But to my eyes, the smartest decision was to include Jones the cat. Jones makes the horror of *Alien* familiar and relatable. While it is infinitely more terrifying, I understand Ripley's decision to run back and find Jones and I think the film is better because of that decision. A perhaps unintended side effect of all of this, though, is that *Alien* has made pet ownership terrifying. I've never had to escape an alien on a space ship, but when I have had to look for my cats in the dark I think of Brett's death as he looked for Jones in the same circumstances.

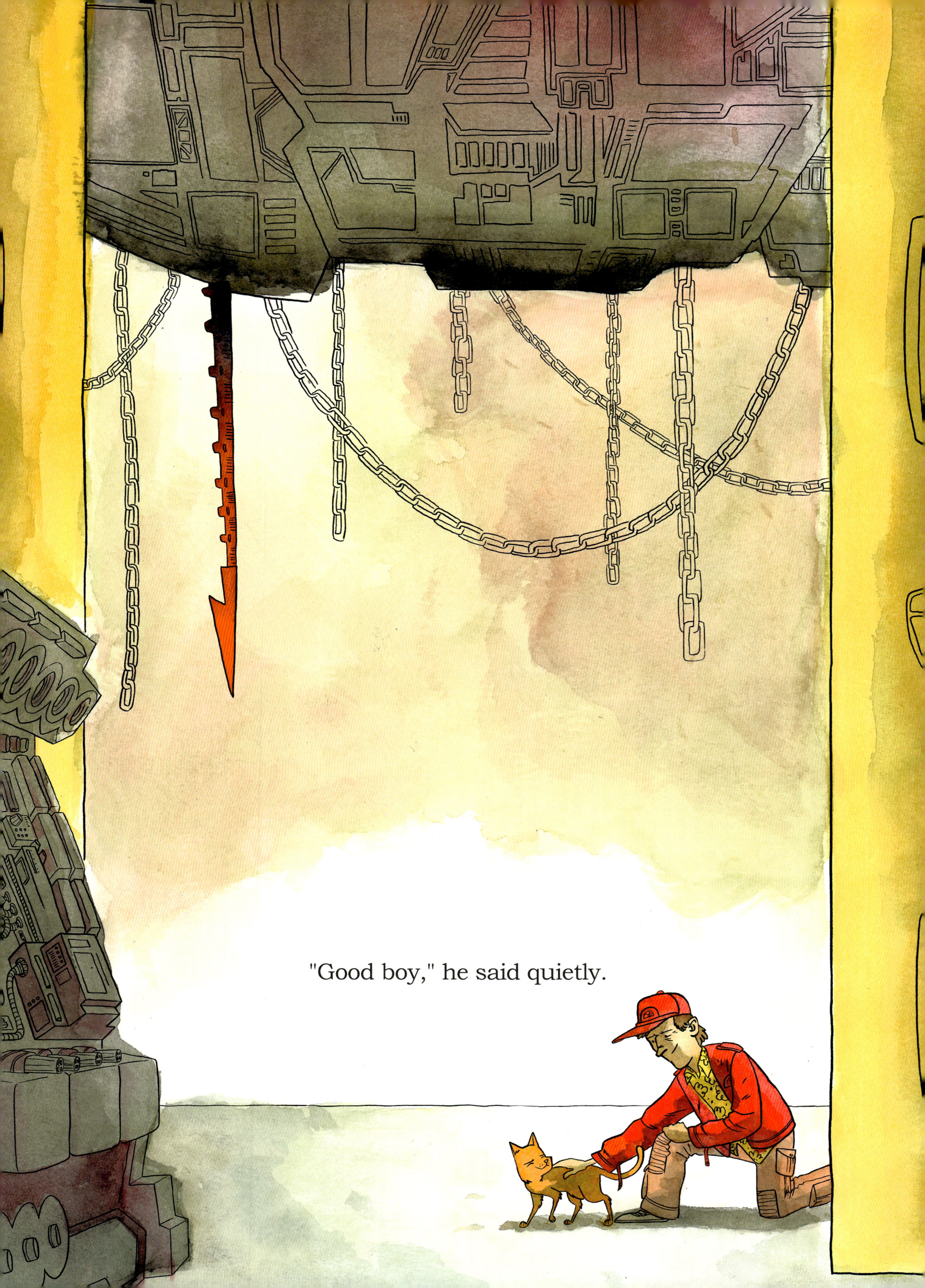

"Good boy," he said quietly.

ALICE MEICHI LI

Yin-Yang | pencil and paint on canvas | 66 x 47 cm

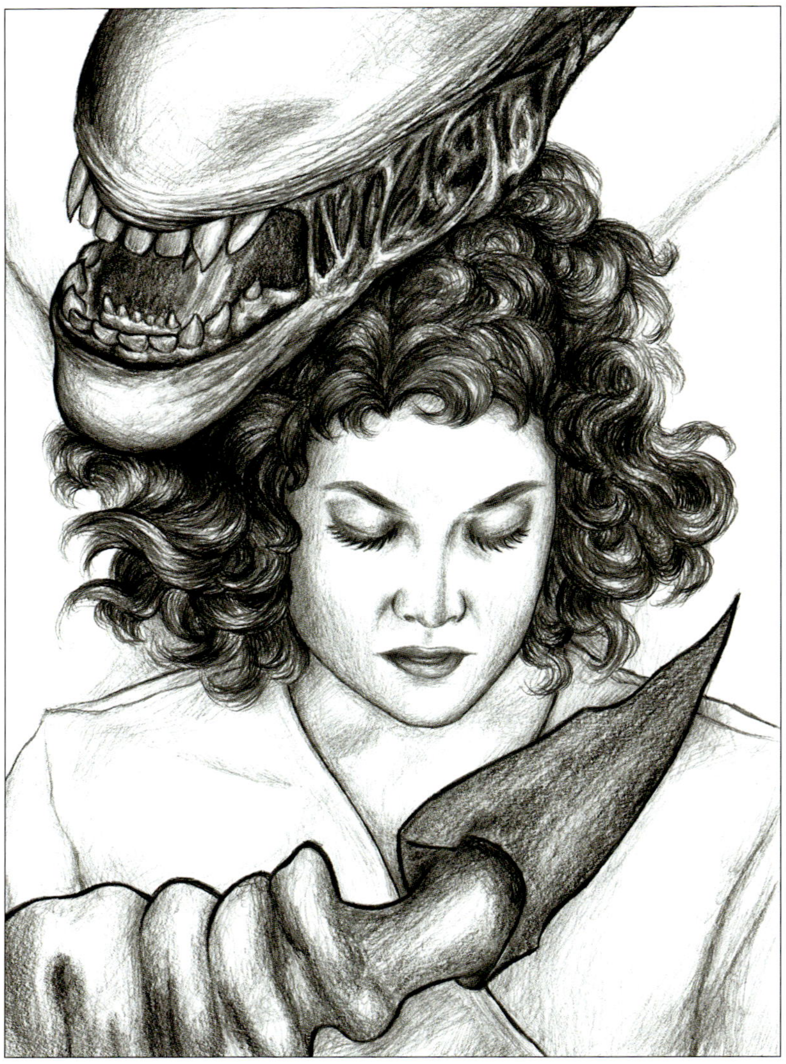

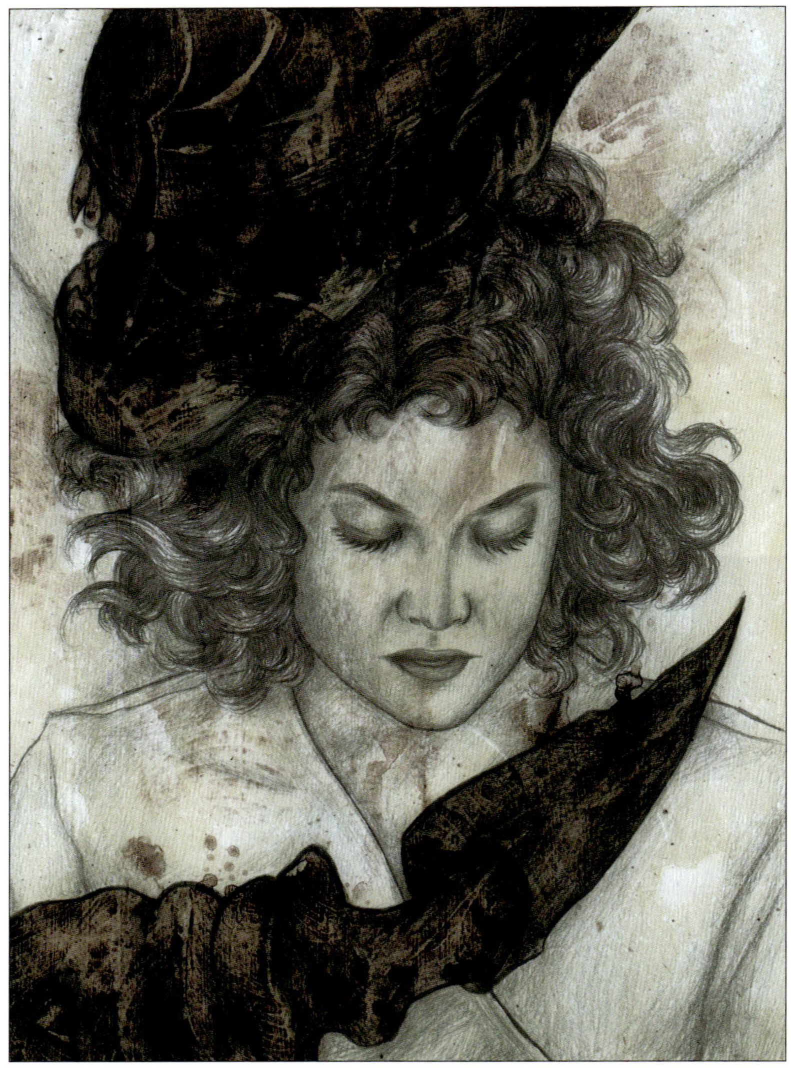

What I find so enduring about the *Alien* franchise is that it taps into primal archetypes, like birth and death, light and dark, male and female, Eros and Thanatos. This is illustrated not only in the themes of motherhood and fecundity that run through the franchise, but also in H. R. Giger's strong imagery that twists and tinges the anatomy of reproductive organs (representing the Natural) with mechanical automobile parts (representing the Artificial) into horrifying monsters.

So many parallels can be drawn between Ellen Ripley and the aliens she battles against. Ripley is a mother who kills out of preservation of herself and her species, and the Xenomorphs' primary drive is to reproduce their species through the parasitic murder of others. This symbolism, combined with the stark visual contrasts between Ripley's peaceful Snow White-like scenes in the hypersleep capsule versus the beautifully grotesque appearance of the Xenomorph, inspired my work greatly.

As a result, I wanted the focus of my piece to be primarily on Ripley herself. It cannot be overstated how much of a pioneering figure she was as one of the first iconic action heroines in cinema, or how important it was for young girls like myself to see a strong female protagonist who wasn't overtly sexualized. From there, I wanted to frame Ripley with the Xenomorph, creeping in around the edges to introduce a contrasting texturally hard and dark element against the soft lightness of Ripley in stasis. The swirling combination of the two nemeses is reminiscent of a Yin-Yang symbol, which serves as a callback to the aforementioned connectedness between the two characters.

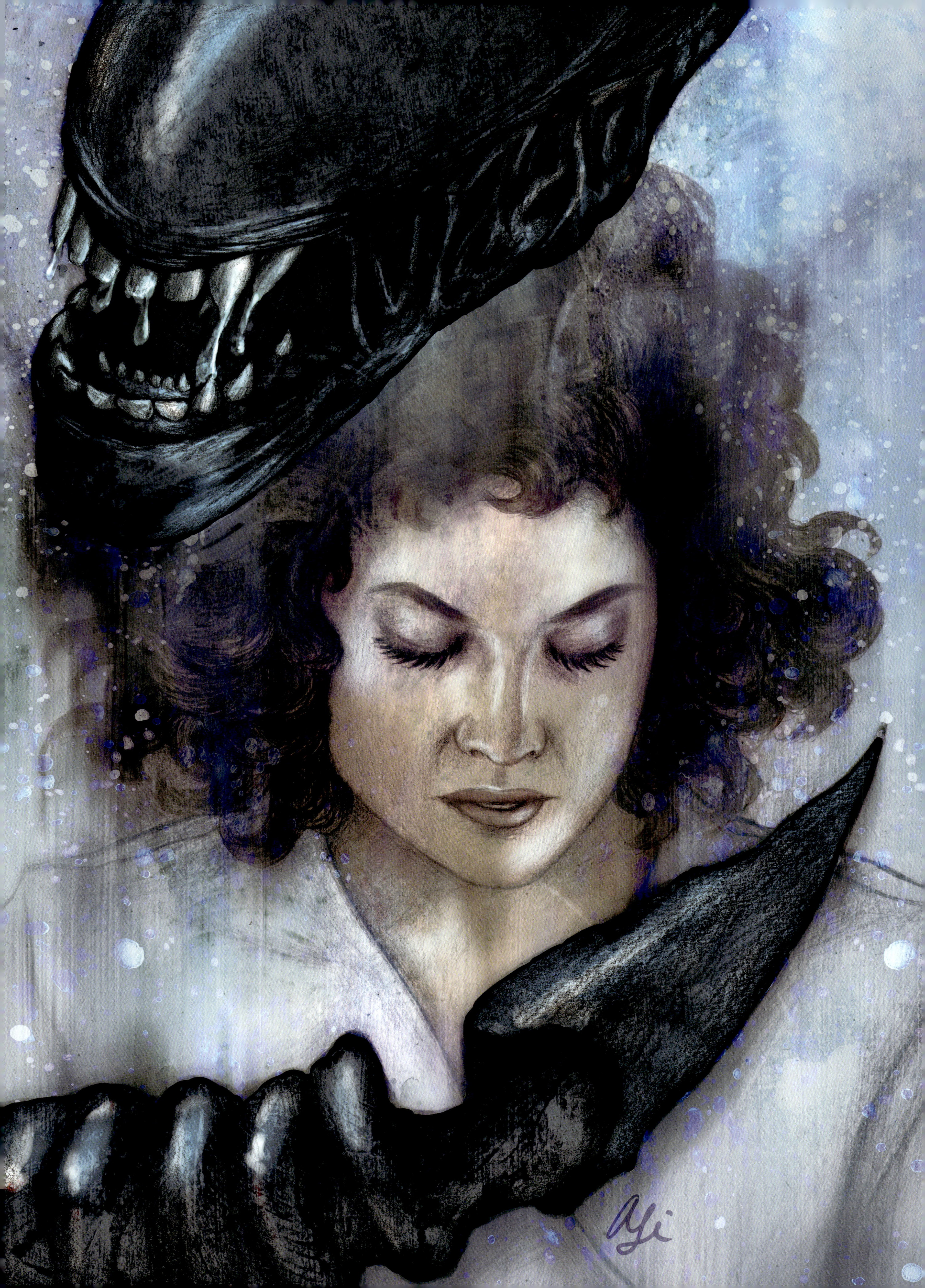

EVAN CAGLE

Still Life | ink on paper and digital | 36 x 25 cm

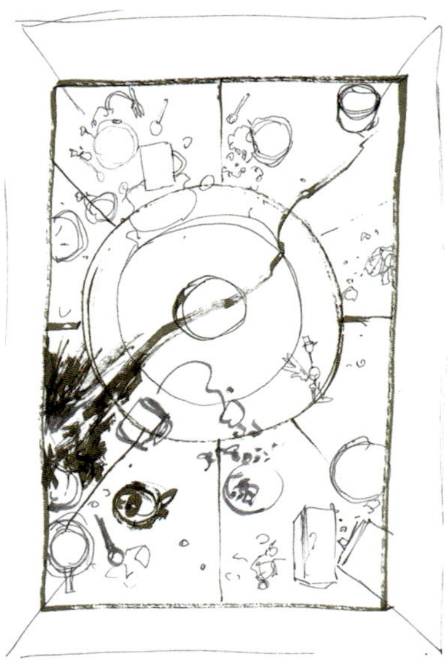

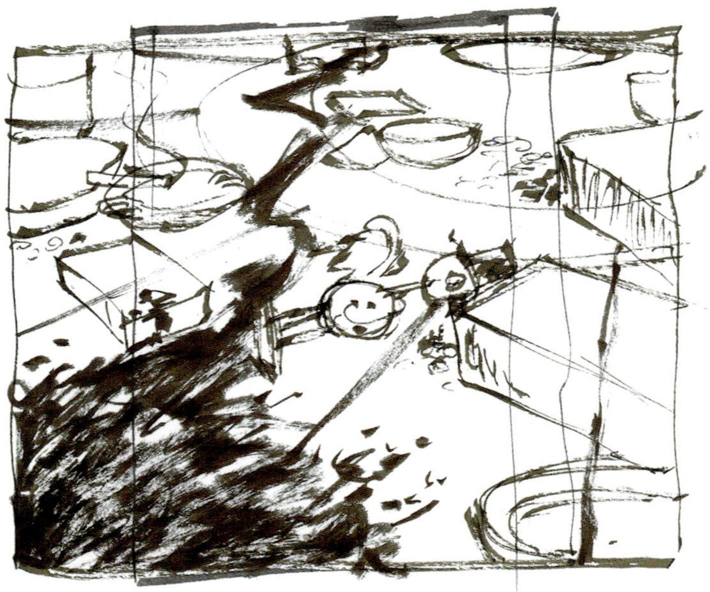

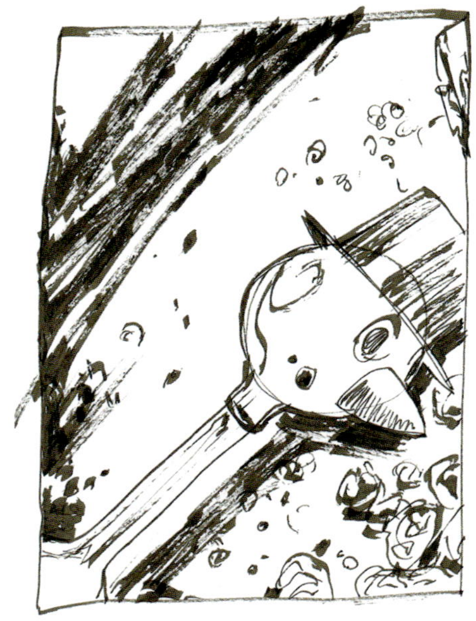

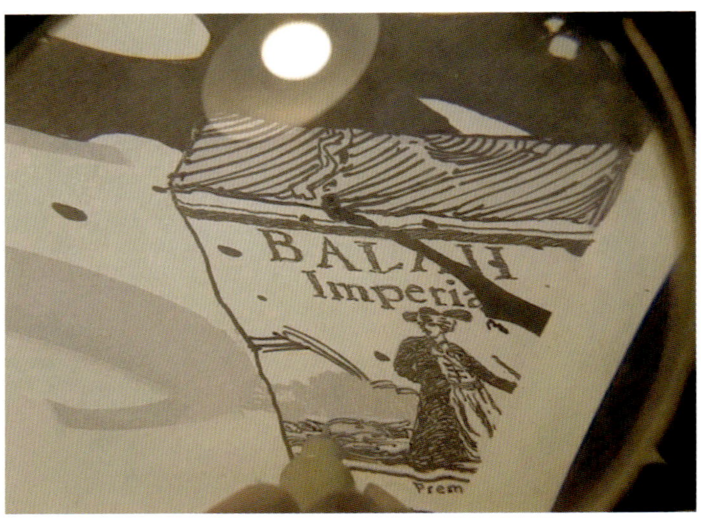

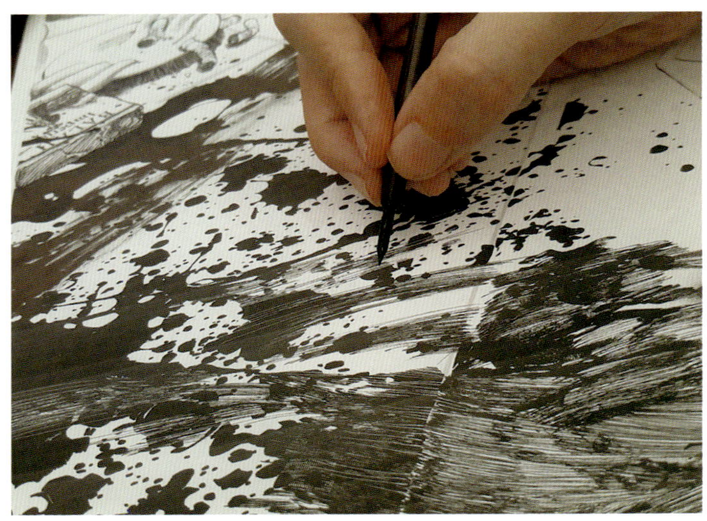

In 2016 I made a devotional piece of *Alien*(s) artwork, *Dragonslayer*, in which I trotted out all the franchise's usual suspects. Ripley is front and center, flanked by aliens and dominated by the alien queen; a facehugger splays across her armored suit; her trusty flamethrower is resplendent. It's a decent enough piece, in my humble opinion, but in it there's a whiff of the kitchen sink. It's an orgy of familiar iconography. And icons, let's be honest, are an odd feature of a property at least nominally concerned with *alien-ness*. How to reconcile so much familiarity – so much that's *recognizable* – with the concept of the alien?

When I began the piece for this book, I knew I wouldn't return to any of my former subjects. No Ripley, no alien in any of its forms. Stripped of these idols, what remains of the *Alien* orthodoxy? I wanted something unexpected, something slightly off-center, like the original film itself. Quiet, and thoughtful… and dangerous.

Still Life is, of course, set at some unseen point just after Kane's death and the alien's birth. The work-a-day grind of menial corporate labor has died, murdered by an explosive new element that demands not just undivided attention, but action. This is the moment between the end of familiar expectations and assumptions, and the beginning of the new, the alien. This, to me, is the moment worth pausing for, worth examining, because with neither characters nor creatures the image feels alien, and paradoxically, somehow all the more *Alien* for their absence.

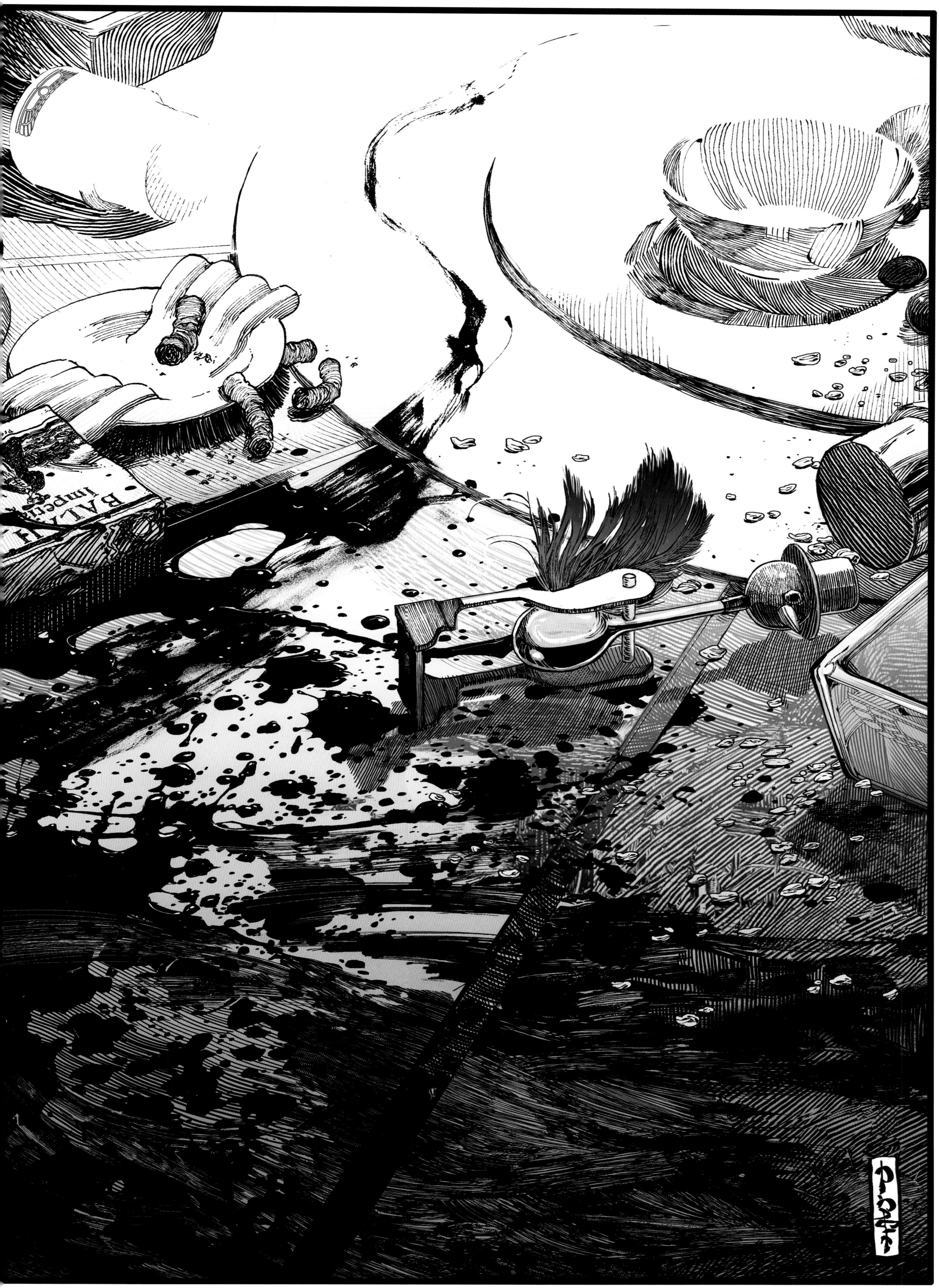

LUIGI 'GIGI CAVE' CAVENAGO

ALIEN | digital | 71 x 57 cm

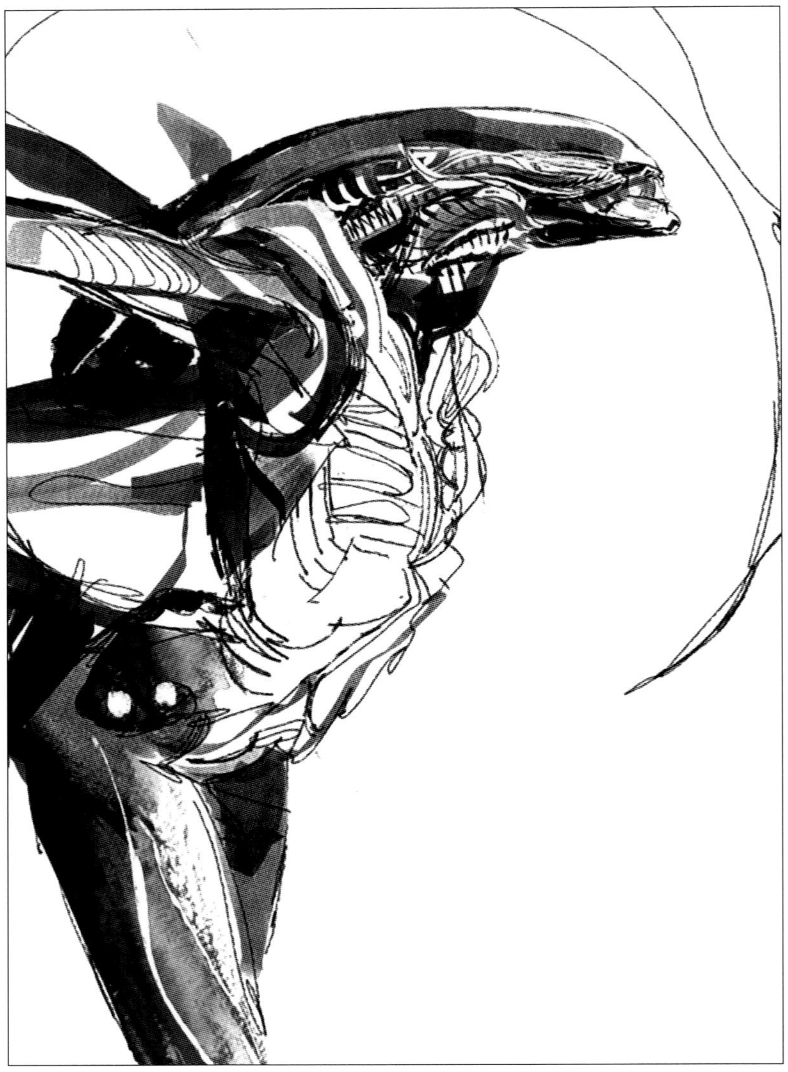

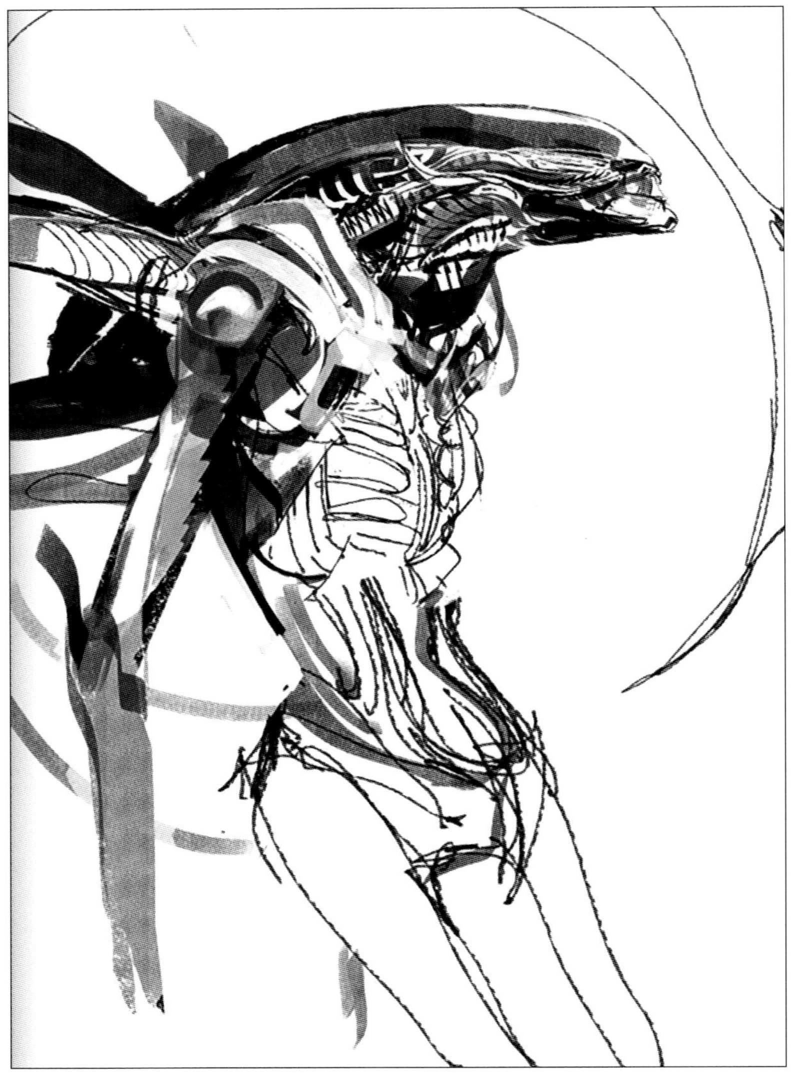

I can trace my love for *Alien* back to summer 1987, when I saw a small article in an Italian Mickey Mouse magazine. It was titled 'Monsters Made in Italy' and the subject was Carlo Rambaldi, one of the main artists in the special effects team on the picture in question. At the time I was five and couldn't read very well, but there was one photo of the Xenomorph head that took all my attention: I immediately fell in love.

I didn't know what that thing was, but still, I couldn't take my eyes off of it.

To me that movie was a miracle, so much so that, to me, the story behind its making is as fascinating as the fantasy world that it describes.

One big contributor to that was, of course, H. R. Giger.

The Xenomorph design made the movie: what used to be the Achilles heel for so many sci-fi movies from that era turned out to be *Alien*'s main strength.

That creature was so unique. It was a great mixture of classic movie monsters, if you think about it: it's ancient and mysterious like the Mummy, it's feral and elusive like the Creature from the Black Lagoon, it's dark and seductive like Dracula, and its biomechanical nature may remind you of the Frankenstein Monster! Too much of a stretch? Maybe so, but that's what great movies do, they make your mind wonder endlessly. Maybe even too much.

Alien planted a very important seed in my brain, and has grown into a very strange shape inside my imagination and, oh man, I'm so grateful for that!

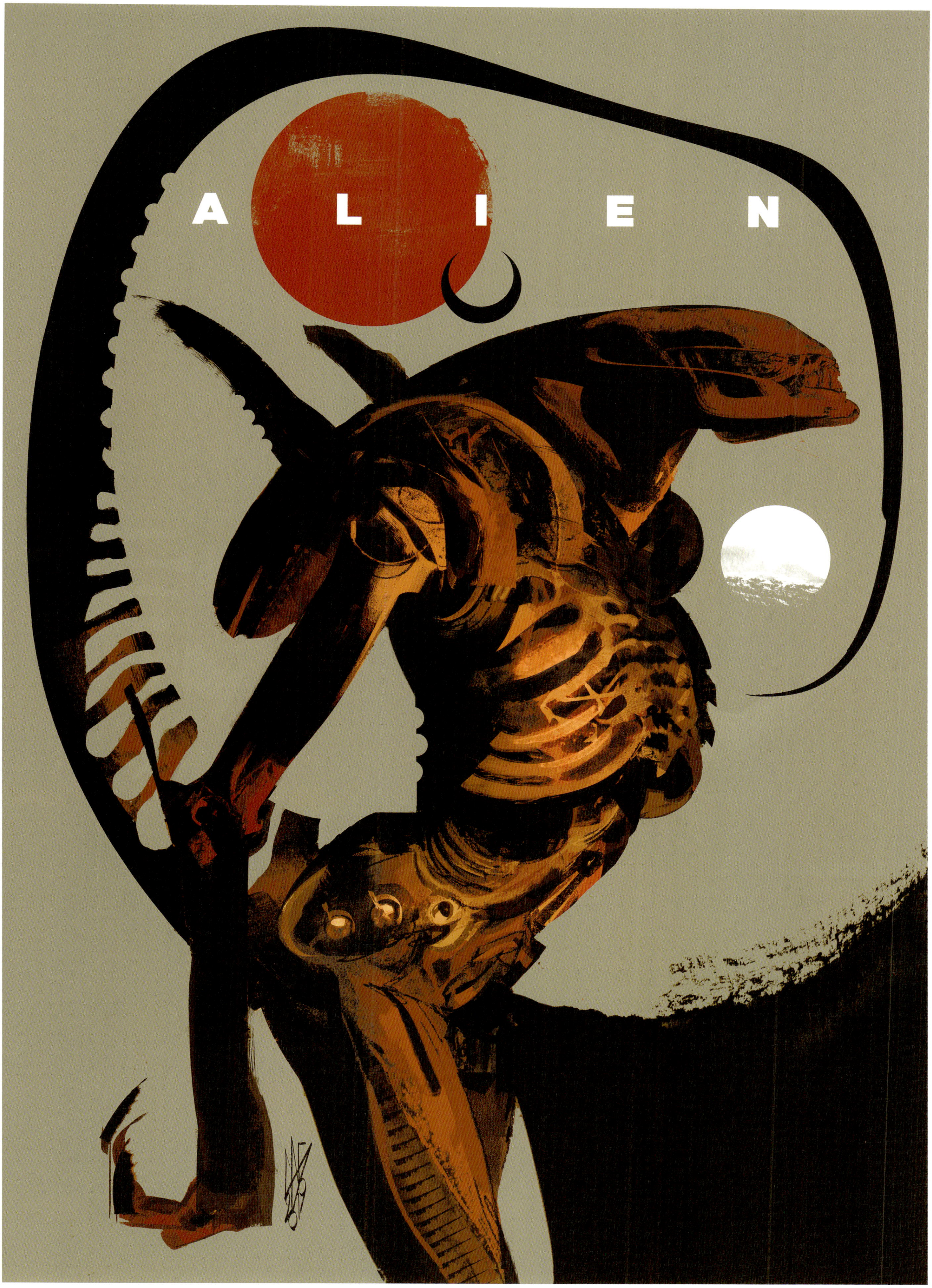
ALIEN

DAVE DORMAN

Alien | oil and acrylic on Bristol board | 37 x 26.5 cm

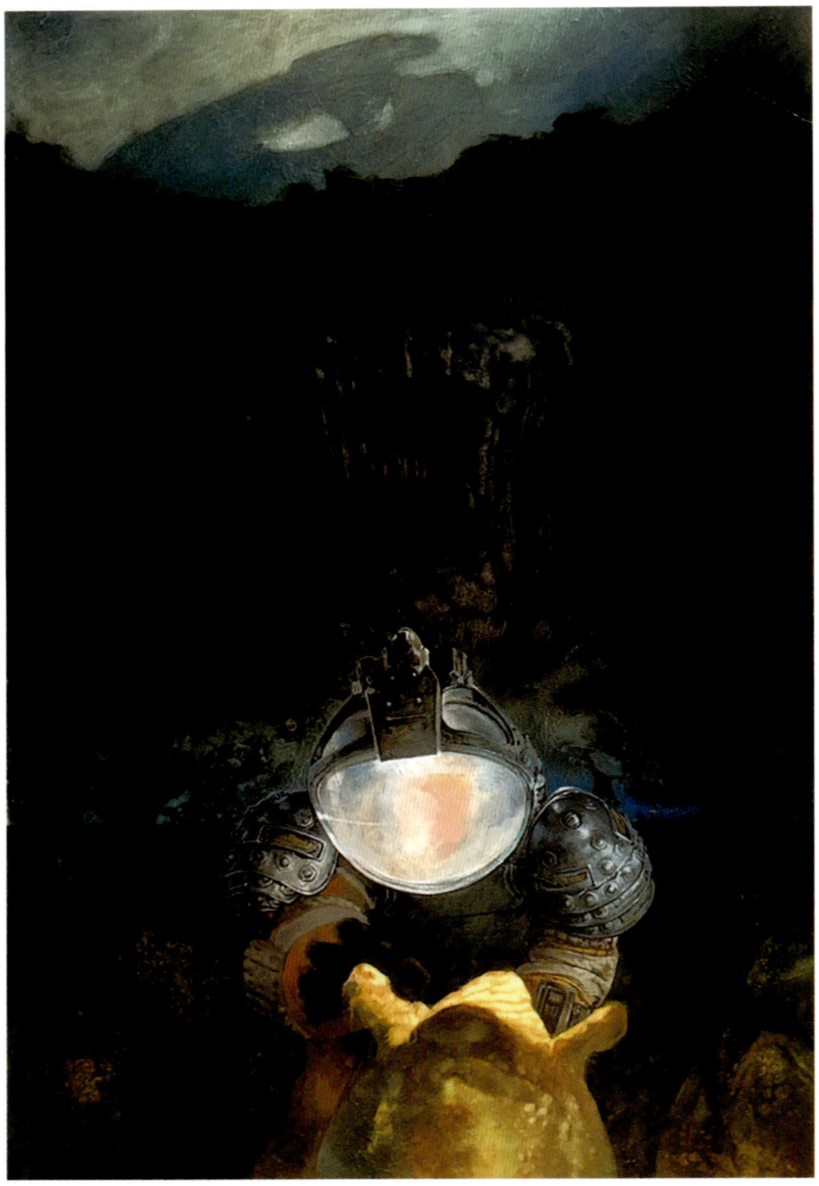

I have found it a wonderful creative challenge to take Mr. Giger's horrifying designs and incorporate them into story-specific illustrations while retaining the otherworldly visage of those creatures. I have been a fan of science fiction and film all my life and it is a great privilege to play in Ridley Scott and H. R. Giger's playground!

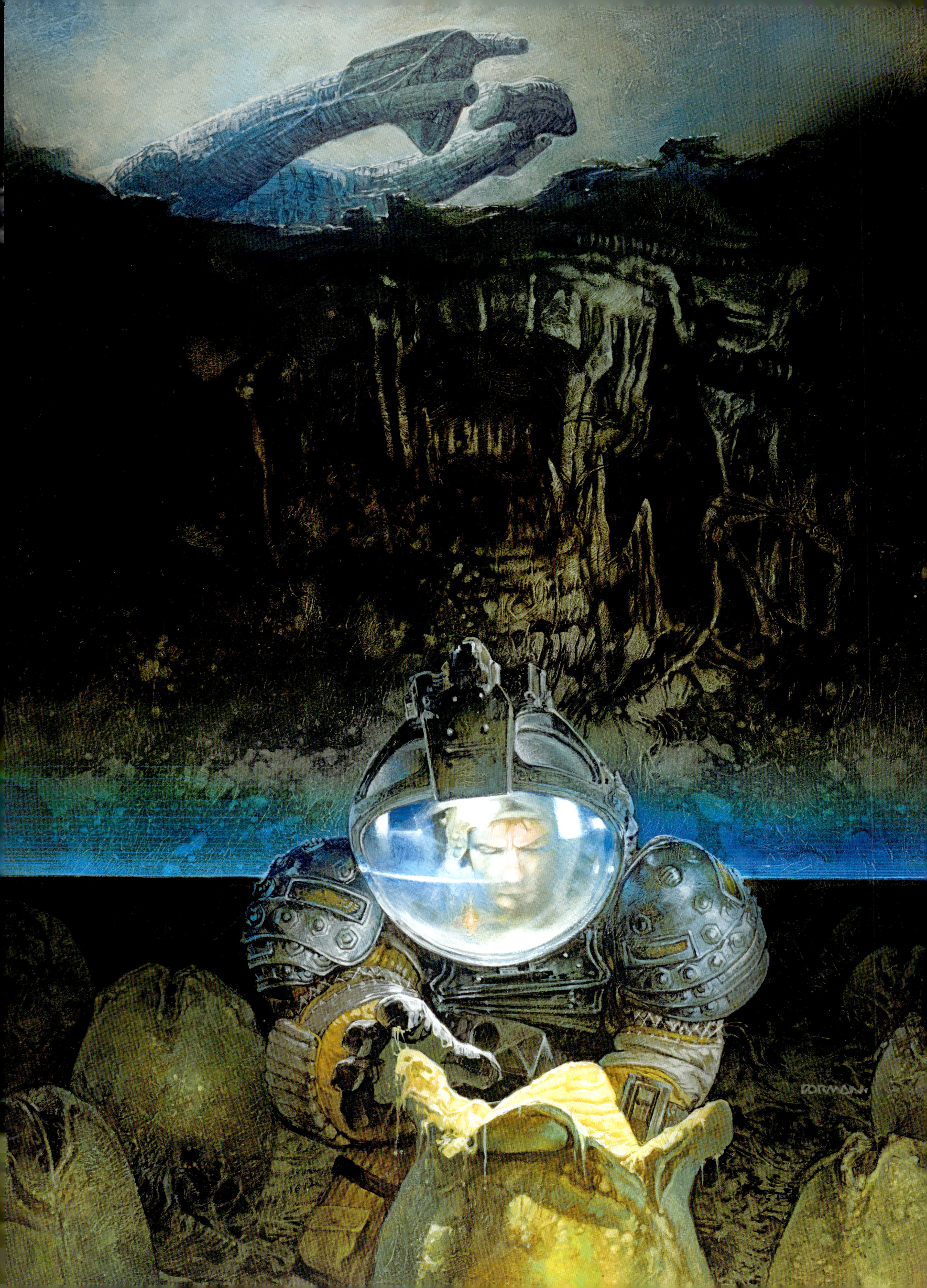
DORMAN

EDWARD PUN

Mech Alien | digital | 36.5 x 26 cm

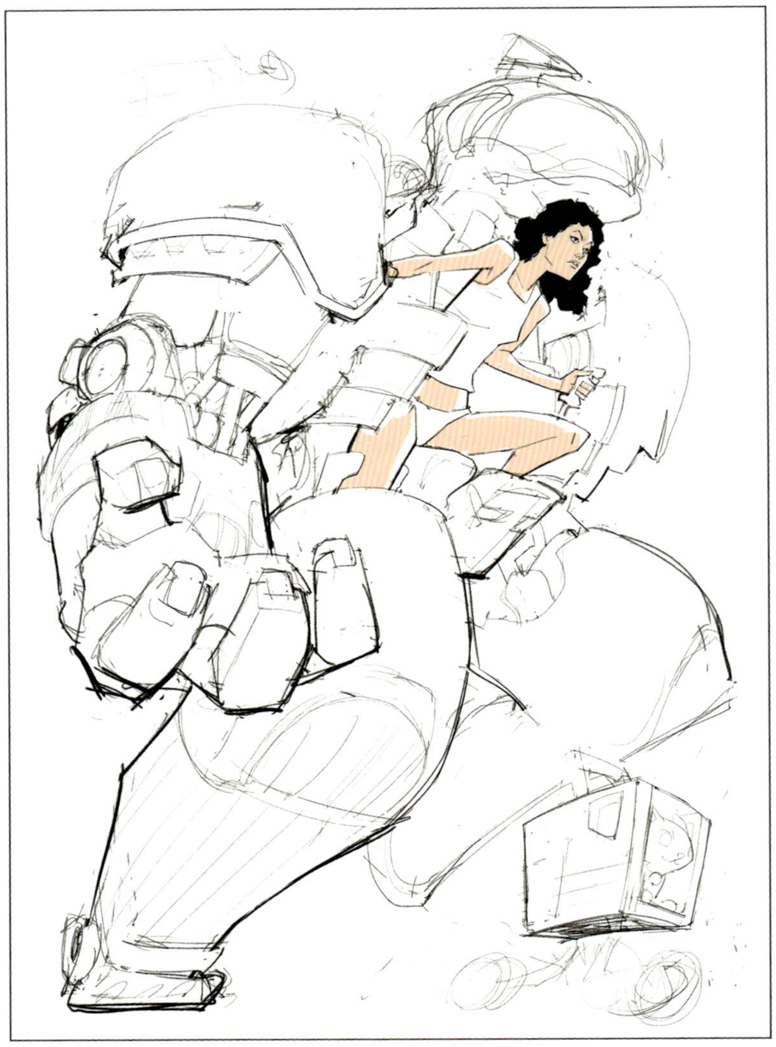

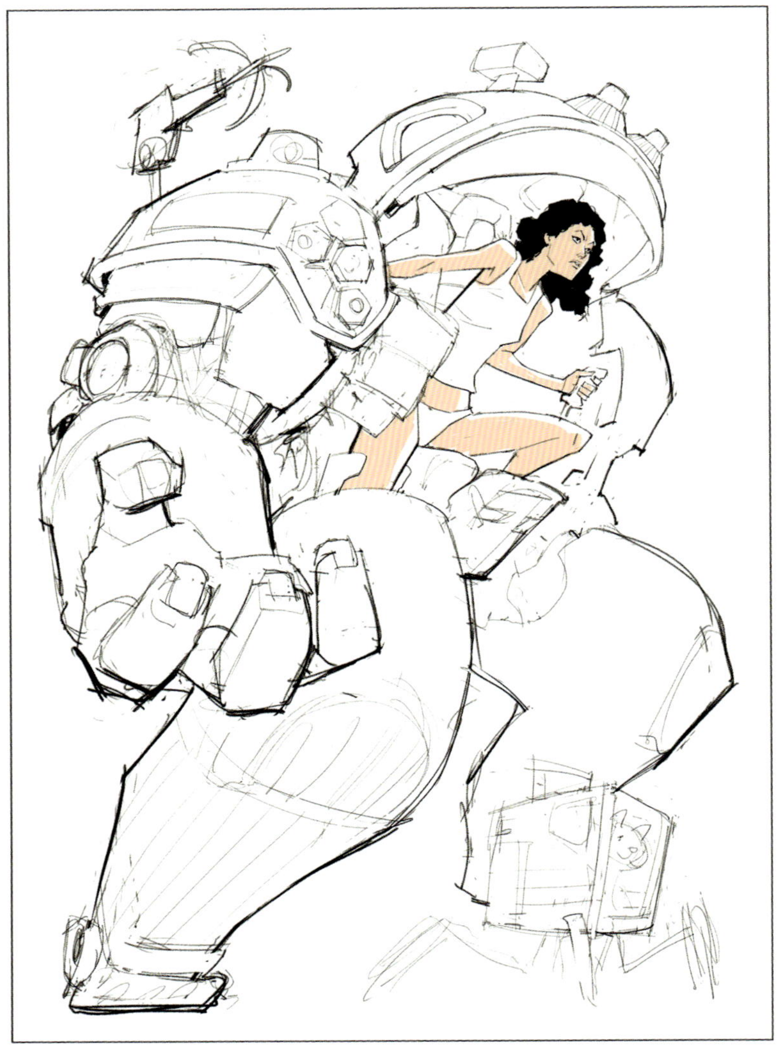

Alien is one of the most influential films from my youth. The sound, visuals, and story all work seamlessly together to produce a movie that is scary as hell. The space ship and the crew, everything looks real and lived in. There's a level of detail, from the messy living quarters to the grimy cargo bay – it's relatable and believable. But when the alien set and creature design appear, it is a shock to the senses, how unsettling and disturbing it looks. The mash-up of sci-fi design with H. R. Giger's unique visuals is why *Alien* is such a powerful movie for me.

Similar to the movie, I wanted to combine different elements to produce an artwork that is familiar and yet different. I chose the iconic moment where Ripley slips on the white space suit to duel with the alien one last time, but with a twist. So I wanted to see what would happen if I combined different genres. I swapped out the space suit for anime-inspired mech armor. It was a blast looking for reference and researching how the space suit comes together, with all the layers of different patterns and designs. After that, it was a big challenge to incorporate those designs into a mech suit. Finally, I couldn't ignore Jonesy. I had to give him a mech suit, too, which is the carrying cage Ripley used to transport Jonesy on to the life craft. With the little mechanical legs that fold out from the side, I can imagine Jonesy scuttling after a facehugger, if any are still around.

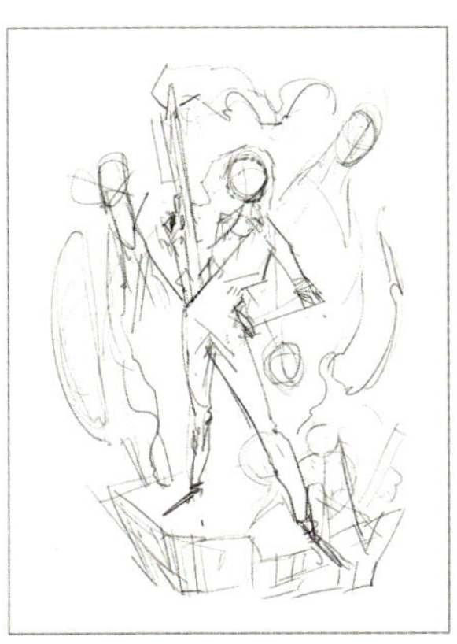

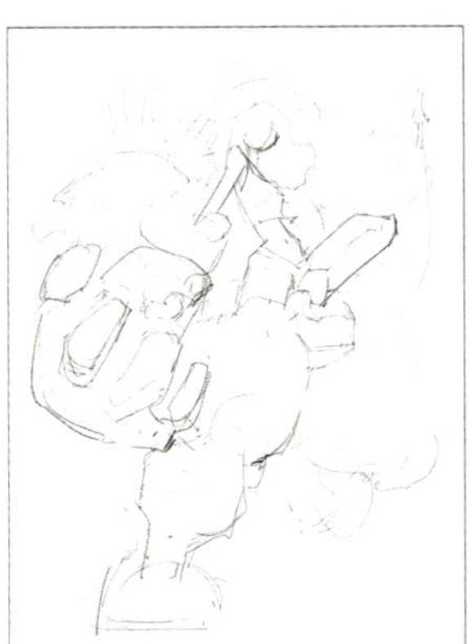

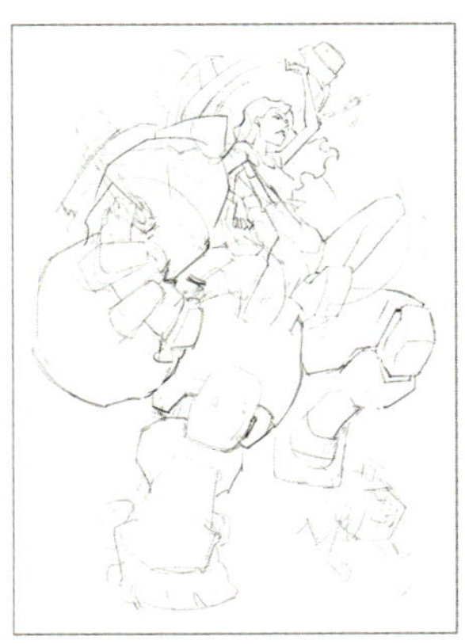

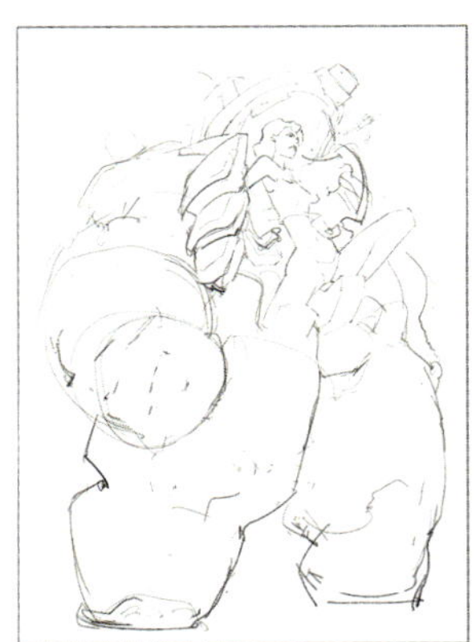

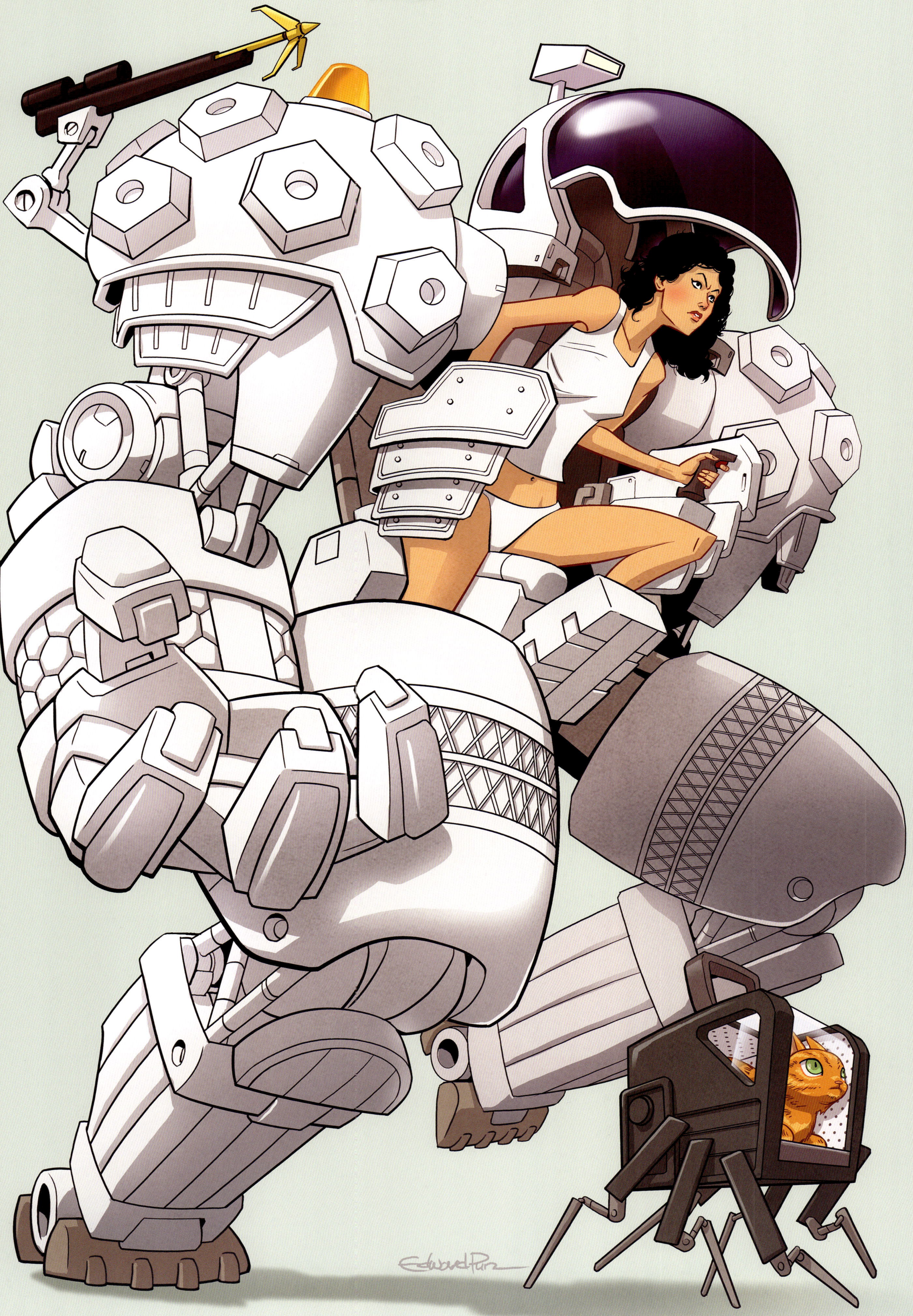

MATT NEEDLE

エイリアン | digital | 37 x 26 cm

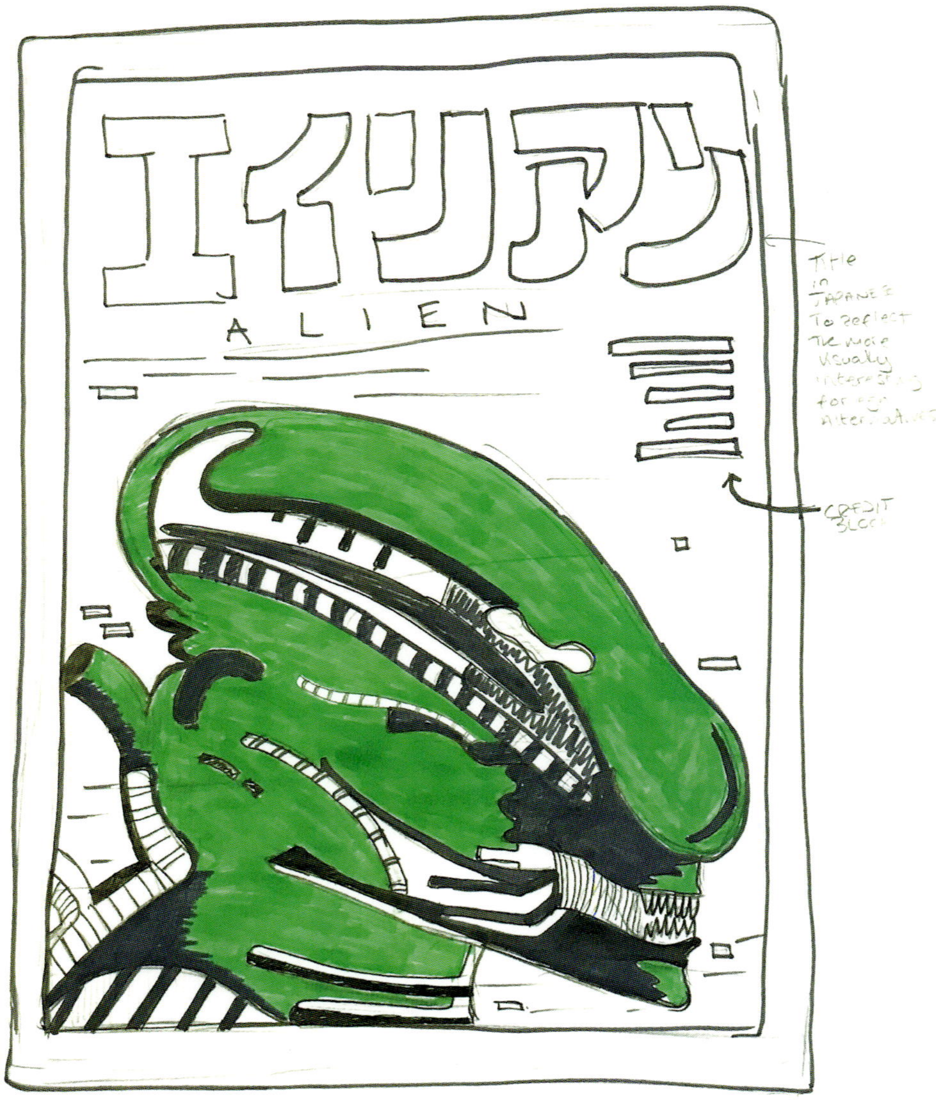

I have been enamoured with the *Alien* franchise ever since I saw it on VHS at a sleepover in the '90s. I was eight or nine at the time, and I thought it was the creepiest and coolest film I'd ever seen.

Throughout the years I grew and watched the subsequent films (and spin offs), but the original has always stuck with me as something special, an iconic movie full of memorable moments and shocks.

I have worked on various *Alien*-inspired pieces of art over the years, but this one is specifically inspired by my love of international film posters and science fiction. I have gone for a tech screen-inspired image, influenced by the computer screens/ displays throughout the *Nostromo*.

My hope was that this piece would mix the blend of organic lifeforms and technology – much like H. R. Giger's original Xenomorph concepts.

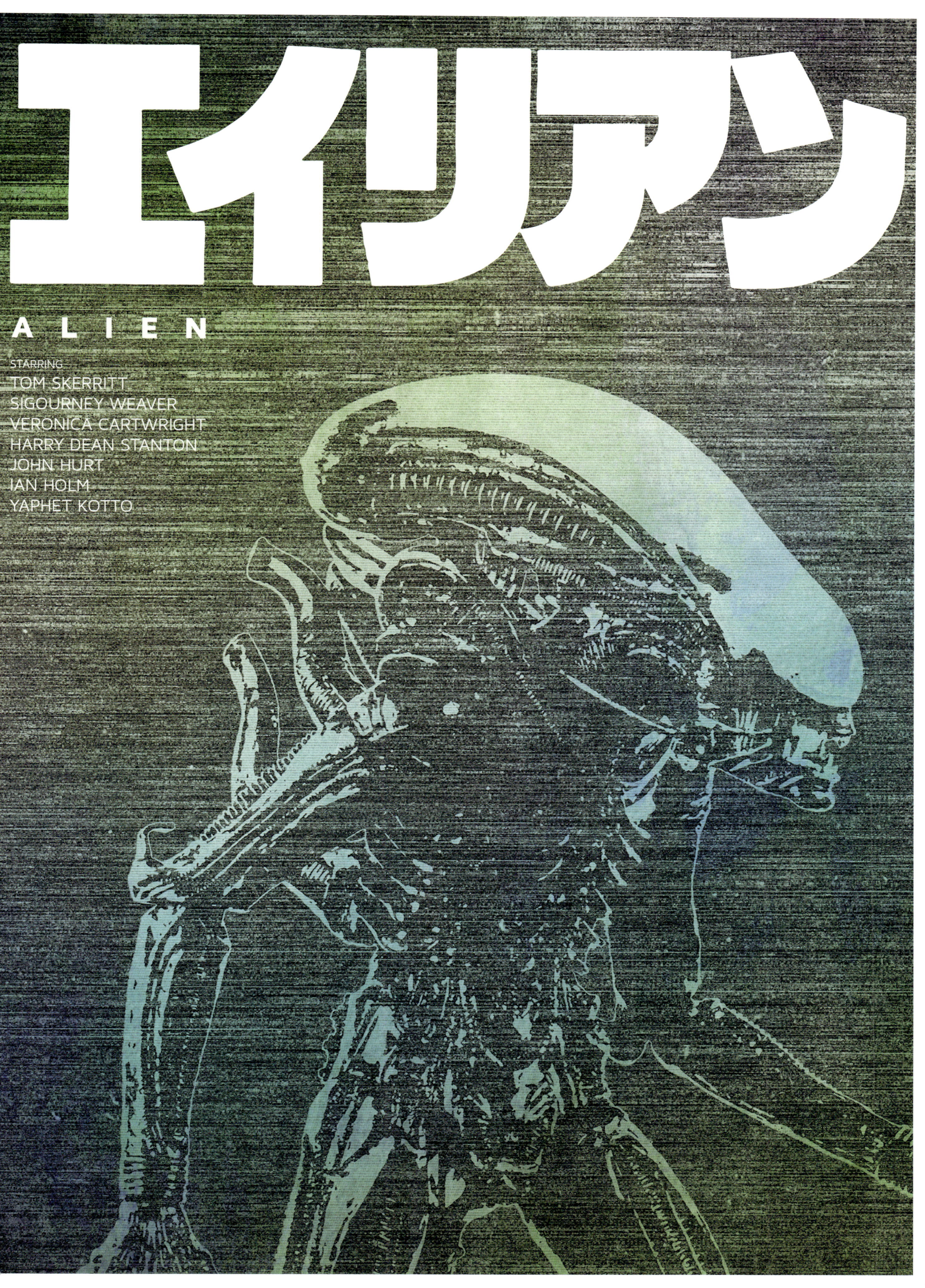
エイリアン
ALIEN
STARRING
TOM SKERRITT
SIGOURNEY WEAVER
VERONICA CARTWRIGHT
HARRY DEAN STANTON
JOHN HURT
IAN HOLM
YAPHET KOTTO

JORDAN VOGT-ROBERTS, JON WILCOX

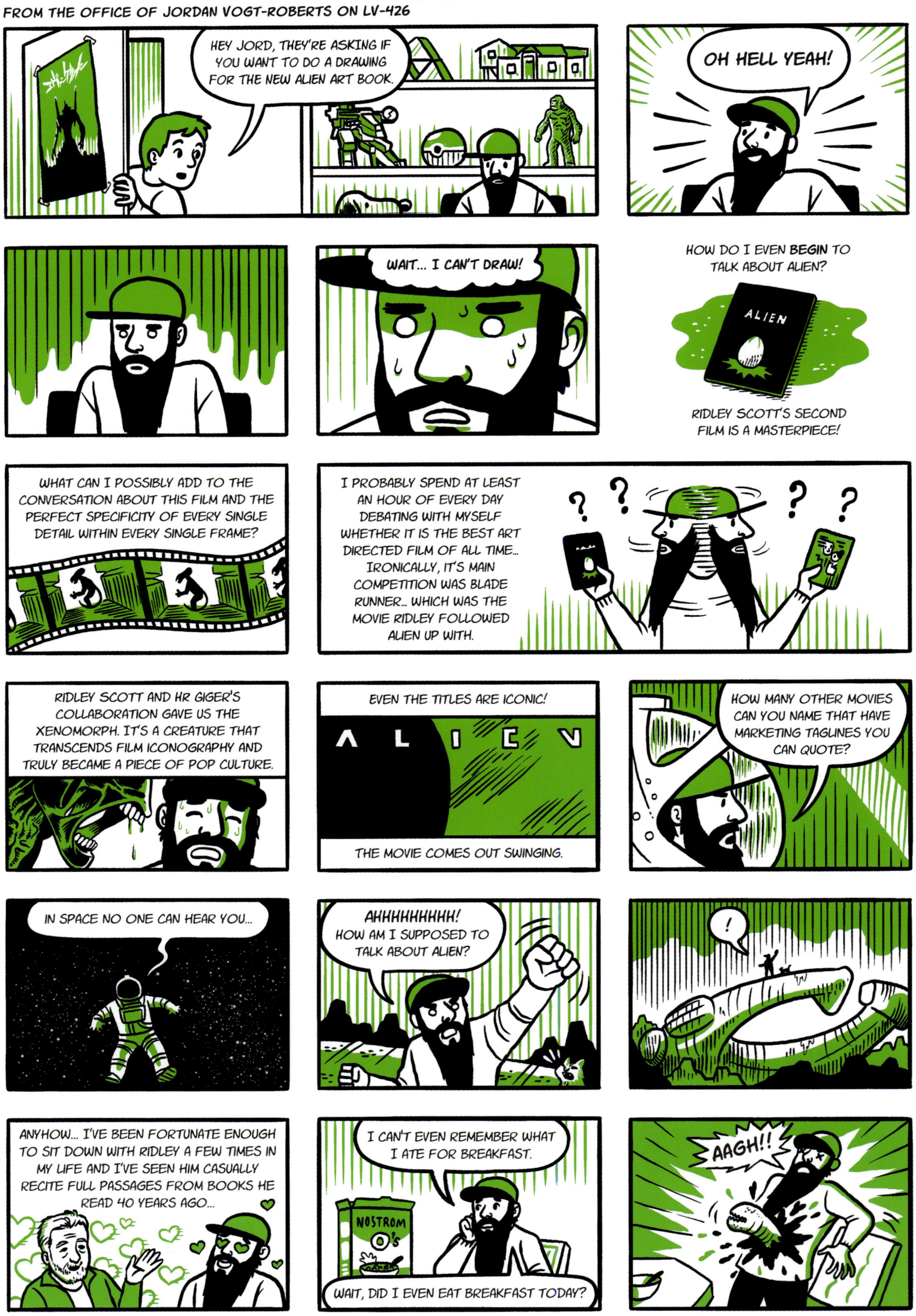

From the Office of Jordan Vogt-Roberts on LV-426 | concept by Jordan Vogt-Roberts, illustration by Jon Wilcox | 49.5 x 72 cm

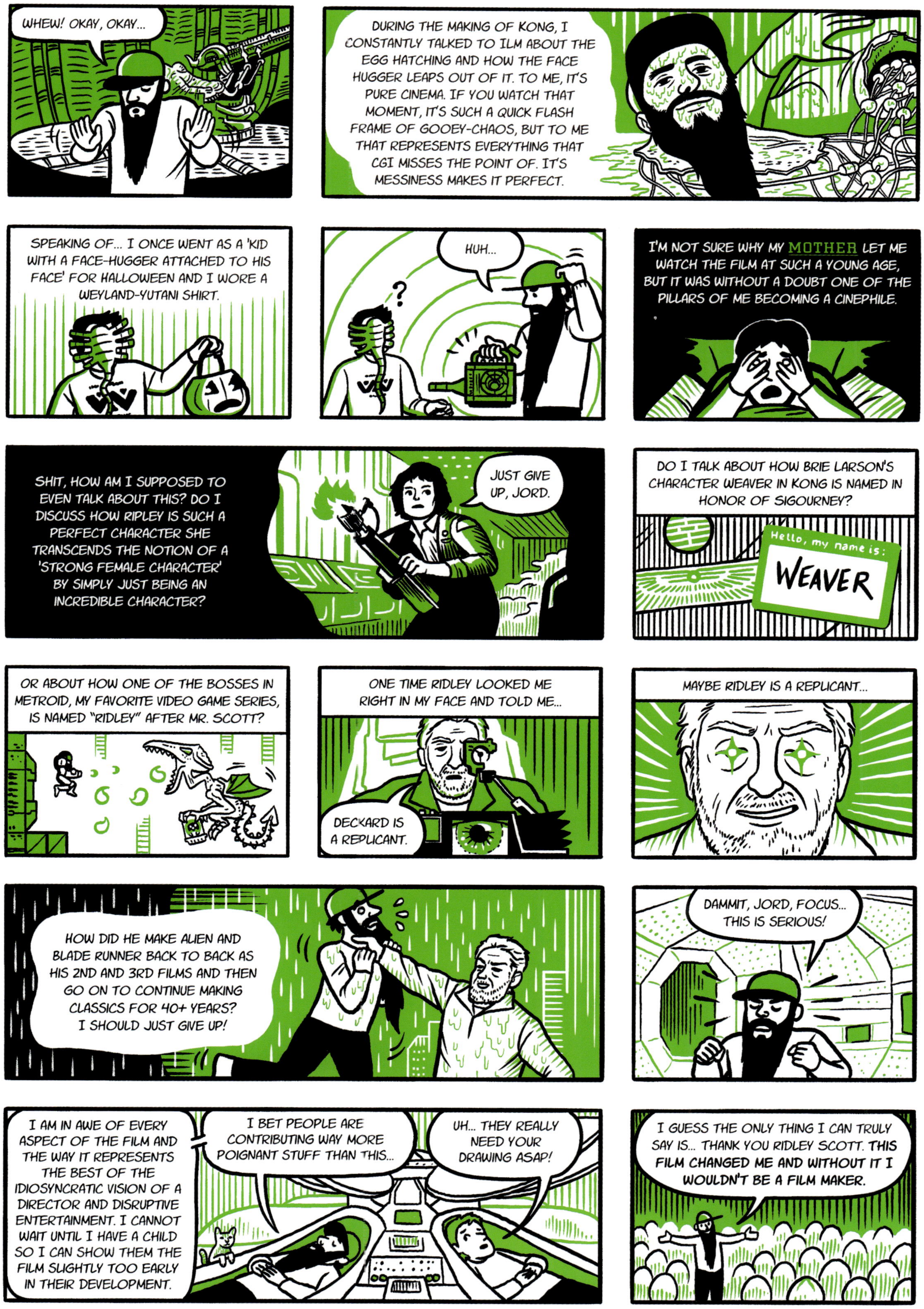

ILLUSTRATED BY JON WILCOX

ALEXANDRA BARBOZA

Lurking in the Shadows | digital | 36.5 x 26 cm

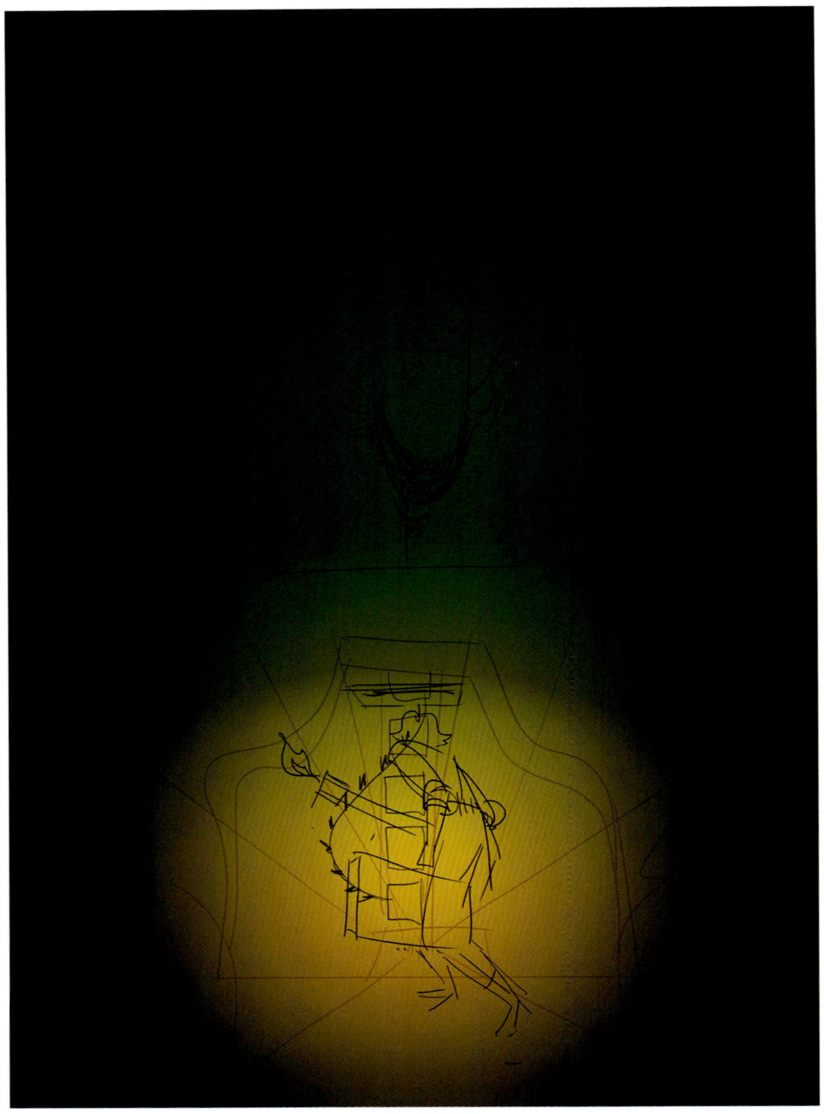

As someone who enjoys sci-fi movies, *Alien* has always been one of my favorites to come back to over and over. It's thrilling, takes place on a space ship, and has a strong female protagonist. What brings me back every time, aside from the thrills, is the *Nostromo*.

It's truly one of my favorite fictional places that I wish I could visit. This piece gave me the opportunity to study the set and interpret it in my own style. I really wanted to do a piece that highlighted the space ship design and also shared the same thrilling feeling I had at the end of the movie, waiting for the alien to drop down and surprise Ripley. She is wielding her weapon of choice, while trying to protect her cat, unaware of the danger that looms above her. I debated drawing a piece with Ripley in her space suit, but we spend so much time in this incredible space ship, admiring the visuals, it basically drew itself.

The realism in the film, I think, mostly comes from the actors – their amazing performances. The design of the alien is iconic and so beautifully done, but their terror and fear ultimately sell the horror of being trapped in space where no one will hear them scream.

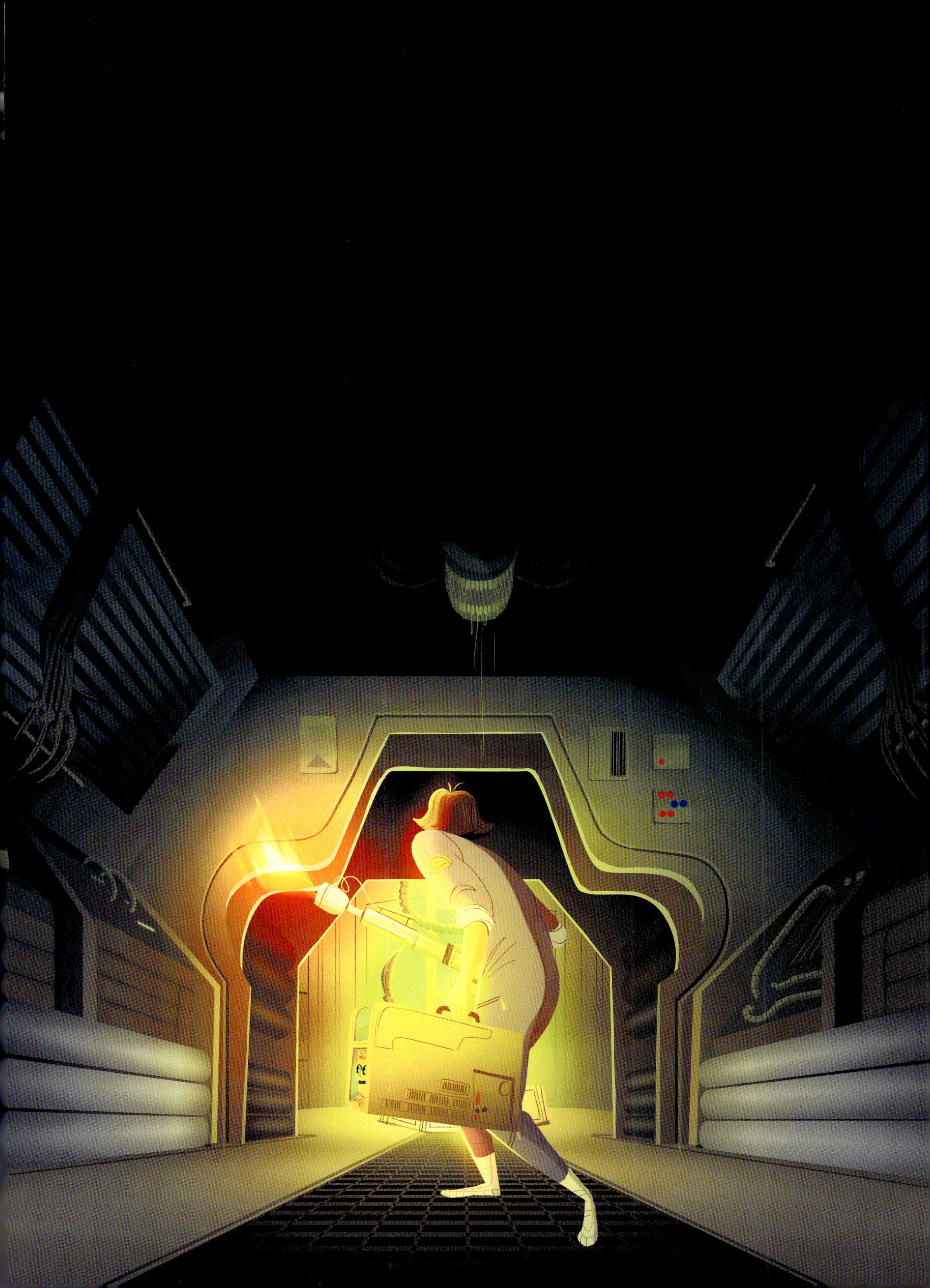

CARRIE ANNE HUDSON

Eye of Providence | ink on paper | 36 x 26 cm

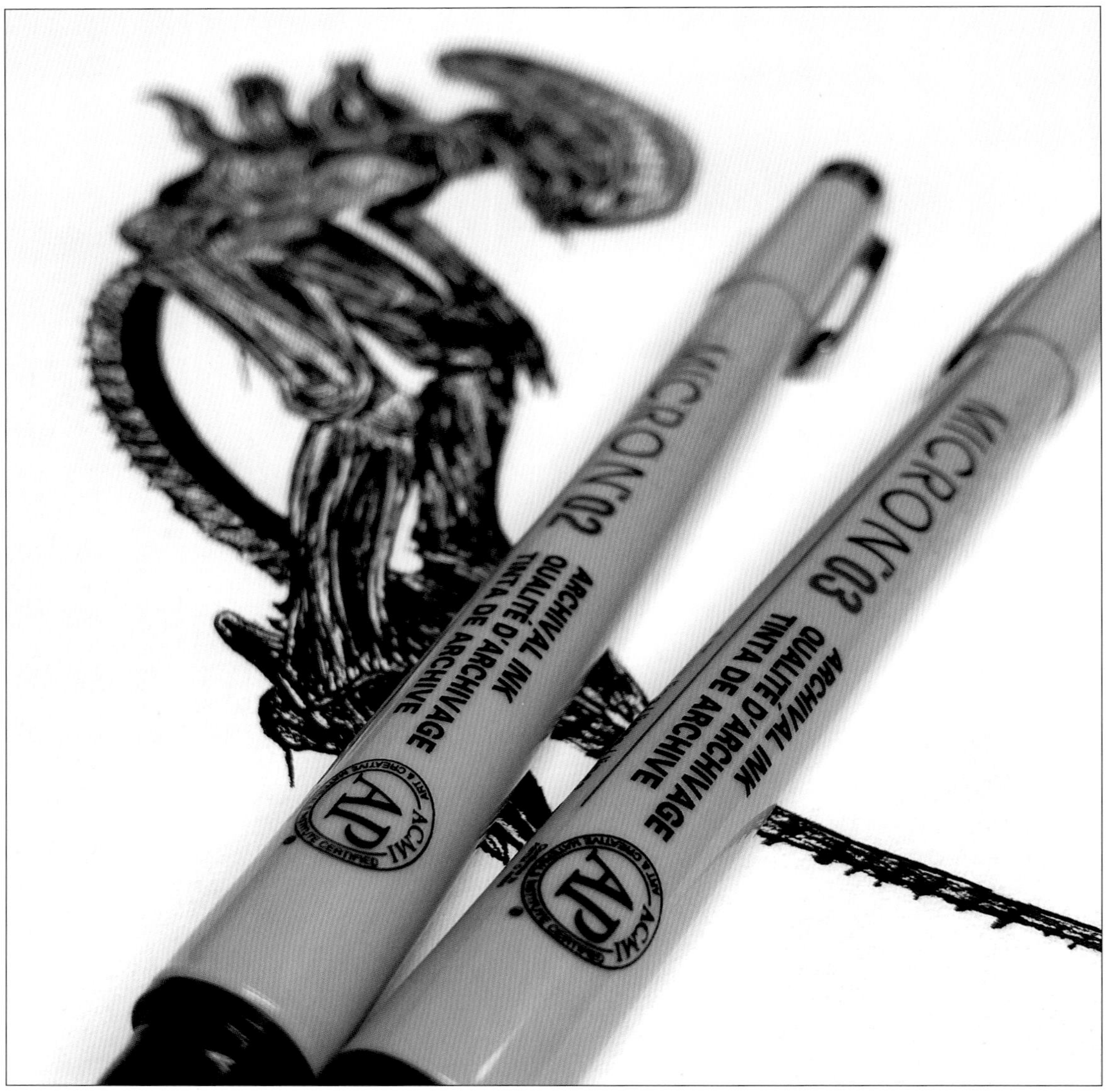

When I was asked to create an art piece inspired by *Alien*, there were no second thoughts about it. *Alien*? *Absolutely!* It is my belief that this classic film not only paved the way for future-thriller sci-fi films, but really set the bar for them with its artistic elements.

There are a few different elements that make up my piece. I wanted to keep the overall look clean, and I wanted to create a piece that honored the late H. R. Giger's design of the Xenomorph. Giger is an absolute legend, and an artist I've personally admired for years. He really set the stage for industrial/organic dark artwork. His artistic design and influence in *Alien* is in a large part what sets the tone of the whole film: Cold. Alone. Terrifying.

As for the background elements, the triangle and eye illustrations in my piece are representative of the Eye of Providence, or "the all-seeing eye". The all-seeing eye is a visual concept of a higher being watching over humanity, or any other omniscient force working behind the scenes, potentially controlling the government, corporations and more. I found this idea fitting with *Alien*. The crew had no idea that there was a robot purposefully planted on their ship the entire time (by their own headquarters!), willing to preserve the alien life form at any cost, even if it meant killing them all. This is still a concept that hits close to home in the modern day. Area-51? UFOs? Is our government lying to us? Who knows, there might be a secret space ship out there right now inspecting a field of alien eggs, and maybe H. R. Giger is with them.

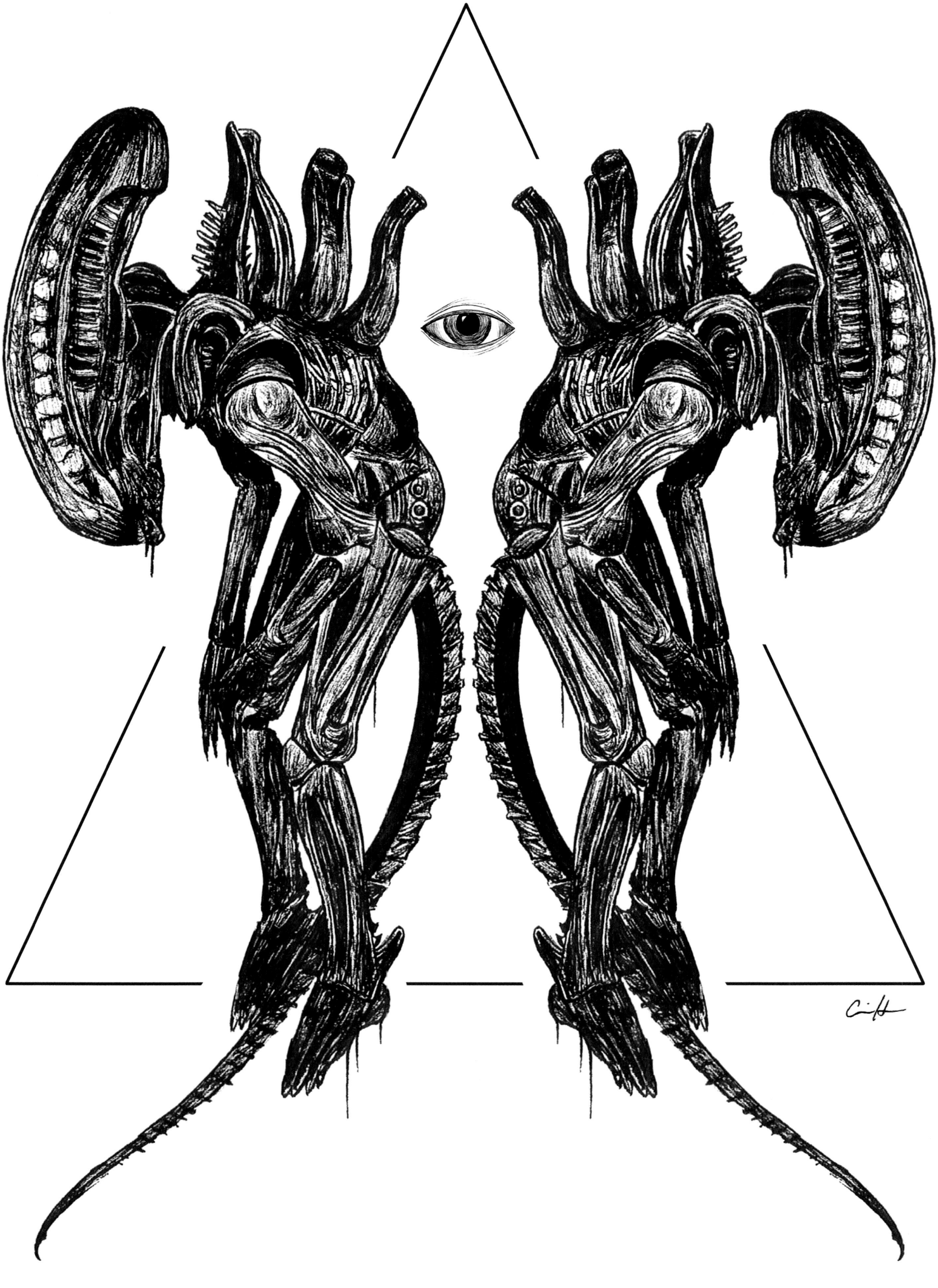

JOEY SPIOTTO

Happy Fortieth Birthday | digital | 36.5 x 26 cm

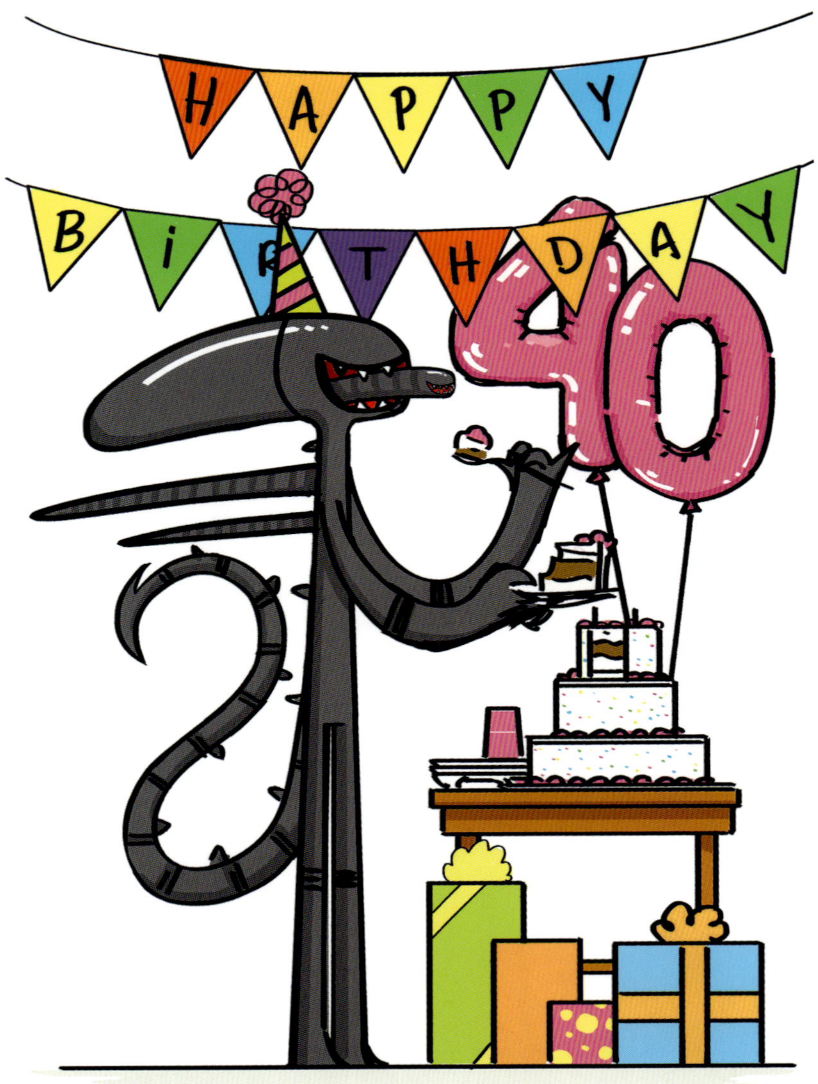

I saw the first *Alien* film when I was much too young to be watching something so scary. My artwork tends to be very kid friendly and when I was approached about the book *Alien Next Door* several years ago, I immediately loved the idea of making a cartoony book about the Xenomorph. The ideas and artwork that I created for that book came to me so easily as I had grown up with this character. I've known the alien for most of my life. I love the films, I love the world and I loved flipping it upside down and making it fun, friendly, colorful and silly while staying respectful of the character. It's a fun challenge to make such a terrifying character approachable, relatable and adorable.

For this book I was asked to contribute artwork celebrating forty years of *Alien* and what better way to celebrate such a monumental occasion than with a birthday party? I have a feeling the alien is no fan of candles, cake, decorations, and presents, and that's why I had so much fun creating this piece. Happy fortieth birthday to the Xenomorph, and here's to forty more!

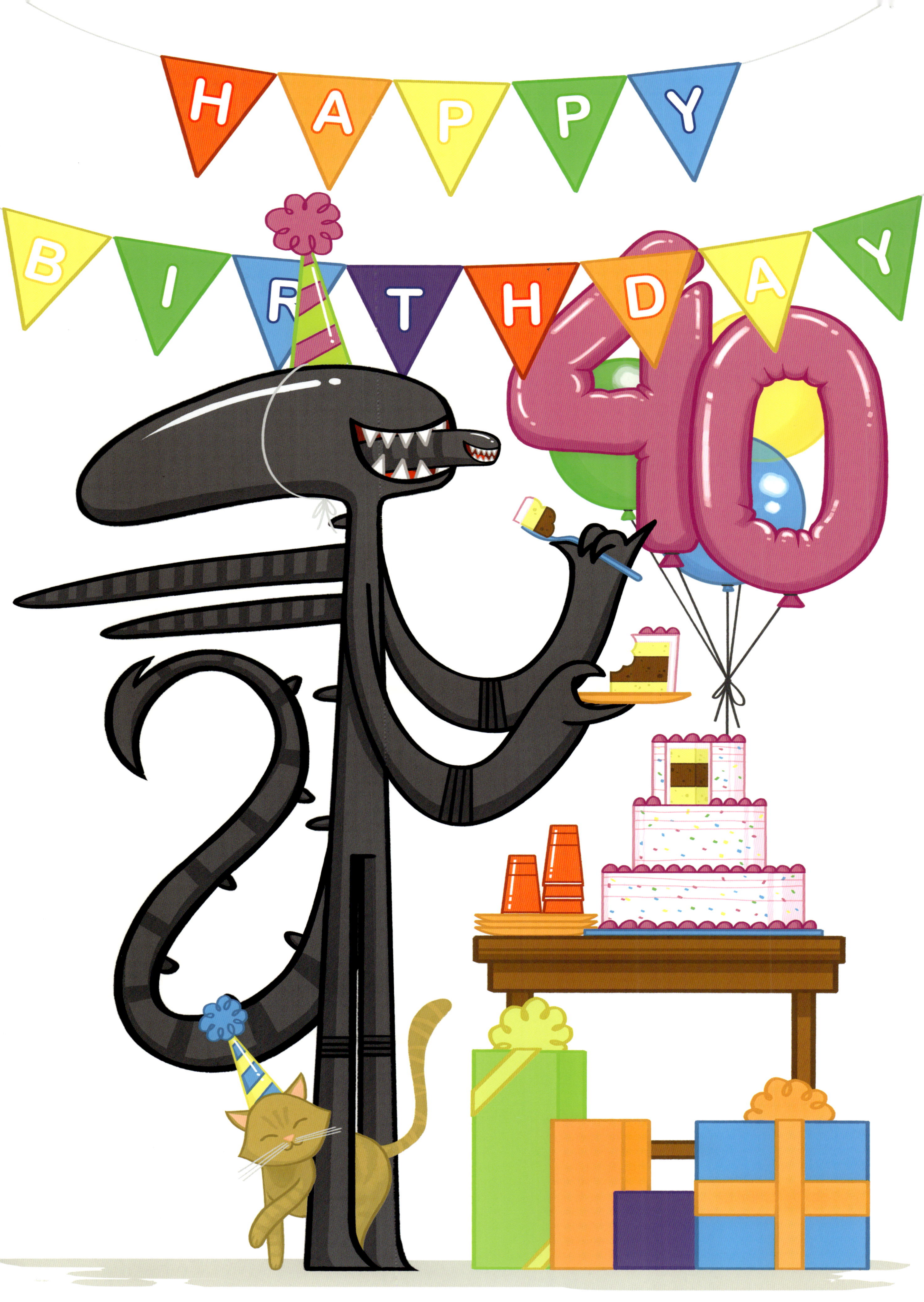
HAPPY
BIRTHDAY
40

ALIEN CONCEPT ART

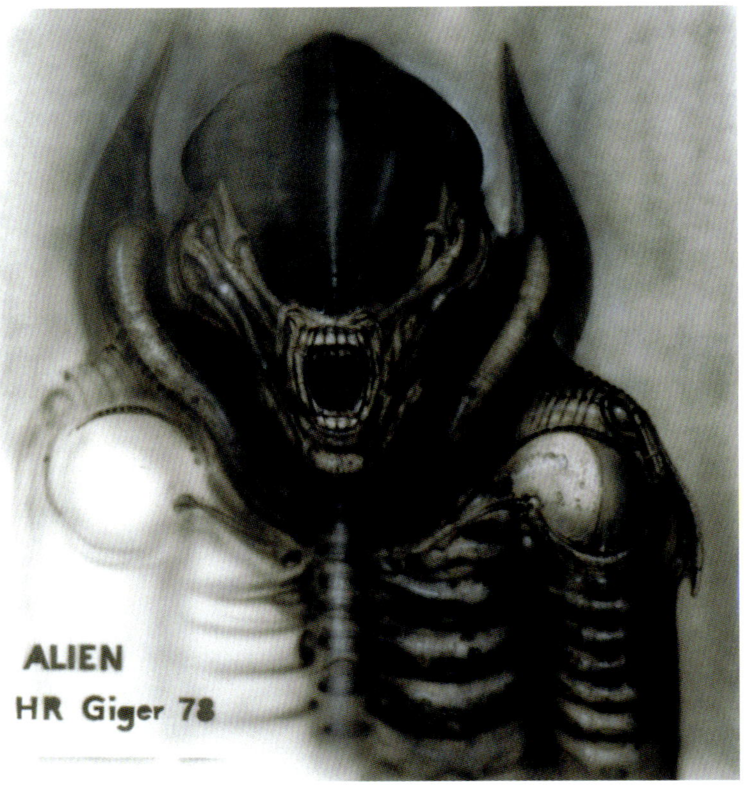

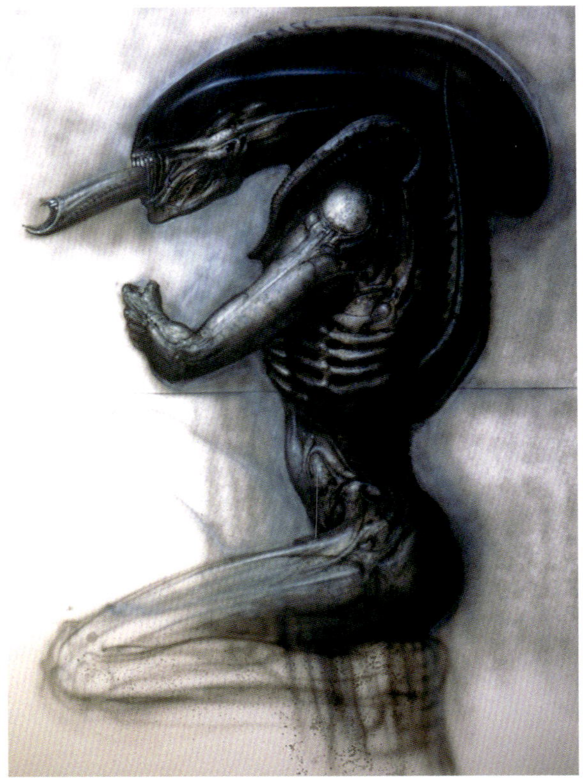

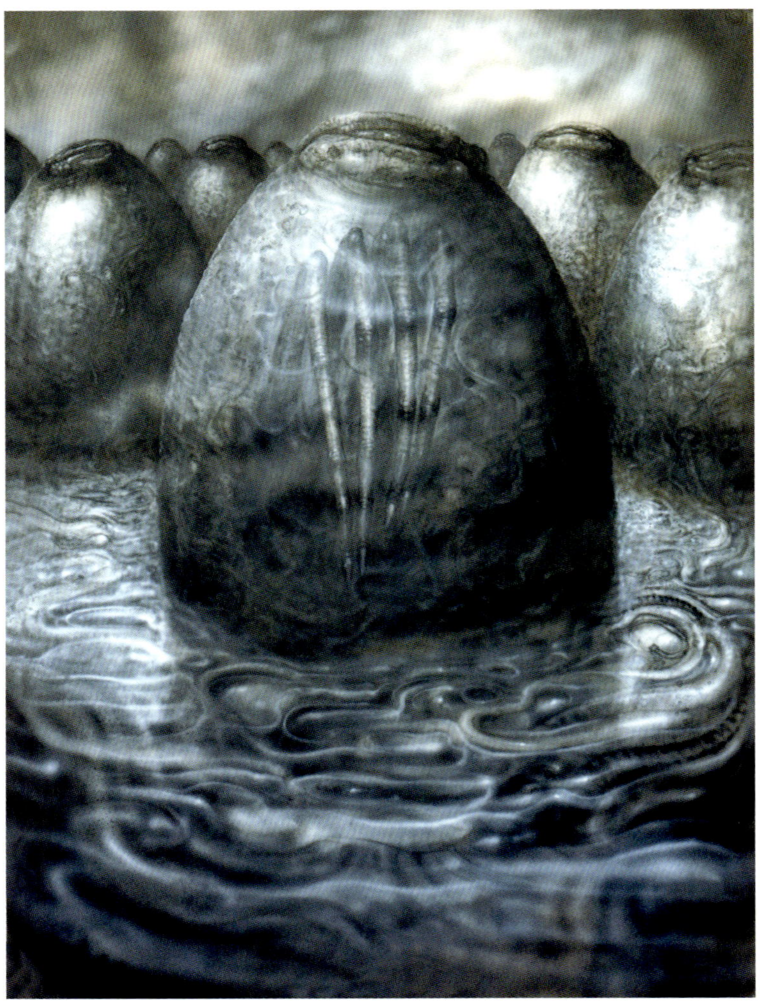

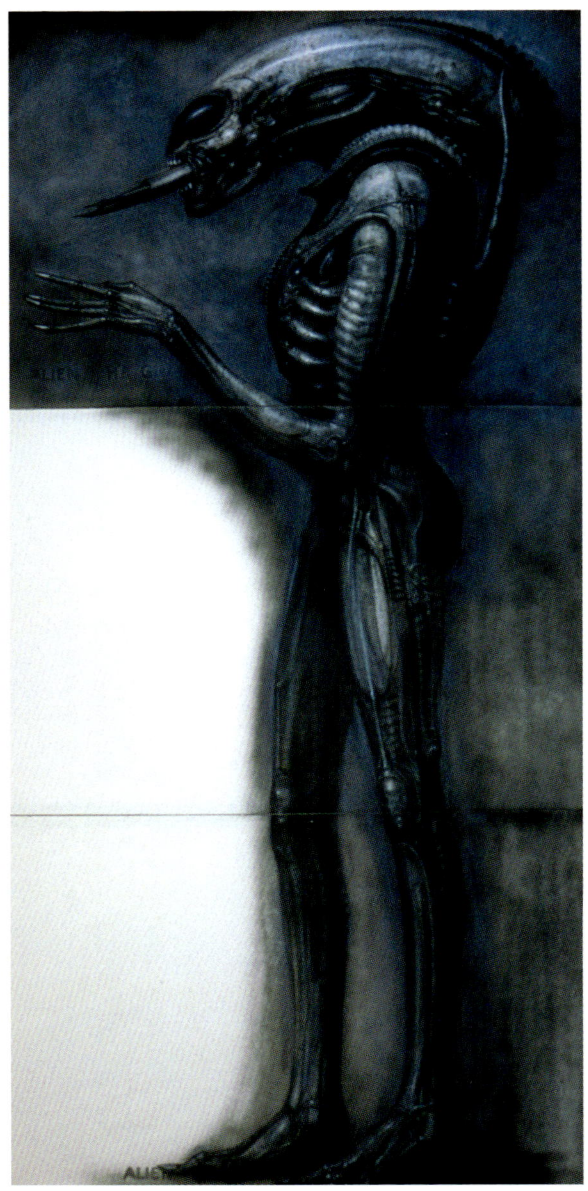

Above: H. R. Giger paintings of the Xenomorph and the egg.

Opposite: H. R. Giger paintings of the facehugger and the Derelict exterior.

ALIEN: 40 Years 40 Artists

APPENDIX 1

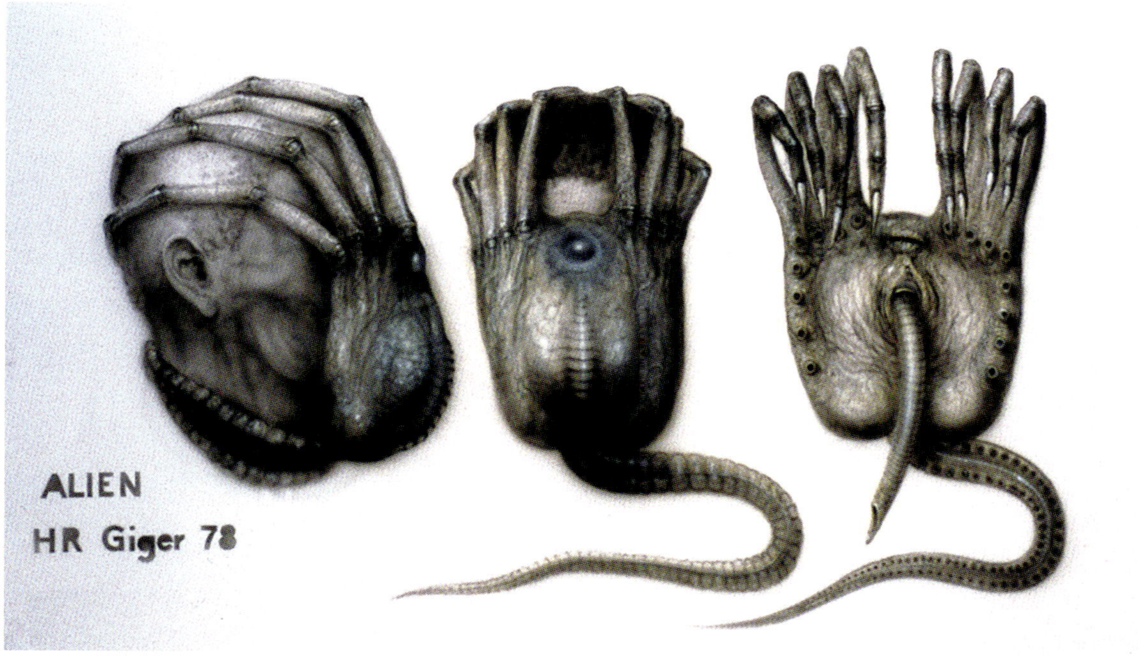

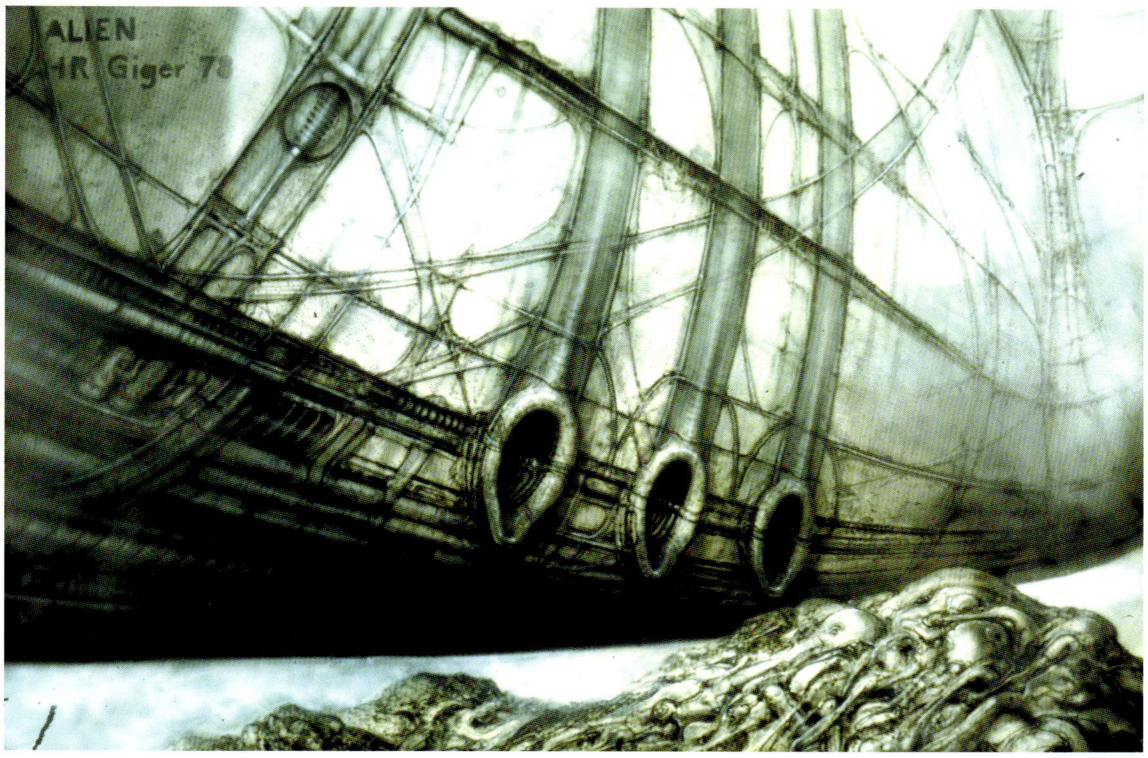

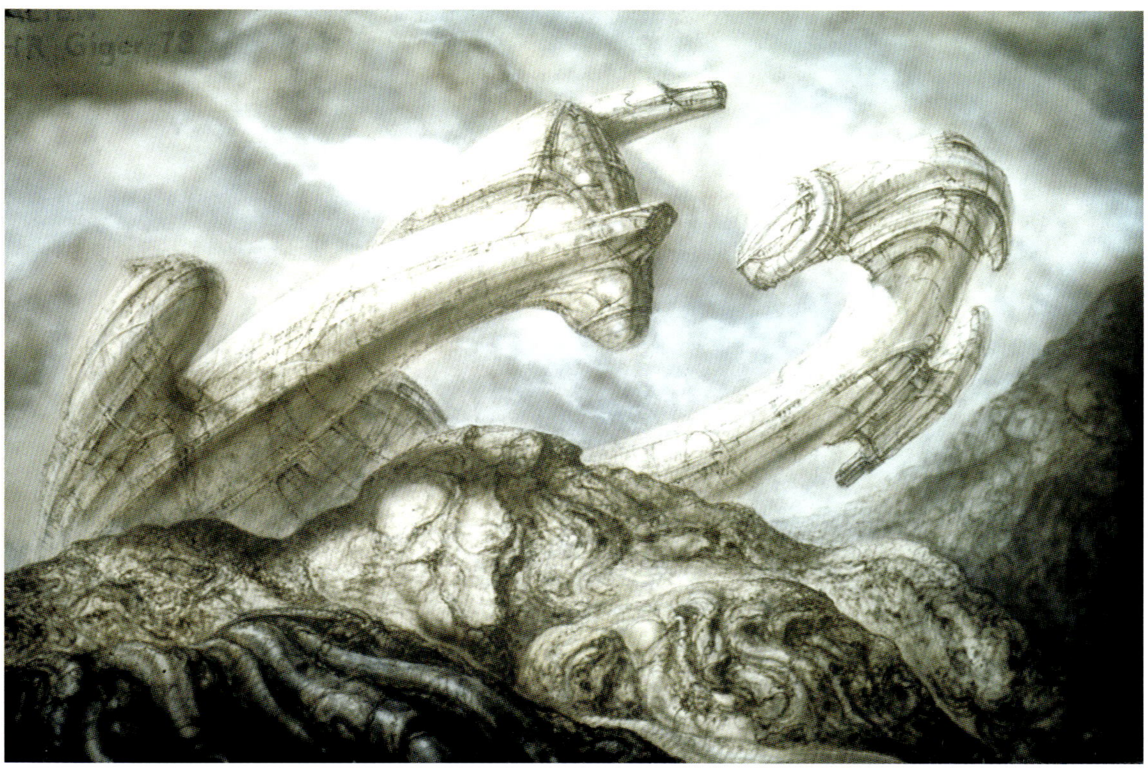

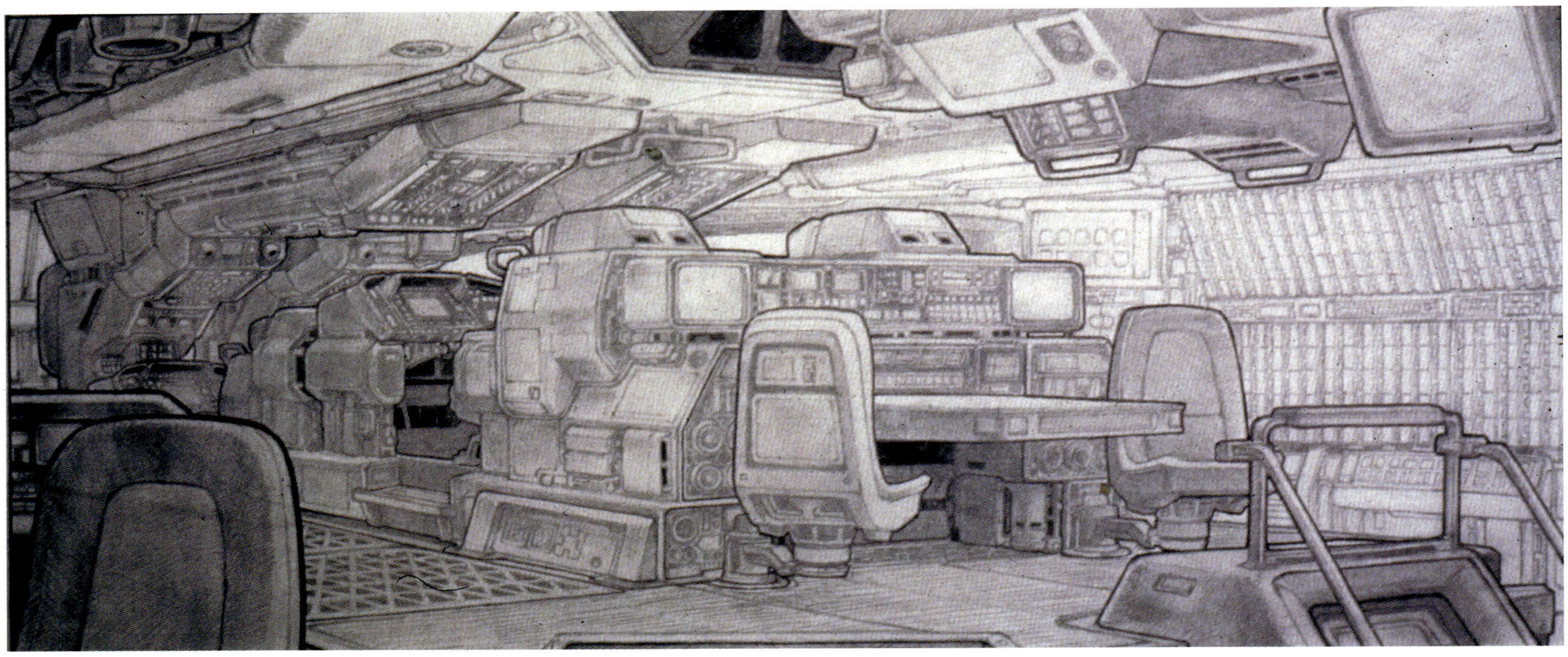

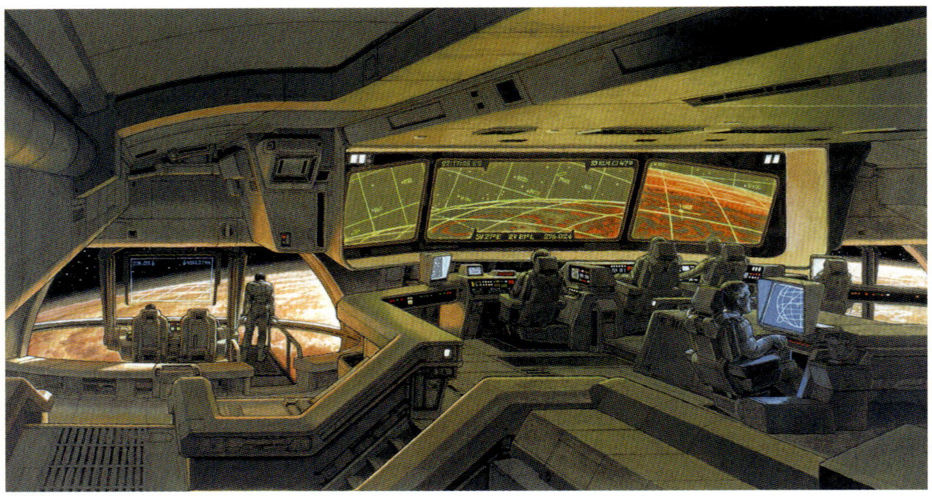

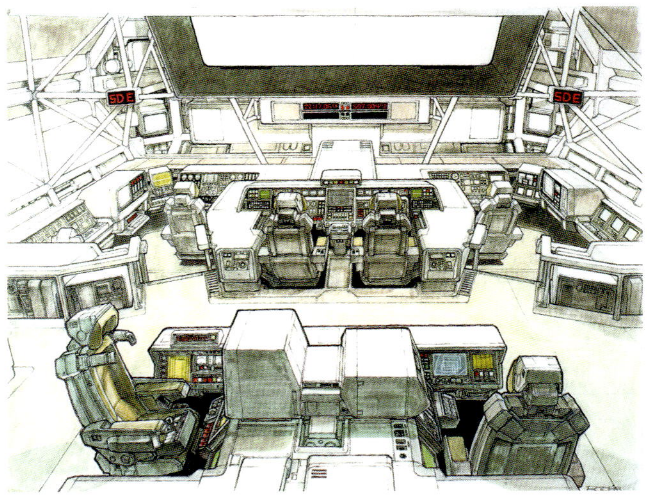

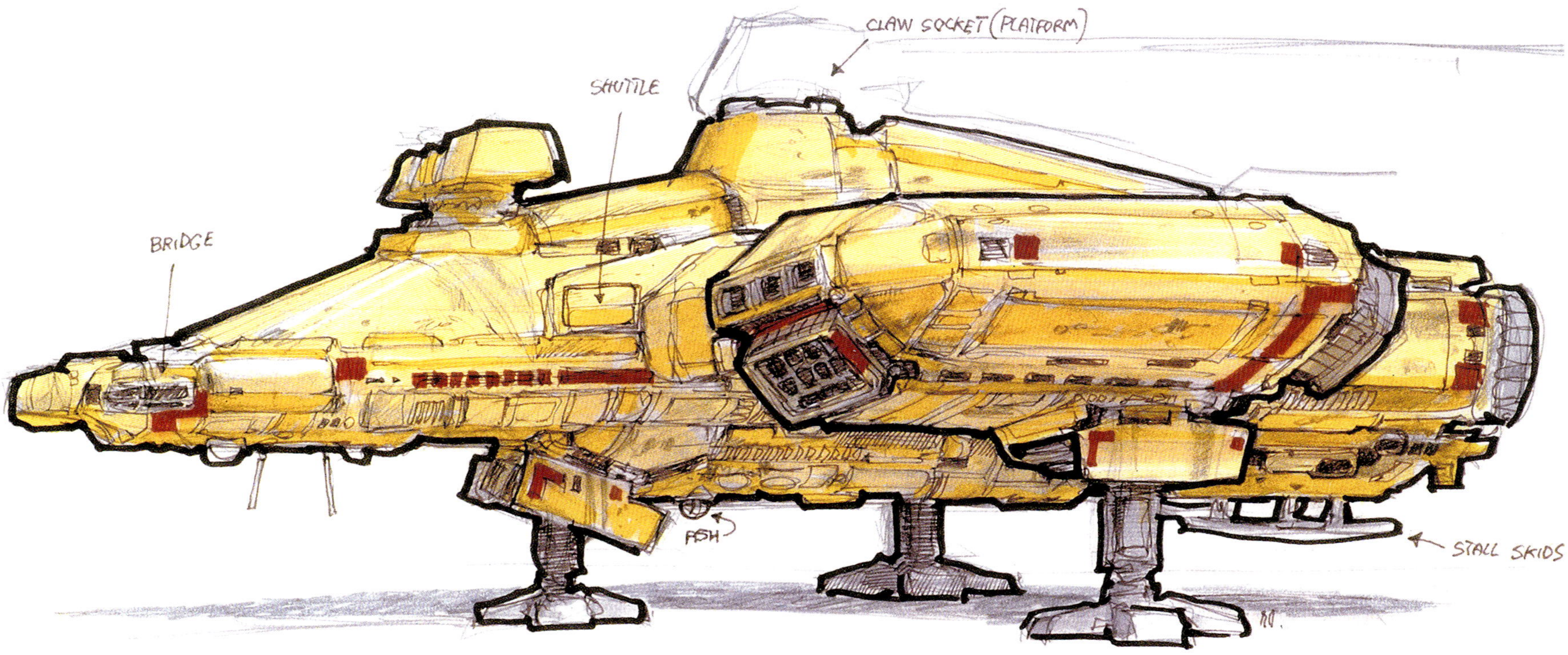

Above: Ron Cobb concepts of the *Nostromo* bridge and his exterior concept approved by Ridley Scott.

Opposite: Moëbius (Jean Giraud) concepts of the space suit.

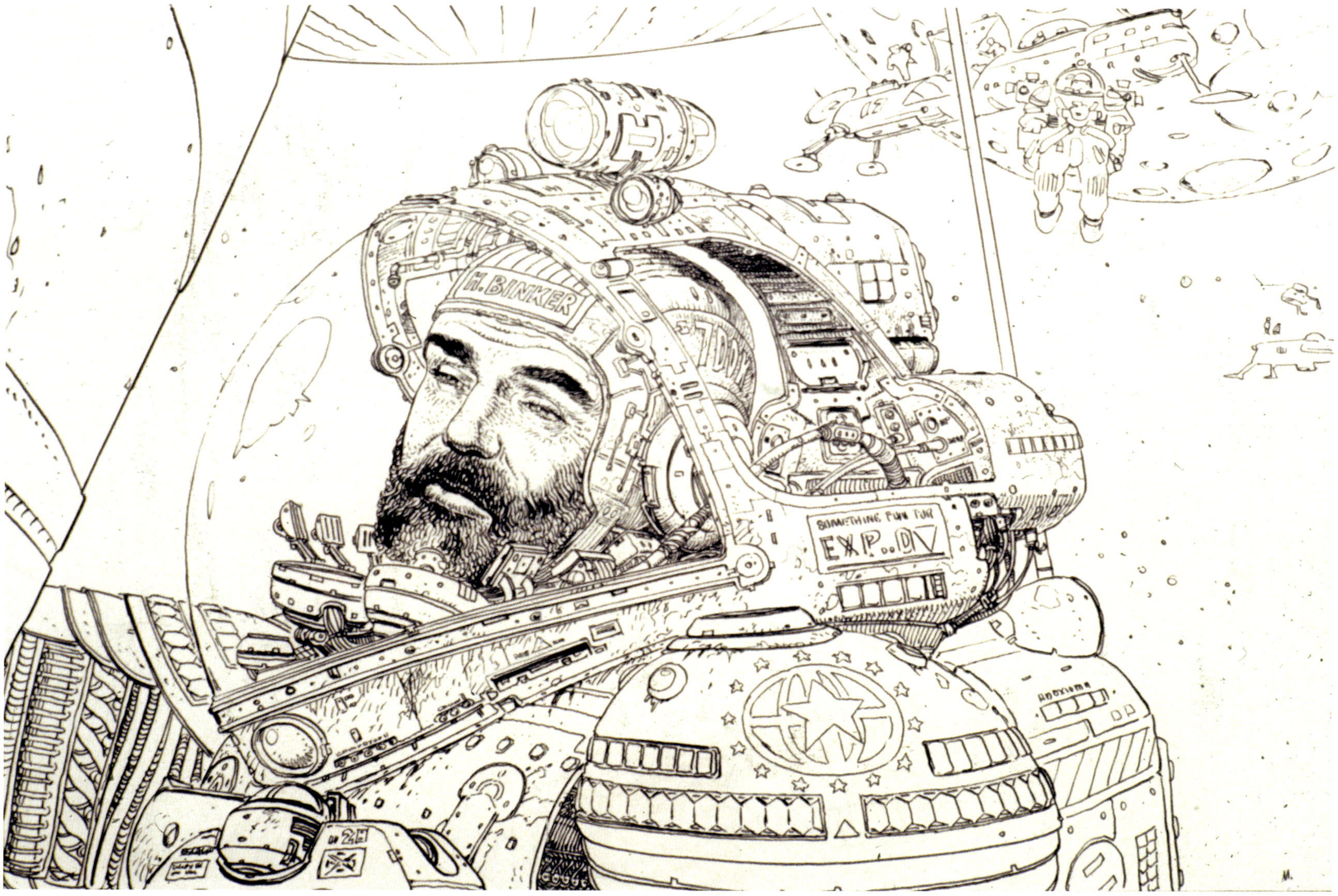
H. BINKER
SOMETHING FUN FOR
EXP..D

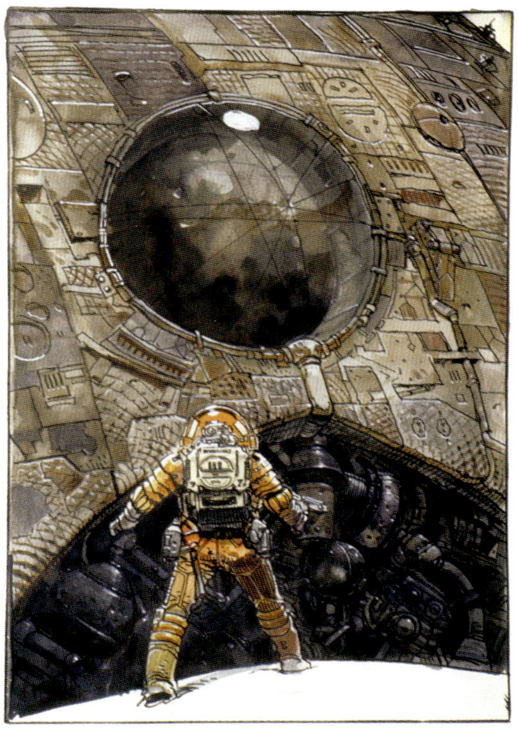

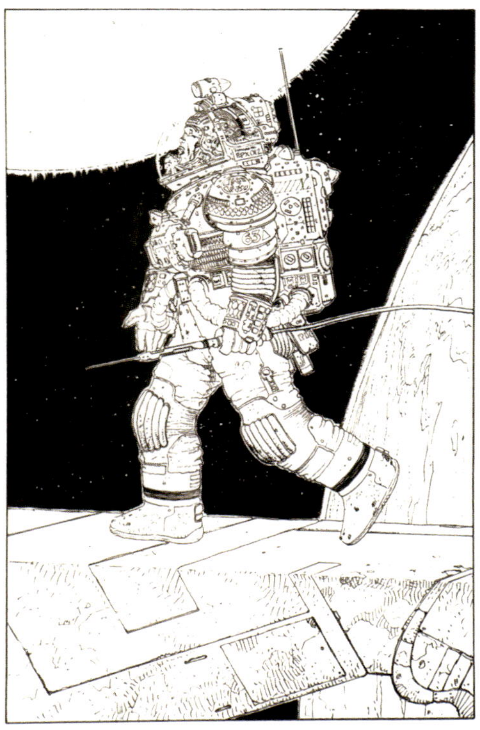

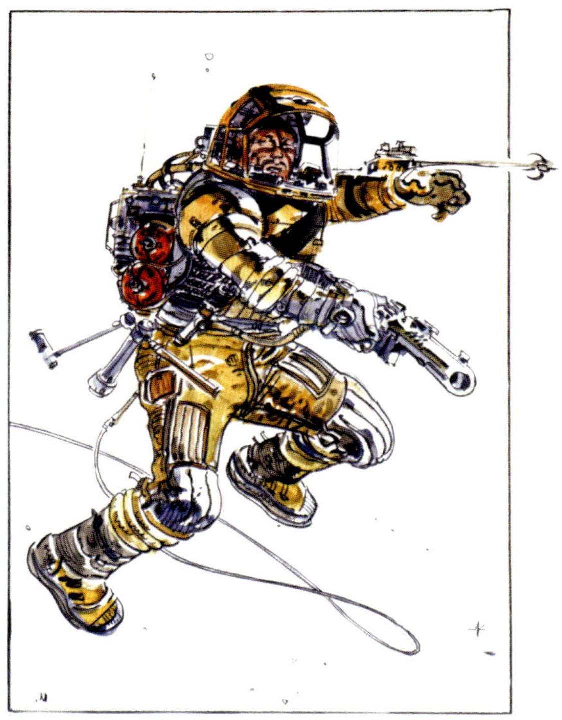

ALIEN POSTER ART

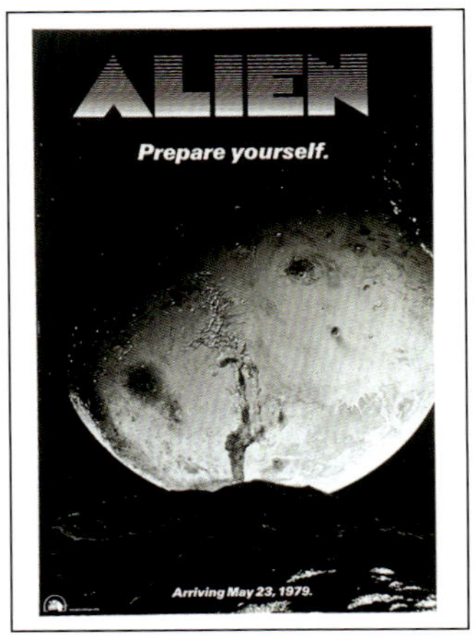

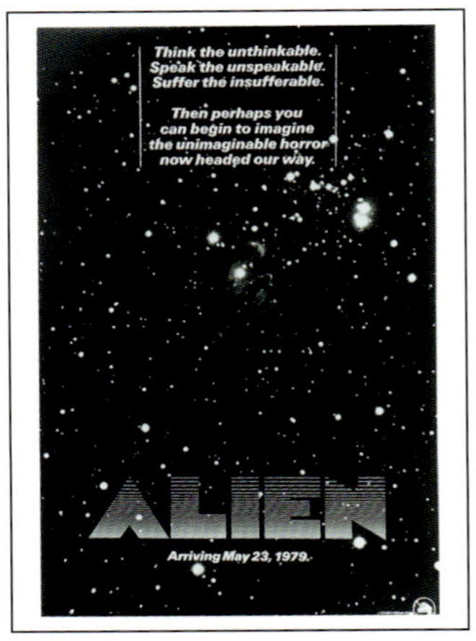

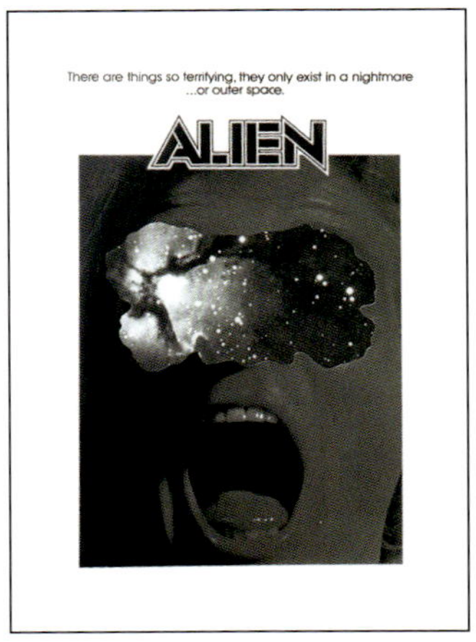

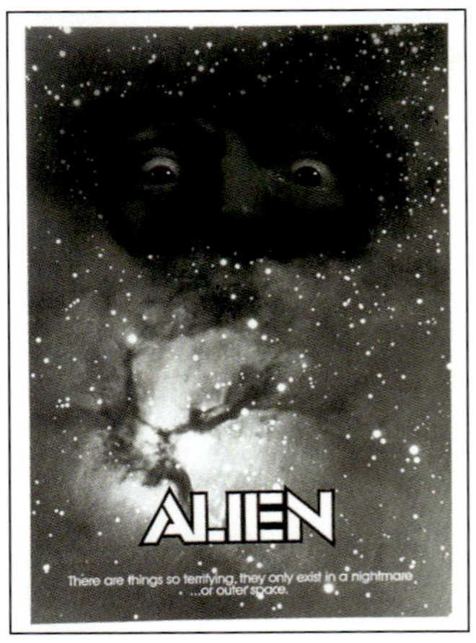

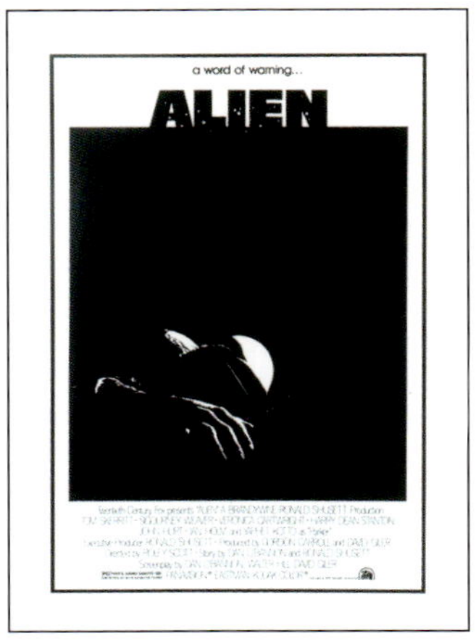

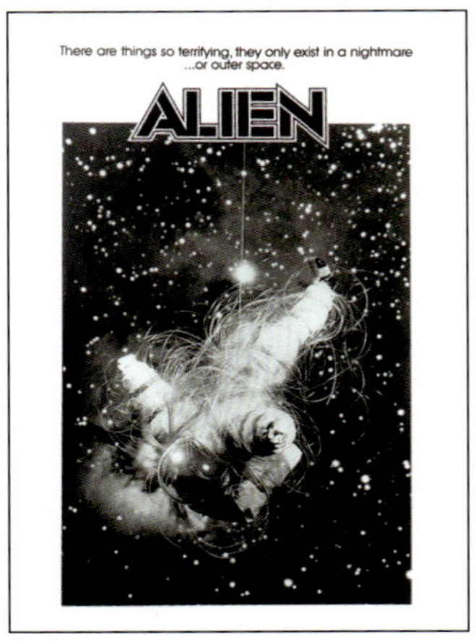

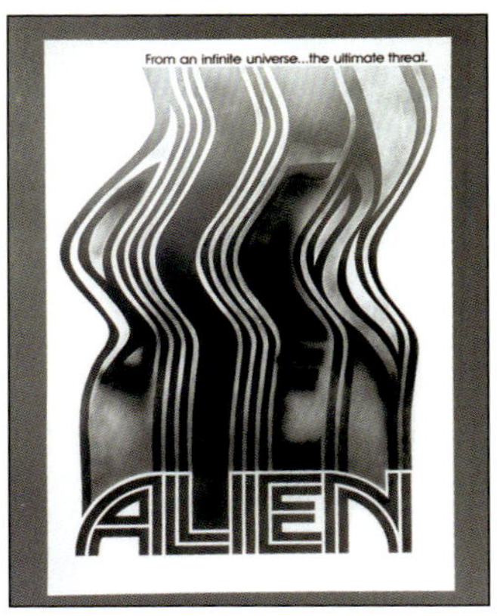

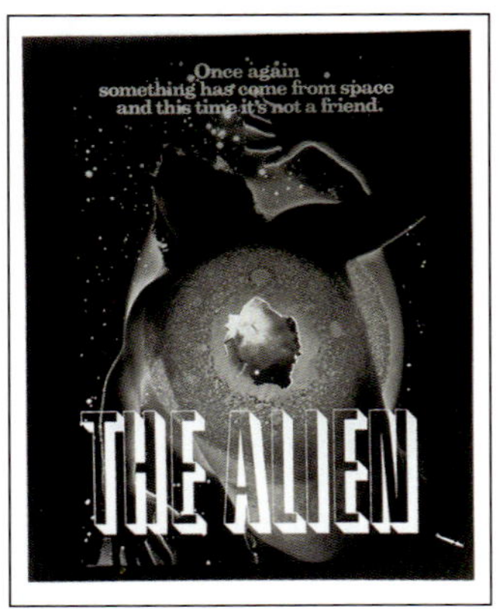

Above: Concepts of the American one-sheet cinematic-release poster.

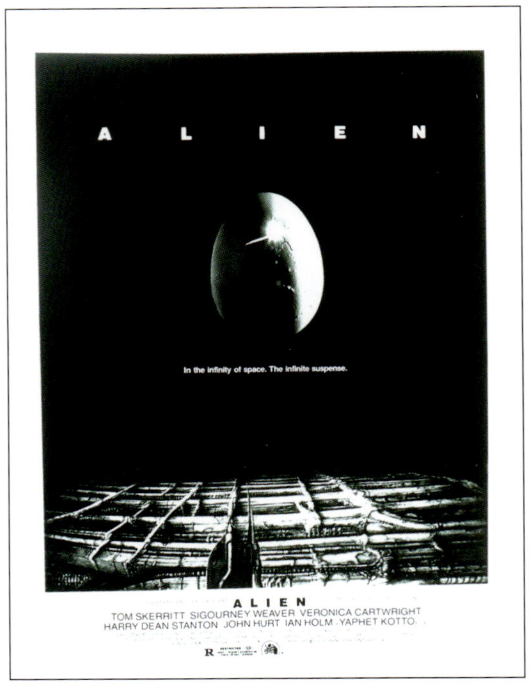

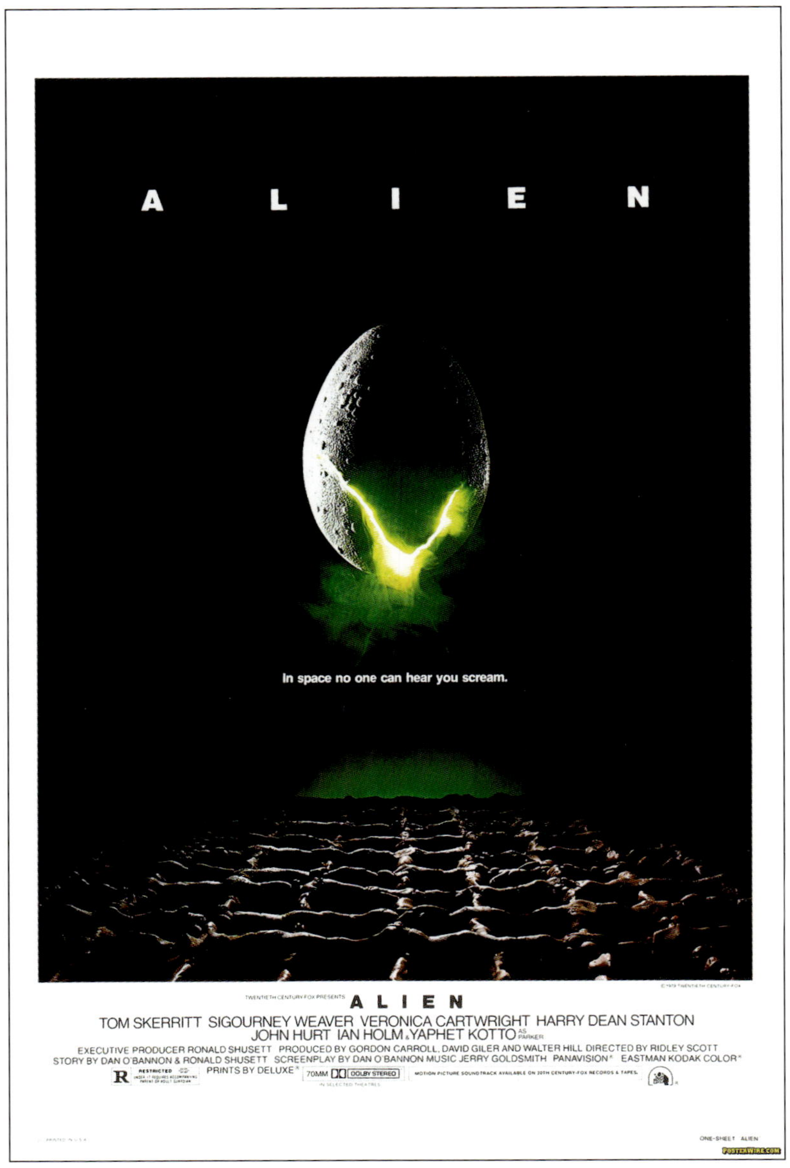

Above: The concept selected and the final one-sheet.

ALIEN: 40 YEARS 40 ARTISTS
APPENDIX 2

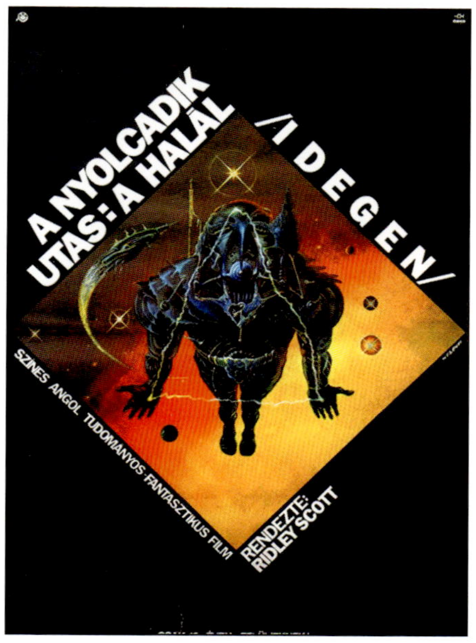

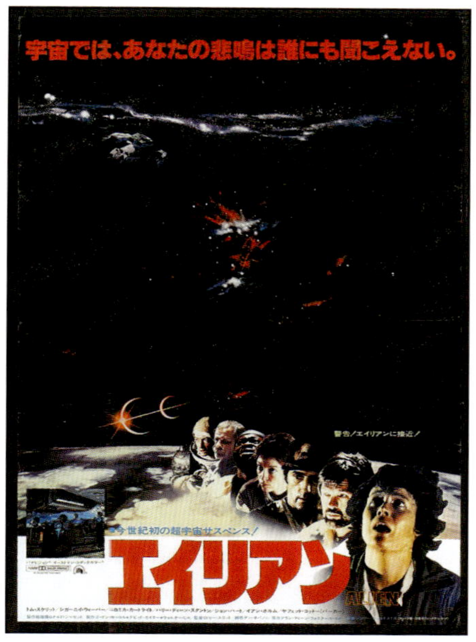

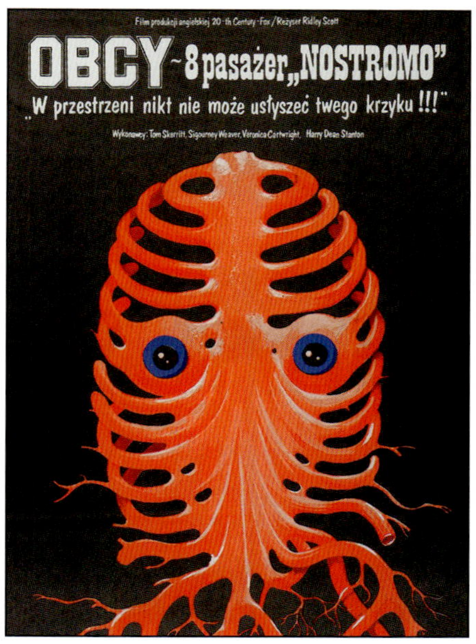

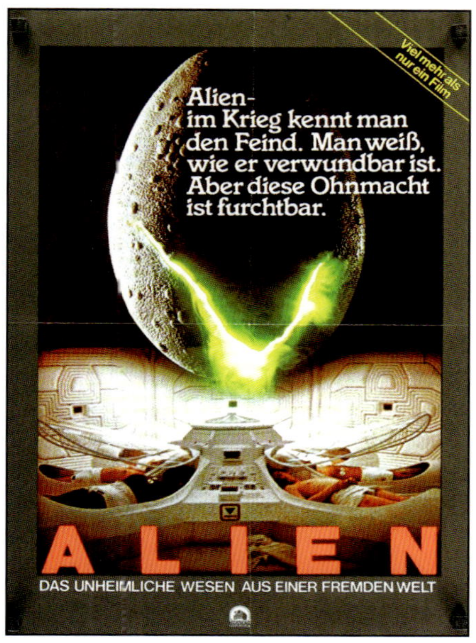

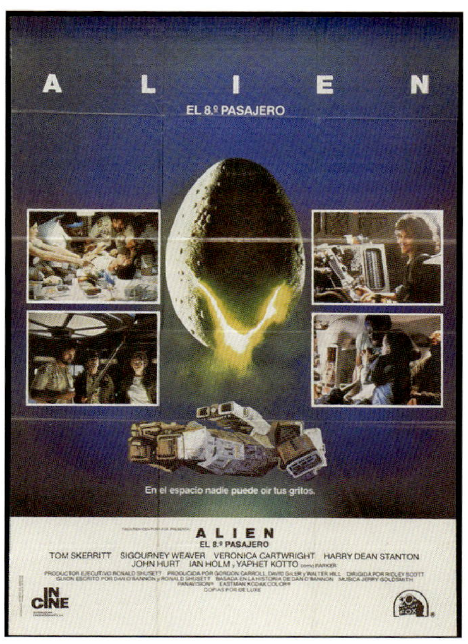

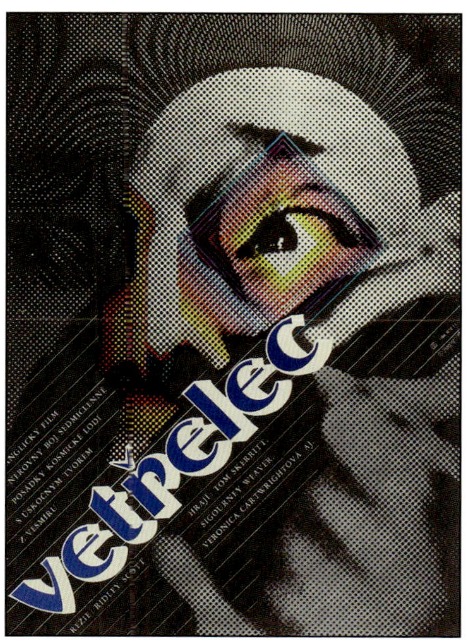

Above: *Alien* one-sheet cinematic-release posters for (clockwise from top left) Hungary, Japan, Germany, Czechoslovakia, Spain, and Poland.

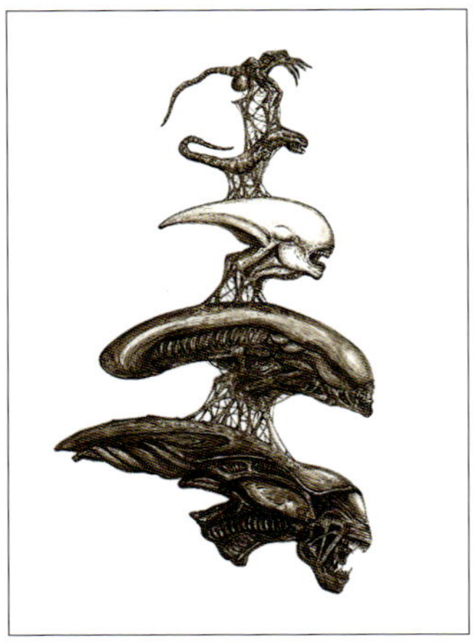

ANSON AGUIRRE FIRTH

A traditional ink and brush illustrator from Mexico City, Mexico. He specializes in ink-based illustrations rendering all kind of creatures; from dinosaurs and dragons to sea monsters and aliens. Anson achieved his BFA in Visual Arts at Emily Carr University of Art + Design in 2013 and has continued to expand his practice around the world. He now lives and works in Vienna, Austria and shows his work at different conventions across Europe and the United States.

Links: instagram.com/aguirrefirth

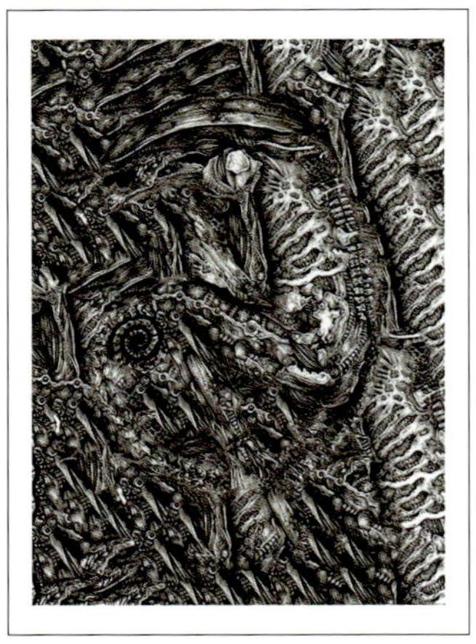

MARTA ALVIM

Aka House of Illustrology. A scientific illustrator based in London/Lisbon who specialises in intricate and detailed illustrations. Her passion for *Alien* and fantastic creatures motivated her to create her own interpretation of a Xenomorph, keeping it dark and visually interesting. She works mainly with biro and gel pens to create her world of (not always) gruesome specimens.

Links: houseofillustrology.wixsite.com/design; behance.net/martaalvim; @houseofillustrology

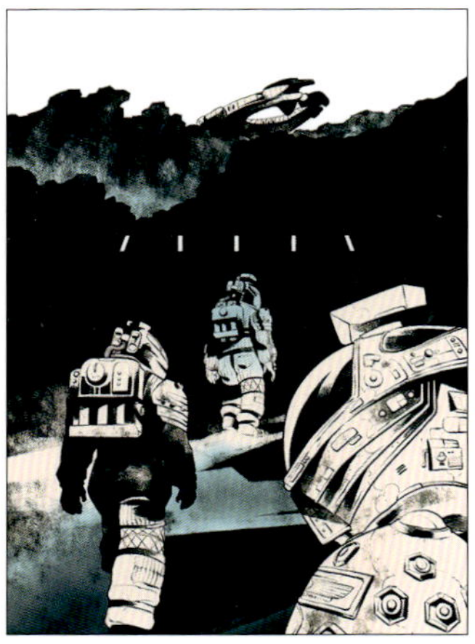

NATHAN J. ANDERSON

A freelance illustrator based in Michigan and part-time professor at the College for Creative Studies in Detroit. Growing up around a family of artists has led him to pursue illustration as a career, with clients including Gale Force Nine, Wizards of the Coast, Laundry LA, The SyFy Channel and Mayer Hawthorne, among others.

Links: nathanandersonart.com

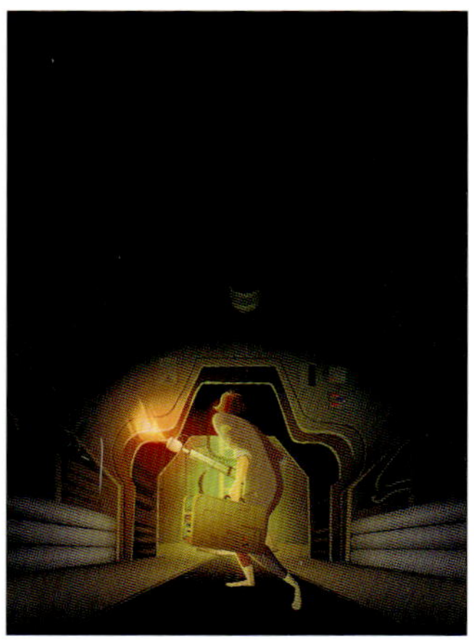

ALEXANDRA BARBOZA

An illustrator and visual development artist from Florida. She graduated from Ringling College of Art + Design in Computer Animation and has been working in animation ever since. From children's books to background painting, she is passionate about animation and creating beautiful visuals to aid in storytelling. In her spare time, she's working on building a sci-fi game!

Links: alexandrabarboza.com

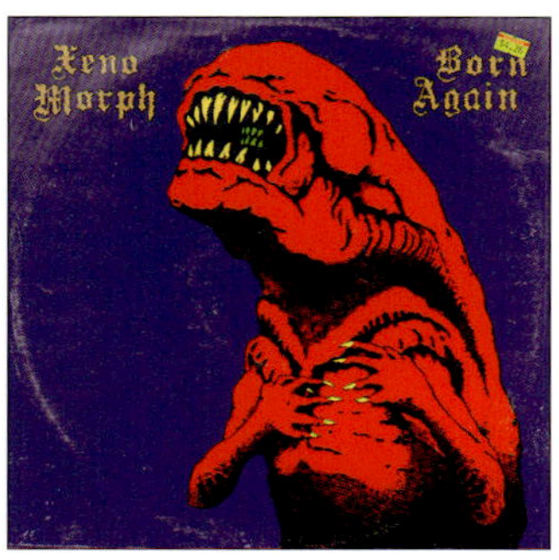

JUSTIN 'VBERKVLT' BARTLETT

He has applied his interpretations of heavy metal and occult symbology to various trades including music, fashion, and entertainment. Most profound in music, his album cover art helped reinvent extreme metal's aesthetics and have been selected for worldwide art gallery exhibitions. Bartlett's work has also cloaked the pages of *Vice*, *Revolver*, *Decibel*, and *Adbusters* magazines, and Taschen books.

Links: vberkvlt.com

ALIEN: 40 YEARS 40 ARTISTS

THE ARTISTS

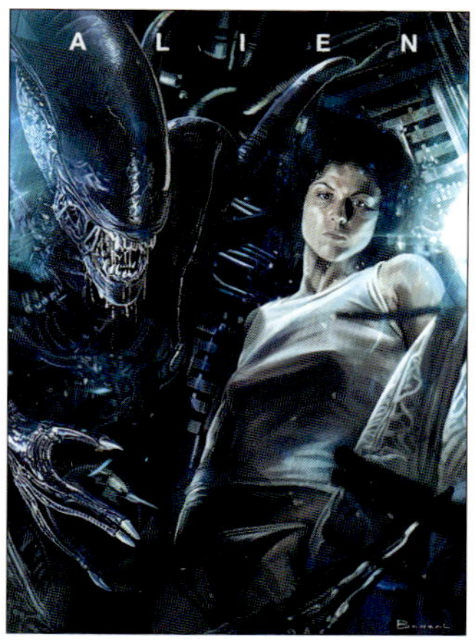

DAVID BENZAL

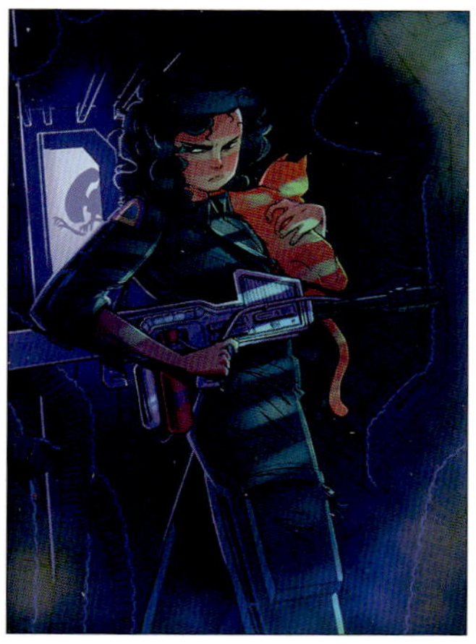

SWEENEY BOO

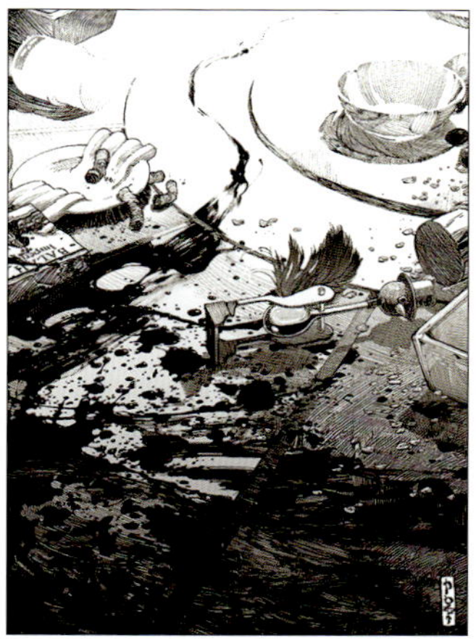

EVAN CAGLE

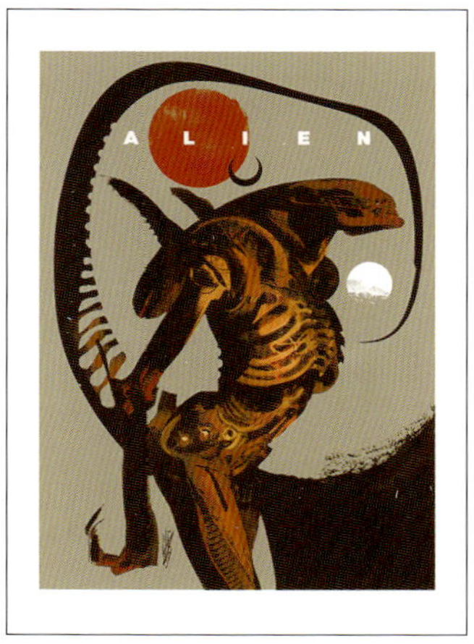

LUIGI 'GIGI CAVE' CAVENAGO

A comic book artist and illustrator based in Italy. He works mainly for Sergio Bonelli Editore as the official cover artist for *Dylan Dog*, one of the best-selling comic books in Italy, as well as on *Orfani* and *Cassidy*. He has received the Gran Guinigi Award and the Attilio Micheluzzi Award for Best Comic Book Artist. He has recently started a collaboration with Netflix.

Links: facebook.com/Gigi.Cavenago; instagram.com/gigicavenago; deviantart.com/gigicave

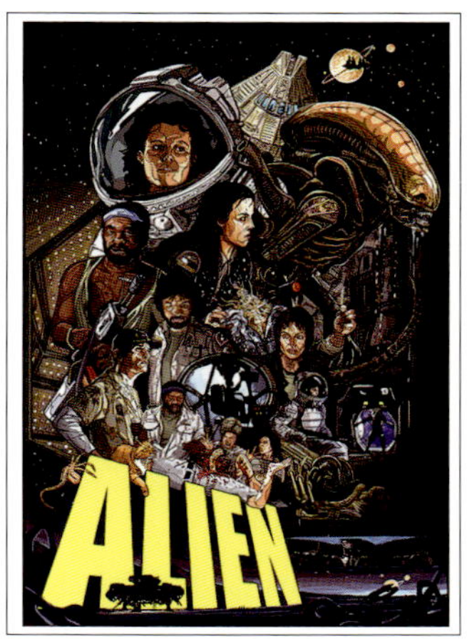

TIM CLINARD

An artist based in Chicago. Skilled in many facets of both traditional and digital art. he has been recognized for his unique composition and character-packed movie posters. Most notably his series of posters from the *Alien* franchise. When not working or painting, Tim enjoys spending time outdoors with his wife, daughter, and their two dogs.

Links: clinartstudios.com; instagram.com/clinartstudios

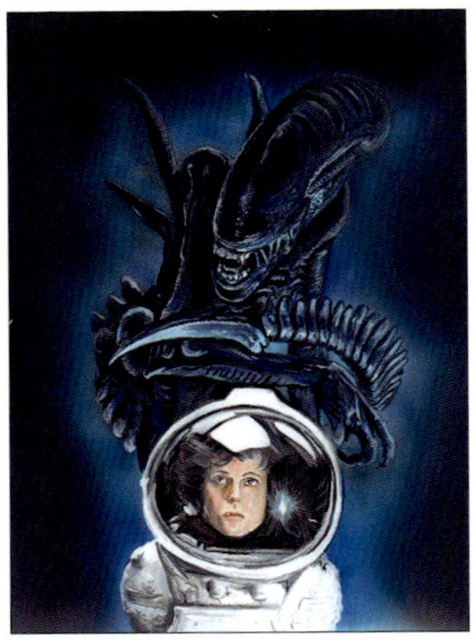

CAROLYN CRAGGS

A self-taught artist from County Durham, England. Whilst growing up she was mentored by renowned local artist and teacher Victor Hair. She works in a variety of mediums, including pencil, paint, airbrush and digital. A self-confessed pop culture enthusiast, Carolyn is also a sketch card artist for popular TV and movie franchises, including *Alien*, *Star Wars*, *Stranger Things* and *The Walking Dead*.

Links: @cjc_artist

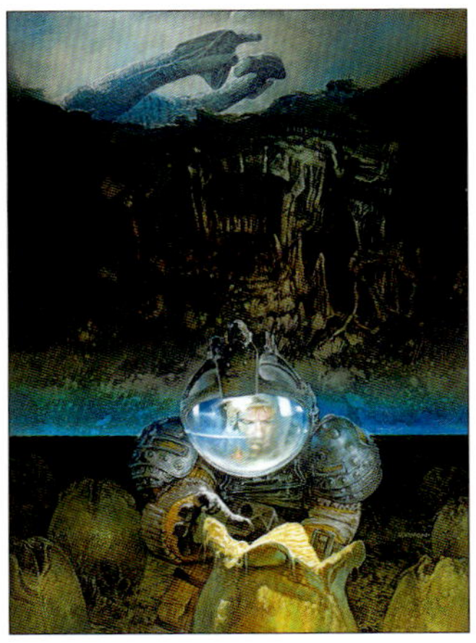

DAVE DORMAN

A freelance illustrator for more than 35 years. Beginning with his first published piece as a cover to *Heavy Metal Magazine*, Dorman has had the pleasure to work with almost every major comics company, as well as numerous game and toy companies. Dorman is the winner of the Eisner award for his outstanding art for *Aliens: Tribes*, an illustrated novel. Dorman was also awarded the prestigious Ink Pot award, given for lifetime achievement in the comics and illustration field.

Links: @DaveDorman; facebook.com/davedormanartist

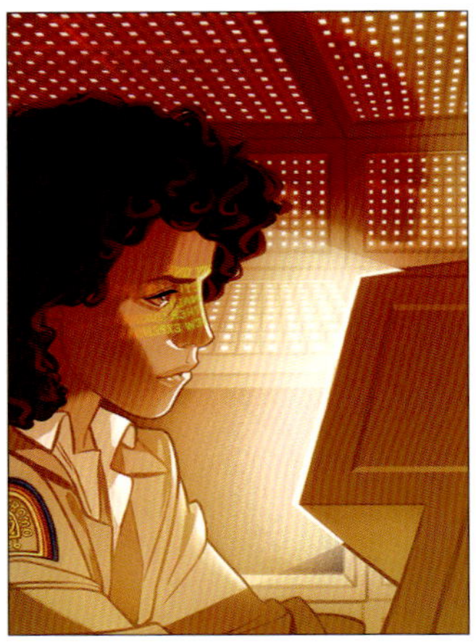

M.J. ERICKSON

A freelance illustrator, comic artist and designer who splits her time between Colorado and Chicago. In addition to her work on comic interiors and covers, she does promotional illustration for books and has Kickstarted a successful line of merchandise based on her original "Creature Conservation" designs, a mash-up of mythology and wildlife rescue programs.

Links: kreugan.com

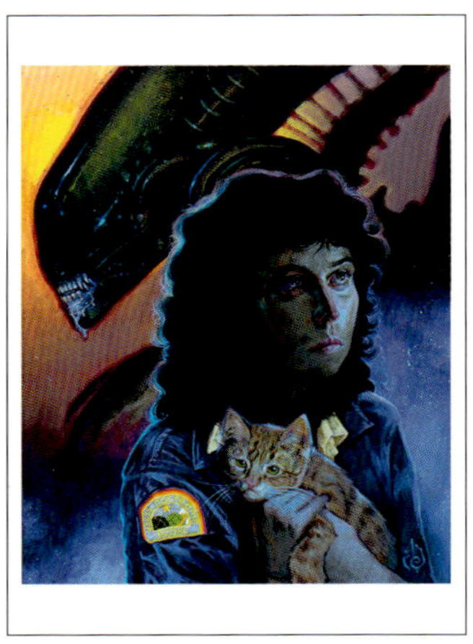

JACQUELINE GALLAGHER

"Painter of Zombies and the Disturbed. Or Disturbed Zombie Painter… I forget which." She received her Bachelor of Fine Arts from the University of Hawaii at Manoa in 2009. Since then, she has exhibited nationally numerous times with 3 solo and countless group shows, specializing in horror, pop culture, and macabre surreal portraiture. In 2015 she relocated to her new home in Portland, Oregon, where she is currently exploring strange themes of sexual augmentation and female identity in a chaotic and alien landscape through paint.

Links: paintdead.com

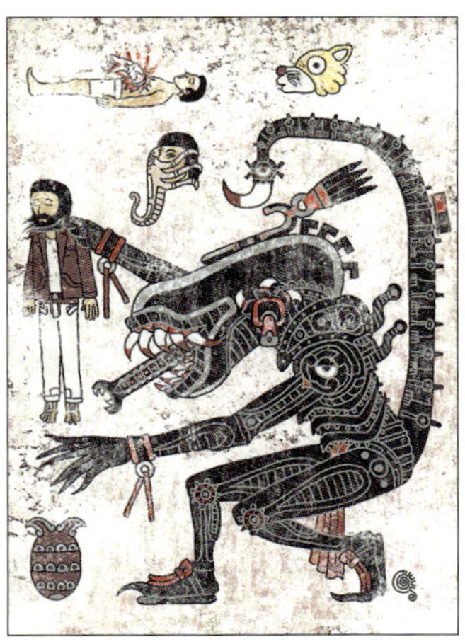

JORGE 'QETZA' GARZA

Aka Qetza. An artist from Northwest Indiana. His work starts from pencil sketches that are scanned and reworked in Photoshop using a drawing tablet. With major influences of comic book art, horror illustration, ancient cultural art of the Americas and screen printing, his work ranges from simple to highly detailed pen and ink.

Links: qetza.com

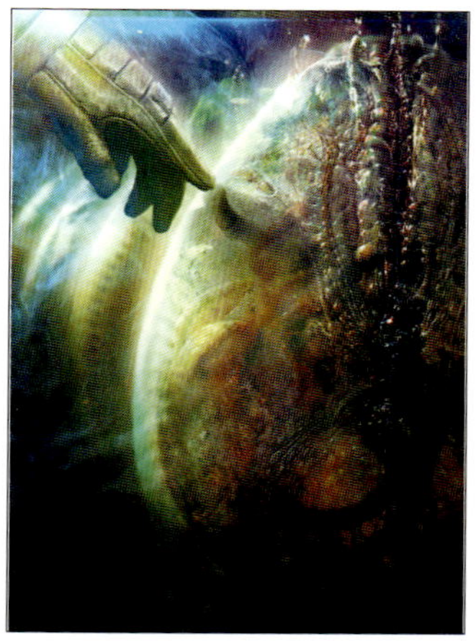

DANE HALLETT

Notable for his unique ability to carry a design from concept to creation, Dane Hallett is an adept concept designer, creature artist and prop maker. In addition to his illustration work featured in *Alien: Covenant*, he has worked on high-profile productions such as *Pirates of the Caribbean: Dead Men Tell No Tales*, *The Wolverine*, *Aquaman* and contributed to several hero vehicles and props for the Academy Award-winning *Mad Max: Fury Road*.

Links: danehallett.com; @dane_hallett_art

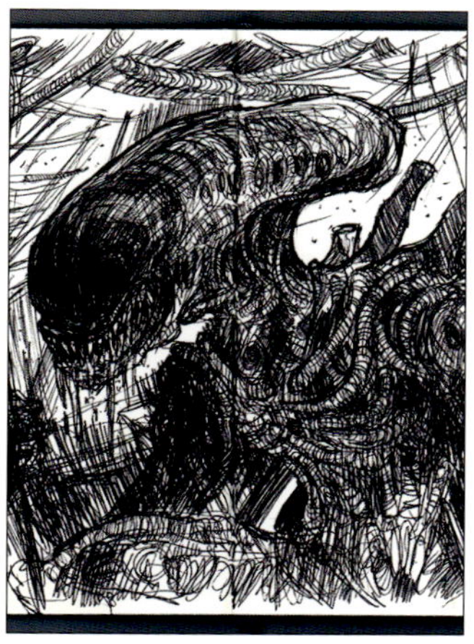

CORIN HARDY

An award-winning filmmaker, illustrator, sculptor and writer, whose visual style mixes the macabre, the beautiful and the epic to visually dazzling effect. Hardy wrote and directed his debut feature, *The Hallow*, in 2015, and his second feature film, *The Nun*, was released in 2018.

Links: imdb.com/name/nm2379028

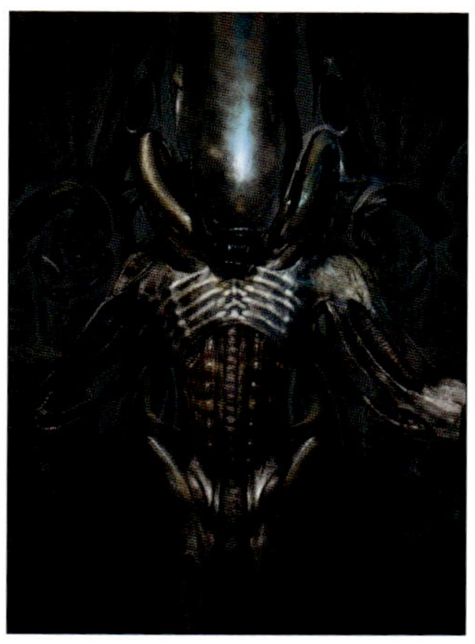

MATT HATTON

Has worked in multiple disciplines and across many departments in film, from character and concept design, props, weapons, set design, set decoration, art direction, VFX, storyboards, and even hair and makeup design for live action, to multiple hats on animation features. In non-movie work he specialises in character and mascot design as well as illustration, graphic design, merchandising, TVCs, marketing, and television work.

Links: @matthatt0n

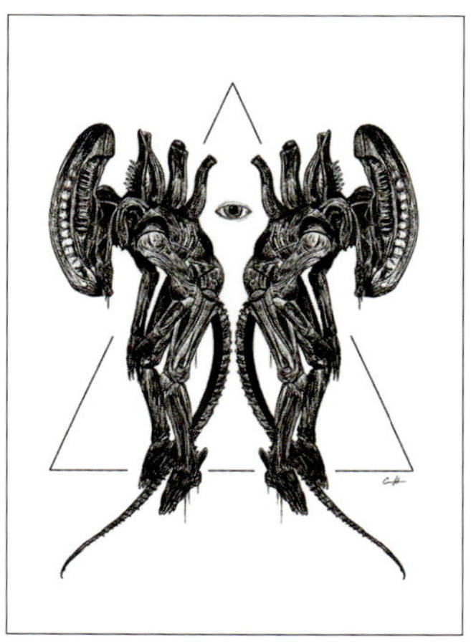

CARRIE ANNE HUDSON

A visual artist from San Diego, California. She describes herself foremost as an illustrator and painter, with a passion for pop culture, pop surrealism, and dark artistries. Touching on themes of death, isolation, and love, she brings an overwhelming sense of passion and wonder to her pieces. Carrie's artwork has been shown in galleries around the globe in a variety of group exhibitions. In the summer of 2014, she was accepted into a month-long artist residency in Transylvania, Romania. In 2017, she was nominated for the Visual Arts Network San Diego Art Prize. And in 2018, Carrie held her first solo show, Haunted, at basileIE Gallery.

Links: carrieannehudson.com; @carriehudson

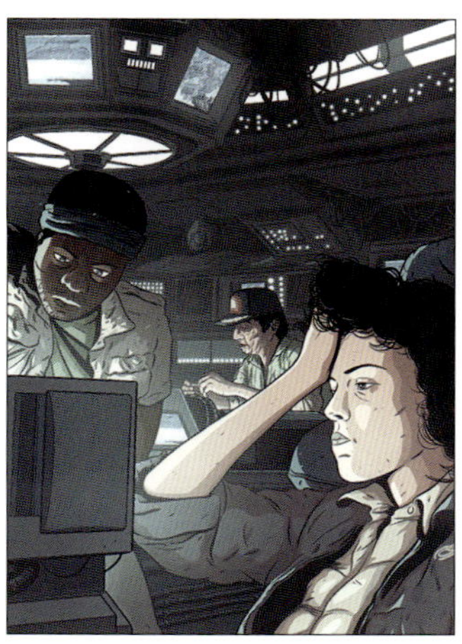

TOM HUMBERSTONE

An award-winning comic artist and illustrator based in Edinburgh. His work has appeared in *Phonogram* (Image Comics), *Doctor Who* (Titan Comics) and the Eisner-nominated *Nelson* (Blank Slate). He writes and draws non-fiction comics for The Nib, *New Statesman*, Vox, Buzzfeed and others. He is also the editor and publisher of the critically acclaimed UK comics anthology *Solipsistic Pop* and the co-editor of *Over The Line: An Introduction to Poetry Comics*. As opposed to Warrant Officer Ellen Louise Ripley, he cannot, in fact, handle himself.

Links: tomhumberstone.com

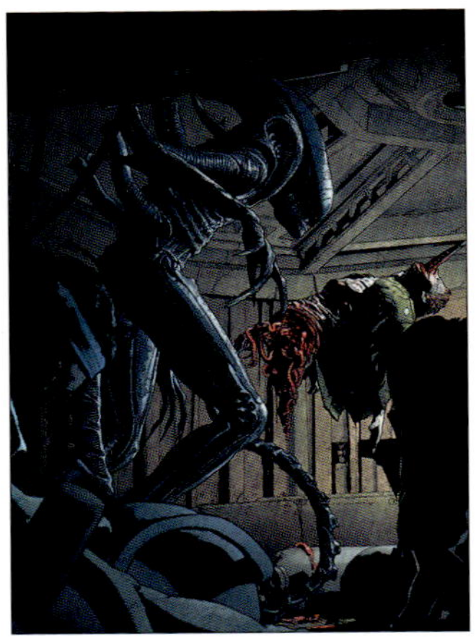

TRISTAN 'T-REX' JONES

A comic book writer and illustrator based in Melbourne, Australia. His work ranges from the *Ninja Turtles*, to the *Ghostbusters* films and comics, *Mad Max* and *Alien*, and companies such as *2000AD*, DC Comics and Image Comics.

Links: @tyrannojones

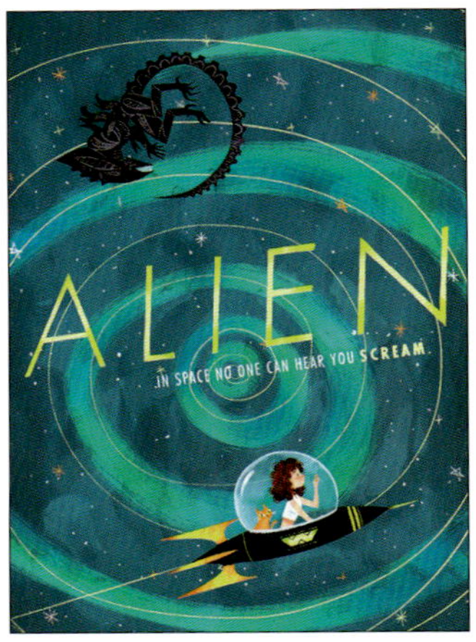

KATHERINE KUEHNE

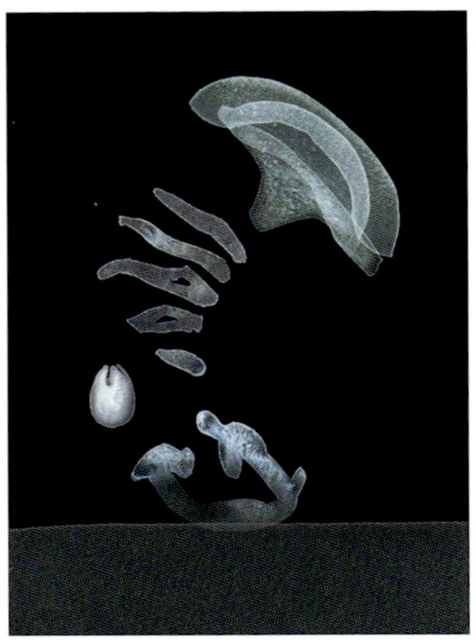

MARTA LECH

A Polish artist and printmaker, who works and lives in Wrocław, active in the fields of drawing, painting and printmaking. Her favorite technique is linocut. She has received the Grand Prize, Bangkok Triennale International – Print and Drawing Exhibition, Thailand 2015; Grand Prix, Split Graphic Biennial, Croatia 2013; Grand Prize, Seoul Space Print Biennial, South Korea 2006.

Links: martalech.wordpress.com

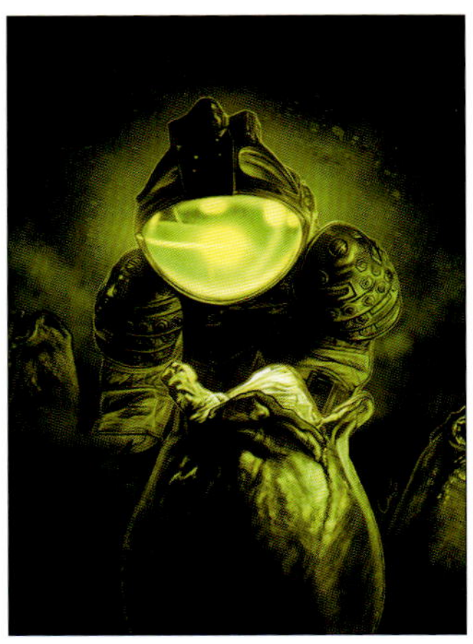

CHELSEA LOWE

A freelance illustrator from East Tennessee. She specializes in poster illustration and she loves drawing everything from creepy horror characters to beautiful endangered animals. Most of her work is digitally created on a Wacom Cintiq and iPad Pro. So far her work has been featured in various art books and art exhibits in the US and UK.

Links: cmloweart.com

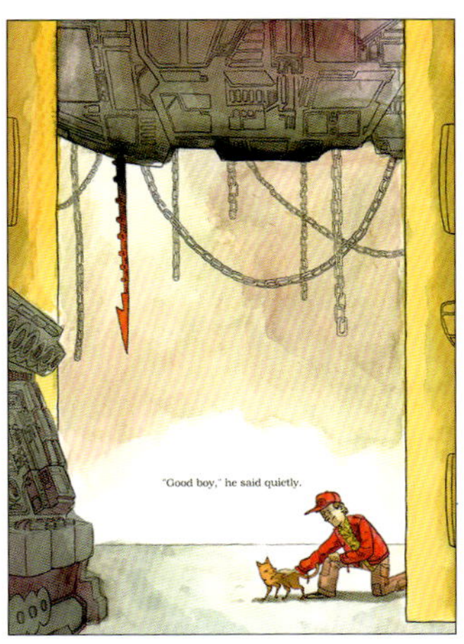

RORY LUCEY

An illustrator and teacher living in New Jersey with his wife and two cats. His first book, *Jonesy: Nine Lives On the Nostromo*, told the story of *Alien* from the perspective of Jonesy the cat.

Links: rorylucey.com

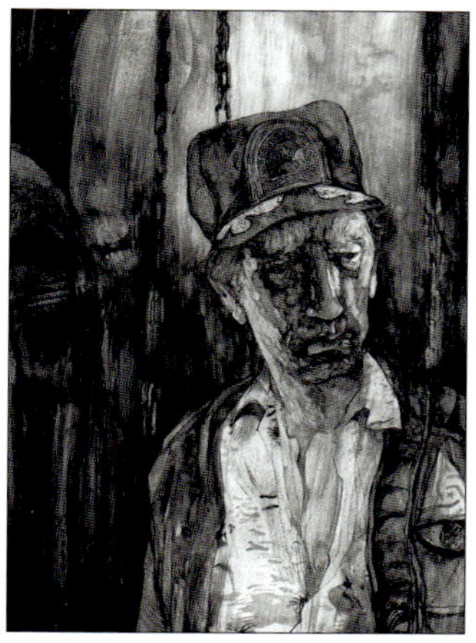

DAVID LUPTON

A London-based illustrator who works with traditional materials. With a lifelong love of film, his illustrations attempt to create a sense of narrative and cinematic atmosphere and he has created work for many briefs, which have included album cover artwork, music video animation, film production design and narrative book illustration.

Links: david-lupton.com

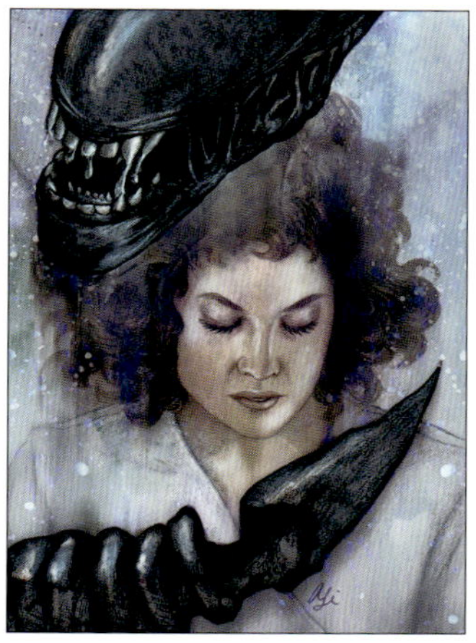

ALICE MEICHI LI

An artist who is originally from Detroit and currently living in New York City. After earning her BFA in illustration from the School of Visual Arts, she went on to create sci-fi and fantasy-inspired artwork for publications such as Oni Press, Archie Comics, Dark Horse, Image Comics, ComicMix, as well as various galleries around the United States.

Links: alicemeichi.com

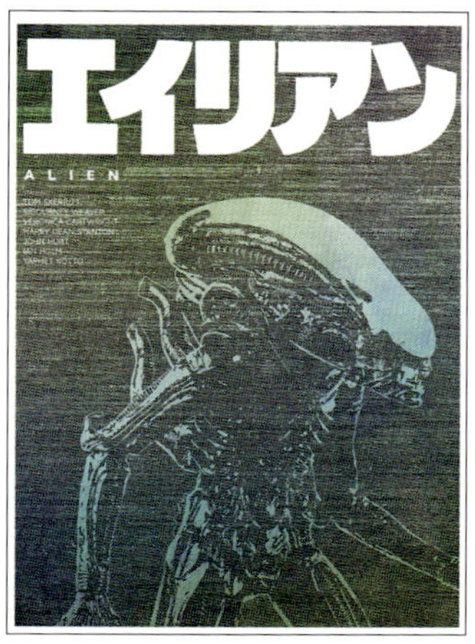

MATT NEEDLE

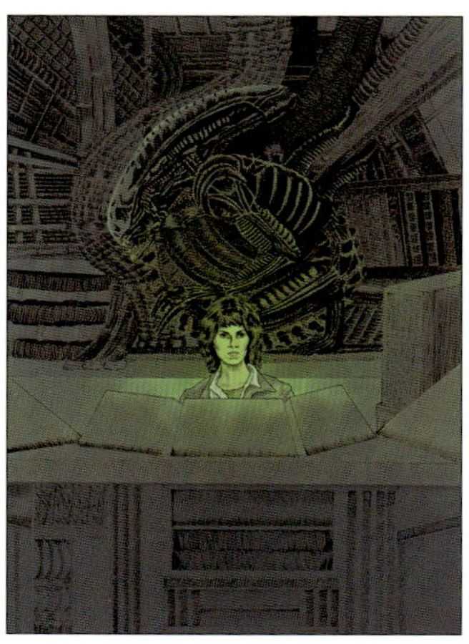

LEONIE O'MOORE

A writer and artist. Her works include comics for *Heavy Metal Magazine* and the original graphic novel *LORD*. She developed the course and wrote the curriculum for the BA Degree in Comics and Graphic Novels at Teesside University, UK. She is also an Art Director for Kymera Press. Originally from Ireland, Leonie currently resides in California.

Links: lomoore.com

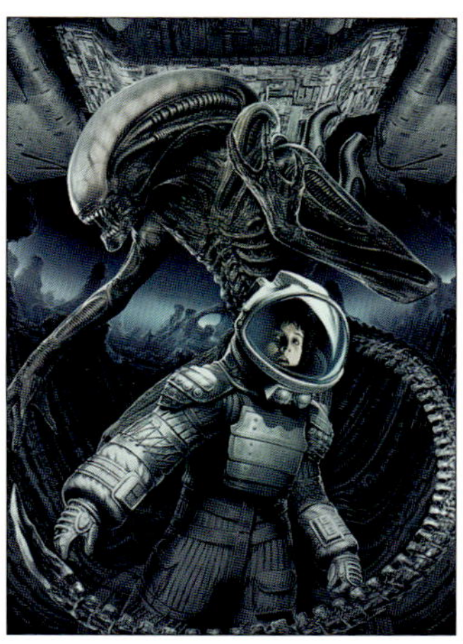

GONZALO 'GENZOMAN' ORDÓÑEZ ARIAS

As a little kid, my father took me to watch *Alien* – "Maybe it's like *Star Wars*," he said – and by the end I was obsessed with Ridley Scott's vision, the mechanical designs of Ron Cobb and Chris Foss, and especially with H. R. Giger's surreal work. The Xenomorph is such a unique design, and it was one reason that impelled me to draw.

Links: genzomancontact@gmail.com; deviantart.com/genzoman; twitter.com/mrgenzoman?lang=en; instagram.com/mrgenzoman/?hl=en; facebook.com/pages/category/Artist/Genzoman-128491607218016

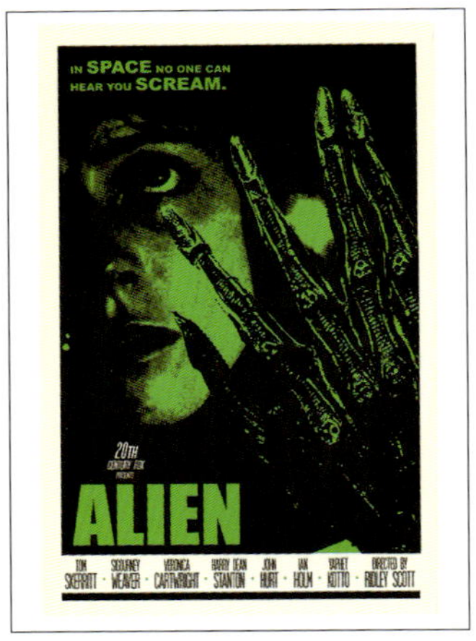

JUAN ORTIZ

Grew up in New York City, where he attended the School of Visual Arts, majoring in editorial illustration. Soon after, he began his career as a designer for various companies within the consumer products and retail business. In 2011 he began a series of retro-styled posters for *Star Trek The Original Series* and has gone on to produce posters for *Lost in Space* and *The Twilight Zone*. Juan currently lives in California in an over-priced studio apartment with an overweight cat.

Links: juanortizart.blogspot.com

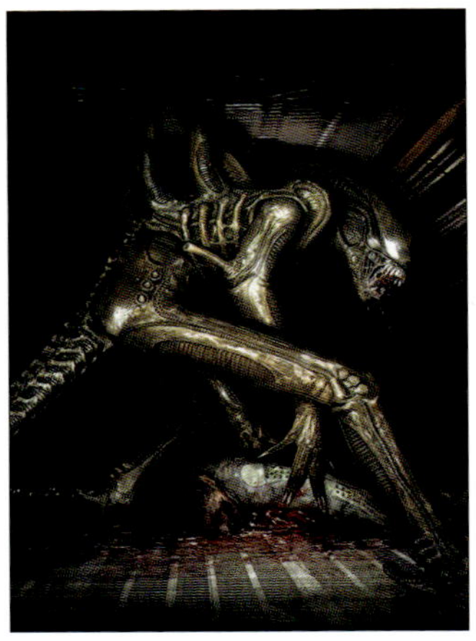

RJ 'ARVALIS' PALMER

An artist based in the San Francisco Bay area of California. Inspired by the natural world, he strives to use nature and science to inform his aesthetic sensibilities. He has become known throughout the world for his inventive and highly thought out creature designs as well as his world-class dinosaur reconstructions.

Links: rj-palmer.com; @arvalis

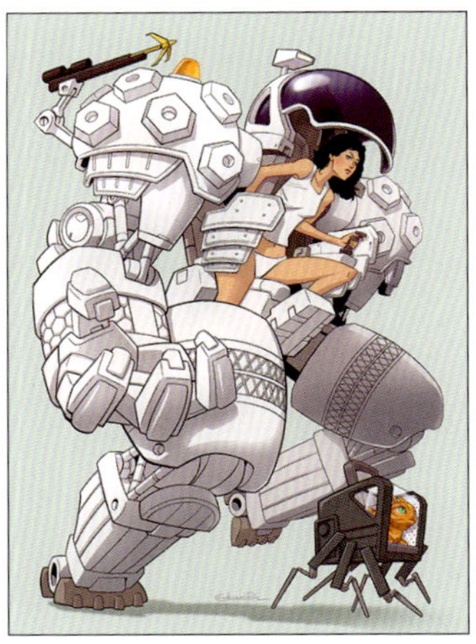

EDWARD PUN

Has worked on video game titles such as *Putt Putt*, *Freddi Fish*, *Sly Cooper*, *Infamous*, and Sony's exclusive soon-to-be-released *Ghost of Tsushima*. As a visual storyteller, he enjoys creating comics and regularly produces fan art, which he posts on his social media accounts.

Links: edwardpun.blogspot.com

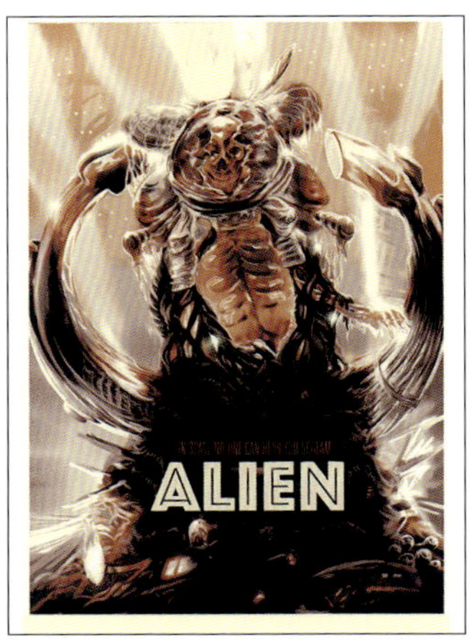

FERNANDO 'FRO' REZA

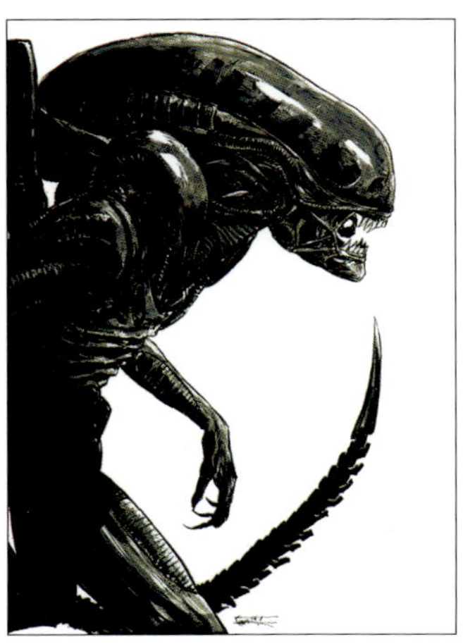

CHRIS 'ZHOURULES' SHEHAN

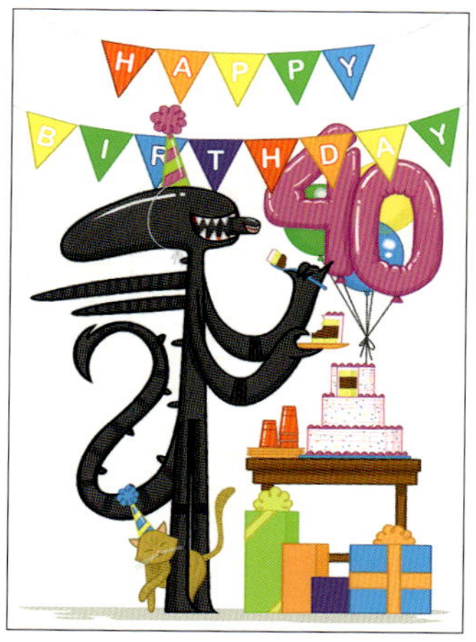

JOEY SPIOTTO

An author and illustrator of *Grumpy Unicorn*, *Alien Next Door* and *Firefly: Back From the Black* from 20th Century Fox and Titan Books. He has created artwork for numerous clients, including Disney, Lucasfilm, Marvel, Microsoft, Rare, and Loot Crate. Joey is a regularly featured artist at Gallery 1988 in Los Angeles where he's had several solo exhibitions. He's also worked as a concept artist in the film and video game industry on such titles as *The Polar Express* for Warner Bros. and *Dead Space* and *The Sims* franchises at Electronic Arts.

Links: jo3bot.com; instagram.com/jo3bot

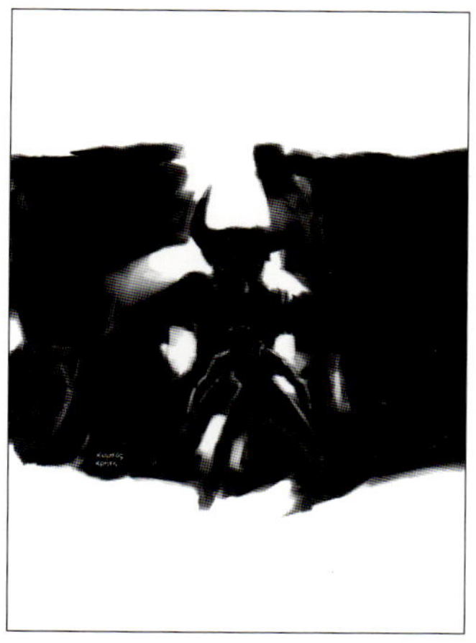

DENIS VILLENEUVE

A French Canadian film director and writer. He started his career as a filmmaker at the National Film Board of Canada. He is best known for his feature films *Arrival* (2016), *Sicario* (2015), *Prisoners* (2013), *Enemy* (2013), and *Incendies* (2010).

Links: imdb.com/name/nm0898288

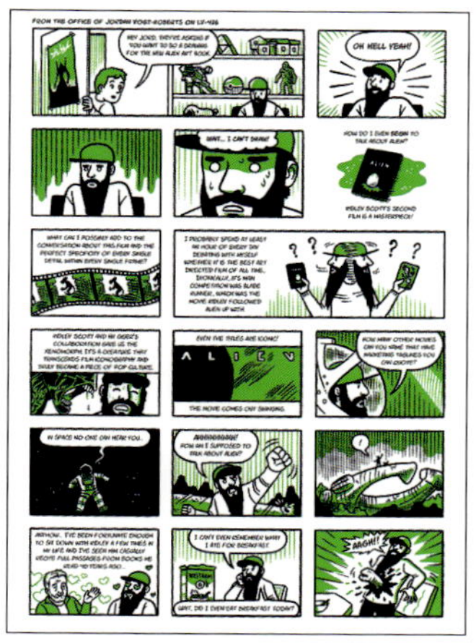

JORDAN VOGT-ROBERTS, JON WILCOX

A director and producer, known for *Kong: Skull Island* (2017), *The Kings of Summer* (2013), and *Successful Alcoholics* (2010).

Links: imdb.com/name/nm3611349

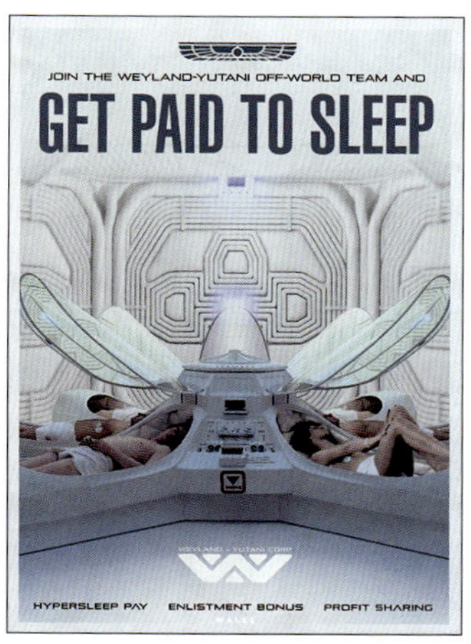

RUSSELL WALKS

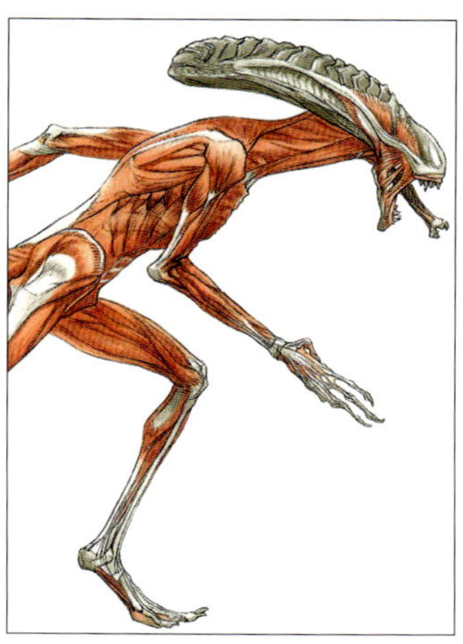

TERRYL WHITLATCH

An American scientific illustrator, who has worked with many major film studios and effects houses as a creature and concept designer, including ILM, Lucasfilm, and Pixar, and with various zoos and natural history museums. Whitlatch also creates and illustrates books, including *The Wildlife of Star Wars: A Field Guide*, and is an international speaker and instructor in animal anatomy and creature design.

Links: artstation.com/terrylwhitlatch

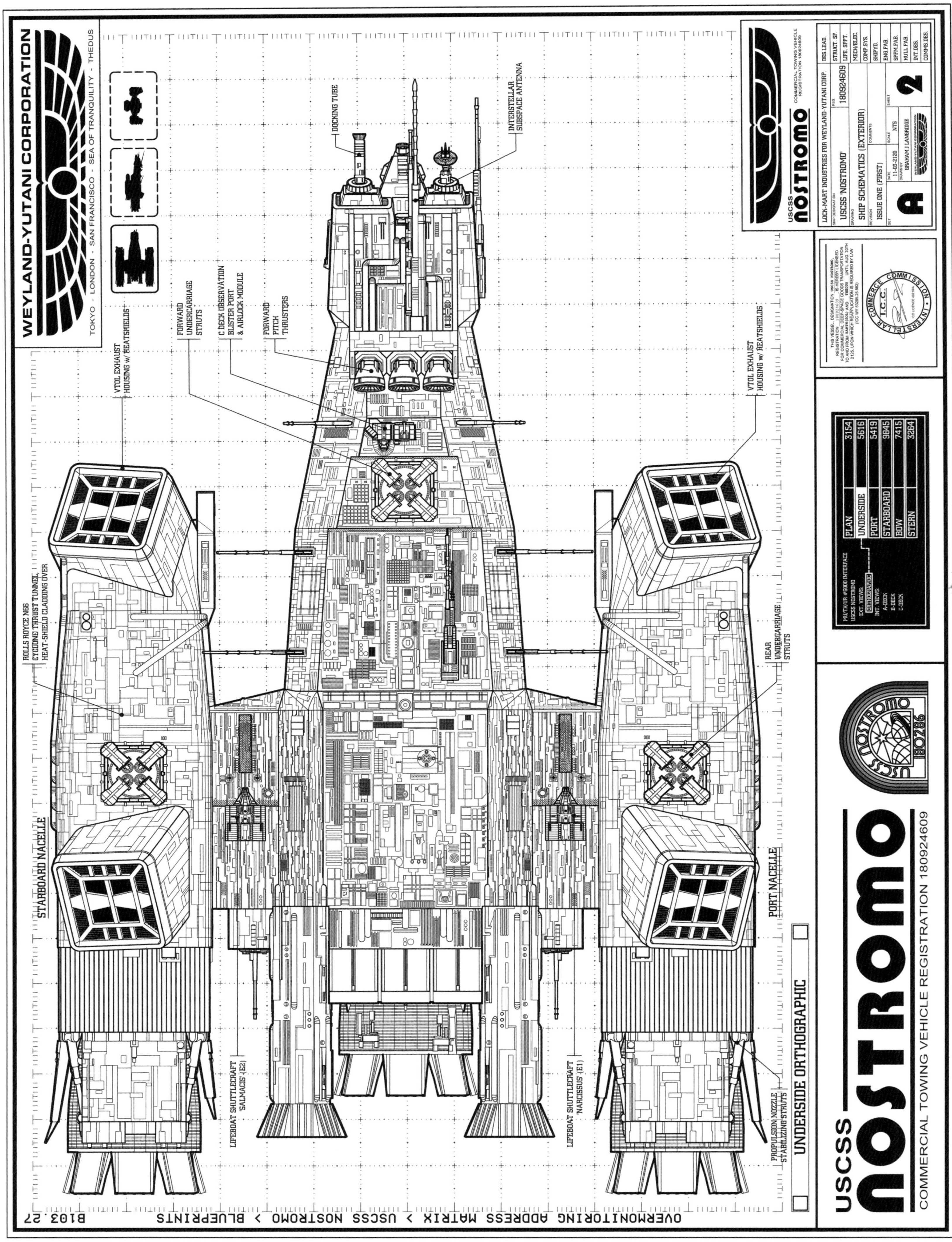

USCSS 'Nostromo' ship schematics (exterior) issue one (first)

from TITAN BOOKS *Alien: The Blueprints* by Graham Langridge

ISBN: 9781785654954